The Revelation of Jesus Christ

to the Seven Churches and to us

chapters 1-11

The Revelation of Jesus Christ

to the Seven Churches and to us

chapters 1-11

by Dave Hagelberg

2014

The Revelation of Jesus Christ to the Seven Churches and to us – published by the Rev. Dr. Ashish Amos of the Indian Society for Promoting Christian Knowledge (ISPCK), Post Box 1585, 1654, Madarsa Road, Kashmere Gate, Delhi-110006.

© Dave Hagelberg, 2013, Revised Edition 2014

All rights reserved. No part of this book may be reproduced or transmitted in any form or by any means, electronic, mechanical, photocopying, recording, or by any information storage and retrieval system, without the prior permission in writing from the publisher.

The views expressed in the book are those of the author and the publisher takes no responsibility for any of the statements.

Scripture quotations are the author's own translation, which is intended to be a word for word translation in order to reflect the original sentence structure.

Order online: http://ispck.org.in/book.php

With a grateful heart this commentary is dedicated to my wife Barbara, whose encouragement and help made this effort possible.

ISBN: 978-81-8465-436-3

Laser typeset by Whyneeta William and the author

ISPCK, Post box 1585, 1654, Madarsa Road, Kashmere Gate, Delhi-110006
Tel.: 011-23866323
e-mail: ashish@ispck.org.in • ella@ispck.org.in
website: www.ispck.org.in

Abbreviations

Bible Versions

HCSB	Holman Christian Standard Bible
KJV	King James Version
NET	New English Translation
NIV	New International Version
NKJV	New King James Version
RSV	Revised Standard Version

Other Abbreviations

BDAG	Bauer, Danker, Arndt, Gingrich Greek Lexicon
EBC	Expositor's Bible Commentary
JETS	Journal of the Evangelical Theological Society
LXX	Septuagint, the Greek translation of the OT
NT	New Testament
OT	Old Testament

Contents

Preface	1
Introduction	2
Authorship	3
Date of Writing	4
Recipients of Revelation	6
Historical Context	6
Revelation as Literature	8
Interpretation	10
Revelation and Systematic Theology	12
The Interpretation of Numbers and Repetitions	15
The Book of Revelation and the Biblical Canon	18
Key Verse	19
Overview and Structure	19
Outline	22
Purpose	24
Exposition of Revelation 1-11	25
I. "What you have seen" (1:1-20)	25
A. Introduction (1:1-8)	25
B. The Vision (1:9-20)	32
II. "What is now " (2:1-3:22)	40
A. Message to the church in Ephesus (2:1-7)	42
B. Message to the church in Smyrna (2:8-11)	53

C. Message to the church in Pergamum (2:12-17)	62
D. Message to the church in Thyatira (2:18-29)	67
E. Message to the church in Sardis (3:1-6)	72
F. Message to the church in Philadelphia (3:7-13)	79
G. Message to the church in Laodicea (3:14-22)	86
III. "What will happen after this" (4-22)	95
A. Vision of Throne Room (4:1-5:14)	97
B. Time of Torment part 1 (6:1–20:3) continued in vol. 2	115
1. Seven Seals (6:1–8:6)	117
2. Seven Trumpets (8:7–11:19)	135
Comments Closing this Volume	157
Appendix: Repetition in Revelation	159
Endnotes	161
Bibliography	193

Preface

Since I believed in Jesus Christ and received Him as my personal Savior in Bogor, West Java, Indonesia in 1975, the Book of Revelation has been an especially significant New Testament book for me. Later when I studied at seminary that attraction grew stronger with a deeper understanding of the structure and the contents of the Book of Revelation. This interest grew even stronger when I began to teach the Book of Revelation in a Bible school on Java and wrote a commentary on Revelation in the Indonesian language.

The importance of understanding, interpreting, applying, and then communicating the contents of the Book of Revelation is becoming increasingly obvious. Although separated by nearly 2000 years, there are remarkable similarities between churches today and the seven churches spoken of in chapters two and three. Certainly the persecution experienced by the congregation of Smyrna and Pergamum, the sexual immorality of Pergamum and Thyatira, and the materialism of Laodicea are painfully evident in too many churches today. In chapters two and three, the Lord Jesus Himself speaks specifically to each church. Then He reveals the secrets of the end of the ages with the intent of strengthening or rebuking each church according to their particular need.

It is my hope that this commentary will help readers to better understand the Book of Revelation so that they are equipped to face temptation, challenge, and suffering in the light of the return of the King. May the living God use His Word powerfully in all our lives

Dave Hagelberg

November 2013

Introduction

If the Book of Revelation is diligently observed, carefully interpreted, and faithfully applied, it certainly can bring great blessing to the reader. This process is made more difficult for two reasons: first, because many things in the book are hard to understand, and second, because the reader might come to the text more motivated by a curiosity about the future rather than a desire to conform to the truth about who the Lord Jesus is and what He has to say about the reader's heart and deeds.

Indeed many things in this book are hard to understand. However, the things that should concern our minds and hearts are not those we cannot understand, but those we can understand but are not applying in our personal lives and in the church of Christ.

Revelation is a great book. It almost goes without saying that it is visionary, but it is also intensely practical. However, before we look at it, this writer would like to suggest some practical "ground rules." In our daily lives we are always observing, interpreting, and applying. We do this as a matter of course. As we read this book we should observe, interpret, and apply rationally and skillfully. Good observations become the foundation for good interpretations, and good interpretations become the foundation for good application. Even so, these things do not actually happen one step at a time. As we read, think, and live the text we can continually improve our observations, interpretations, and applications, which in turn all help us to better observe, interpret, and apply. And the deep benefits of this book only come from good application!

Authorship

This writer's understanding is that the entire Book of Revelation is the product of the inspiration of the Holy Spirit working through the Apostle John,[1] as described in 2 Peter 1:21. That work of the Holy Spirit was accomplished in different ways in different parts of the book. For instance, the text tells us that the words of chapters two and three were dictated word for word to John by the Lord Himself, but in other parts of the book John experienced visions from the Lord which he, guided by the Spirit, wrote down. Therefore it is somewhat futile to compare the style of the language of the Book of Revelation to the style of the language of the Gospel of John or the Epistles of John. This is true despite the opinion to the contrary of Dionysius, Bishop of Alexandria, in the third century. He observed that the vocabulary and grammar of Revelation is different from that of the Gospel of John or John's letters. He said that the Greek used in the Gospel of John and John's letters was refined and beautiful, but the Greek used in the Book of Revelation was not standard, including "idioms that were uncivilized."[2] It is true that the language used in the Gospel of John and his three letters is different from the language used in Revelation.[3] Standard rules of grammar are often "violated" in the Book of Revelation but those "violations" are not random. The "violations" of the rules of grammar in the Book of Revelation are intentional, in accord with the author's purpose.[4]

Prior to Dionysius, Justin Martyr in Dialogue with Trypho (about 135 AD) affirmed that John the Apostle was the author of Revelation. That is particularly significant, because of that early date and because for several years Justin lived in Ephesus,[5] where strong tradition places John for many years. There is a tomb said to be the Apostle John's tomb, on a hill that overlooks the site of the Temple of Artemis of Ephesus. Eusebius, Irenaeus,[6] Clement, Origen, Tertullian, and Hippolytus all affirm that the Apostle John wrote Revelation.

The book itself, in 1:1, 4, 9; and 22:8, claims to be written by "John." If another man named John wrote it, one would hope for clarification to that effect. With no clarification to the contrary, it is fair to say that the book was written either by the well-known Apostle John, or else by an impostor.[7] It seems most unlikely that there was another John that was so well-known to the church in Ephesus and the entire Roman province of Asia that he could call himself "John" and expect to be understood.

Letter writers were often helped by a secretary. This custom is clear in 1 Corinthians 16:21, where the Apostle Paul writes, "With my own hand I write this: Greetings from Paul."[8] The details of how the letter writer and his secretary worked together were not usually disclosed. If the owner of a business told his secretary to prepare an invitation for a meeting the following week, the contents of that invitation could be fully written by the secretary and just signed by the owner. On the other hand, the owner might dictate the contents of the invitation word by word. Writers at the time of the Apostle John had a similar choice. Ladd[9] brings up the possibility that the Gospel of John was written by John with the help of a secretary who was one of his disciples. This writer believes that Revelation was written without a secretary, because on the island of Patmos there was probably no secretary to help the Apostle John. The Lord Jesus appeared to him and began dictating to him and revealing things to him, apparently without a warning that would enable him to call a secretary to help him!

Further, the arguments of Dionysius and other scholars that do not believe the Apostle John wrote Revelation do not really make sense. What kind of Greek was written by a person who "fell at His feet as though dead"? Surely if a man is writing in such extraordinary circumstances about a topic that is so extraordinary, at the moments when he is not writing the exact words given to him by revelation, he will use vocabulary and grammar that are also extraordinary.

This writer takes the statements of Revelation 1:1, 4, 9; and 22:8 at face value, and understands the Apostle John to be the author of the Book of Revelation.

Date of Writing

The Lord's message to the congregation in Smyrna indicates that they had been and would be persecuted. Antipas had been killed. John had been exiled to Patmos (note especially in Revelation 1:9, 2:10, 13, and 3:10). Even though Nero persecuted Christians in Rome, and several emperors were worshiped as divine, it was not until the reign of Domitian, who required that others address him as *Dominus et Deus*[10] ("Lord and God"), that Christians were persecuted because they would not participate in the worship of the emperor.[11] This suggests that the book was written during his reign, which was from 81-96 AD.

Besides the issue of persecution, there are several other factors that support dating the writing of Revelation late in Domitian's reign:

1. Irenaeus said that Revelation was written at the end of the reign of Domitian.
2. The seven churches of Revelation all had some history. They were not newly planted churches. If (as some suggest) Revelation was written during the reign of Nero (54-68 AD), there would not have been time for the decline of the congregations of Thyatira, Sardis, and Laodicea or the commended perseverance of the congregations of Ephesus, Smyrna, and Philadelphia which are all mentioned in chapters two and three. Specifically, if Revelation was written in 54-68 AD during the reign of Nero, it is doubtful that the congregation of Ephesus would have had time to leave their first love, considering that Paul's letter to the Ephesians, which gives no indication any spiritual problem, was written about 60 AD?
3. Although in 3:17 Laodicea is physically rich, the city was very badly damaged by an earthquake in 60 or 61 AD, and it would have taken some time for the city to rebuild itself.
4. If the book was written during the time that Paul was serving there, it is strange that neither he nor any of his coworkers were mentioned.

So for these reasons, conservative biblical scholars usually date the writing of this book at about 95 AD. It is usually placed during the reign of the Emperor Domitian, 81-96 AD. If John was born in 10 AD, he was about 23 years old when he walked with the Lord Jesus in Israel, and he would have been 85 years old in 95 AD. Tradition holds that he lived a long life, and was the only one of the apostles to die a natural death.[12]

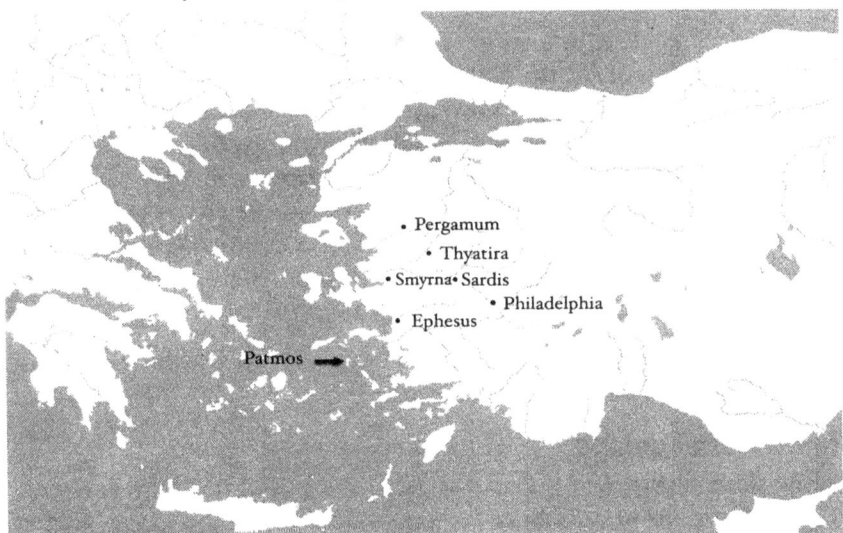

Recipients of Revelation

This book was written to seven specific congregations in seven cities in the Roman province of Asia in the western part of what is now called Turkey (1:11). Each of the seven cities was located on a certain postal road and each had a post office.[13] The nearest two cities along that road were Philadelphia and Laodicea; they were 43 kilometers (27 miles) apart. The longest distance between two cities on that route was 152 kilometers (94 miles),[14] the distance from Ephesus to Laodicea. Each of these seven congregations had their distinct characteristics, and it is very interesting how the Lord draws upon those distinct characteristics as He sends the messages to those seven churches. These were real people in real churches in real cities.

As a part of the Bible, this book was also written to all Christians (Revelation 2:7, 17, 29, etc.).

Historical Context

Ethnic and Cultural Background

Prior to the conquests of Alexander the Great in 334 BC, this region was dominated by various ethnic groups including the Lydians and the Phrygians, but Alexander the Great's victories brought Greek settlers and influence. After 334 BC Greek language and culture grew more and more predominant. By 133 BC Rome controlled the entire region, but the Latin language and Roman culture did not overturn that Greek influence.

Social Background

The wealthy of that era were incredibly wealthy. Eating off silver plates was despised by the upper classes; gold plates were required. One emperor had a meal of peacock tongues. For a victory parade one emperor clothed his entire army in silk, brought overland from China. In 18:11-17 the list of the great wealth of Babylon is very similar to the great wealth of the upper classes of Rome at the time the book was written. Many were also very poor. Instead of a middle class, there was an enormous gap between the rich and the poor. Slavery was common. A slave was not considered human; he was property.

Although Jews were already dispersed in the region, the destruction of the Temple in 70 AD increased that dispersion.

Political Background

In the Roman province of Asia the worship of the emperor was strong. Refusing to worship the emperor, to burn the incense and to say "Caesar is Lord," could easily result in death or banishment to a prison island, depending on the official's whim. The emperor Domitian enforced emperor worship, but we have no documents detailing how he enforced it. There had been persecution against Christians before the book was written (Antipas's martyrdom is mentioned in 2:13) and directly after it was written (in 2:10 we read "what you are about to suffer... prison... suffer persecution").

Early on the morning of July 19 in the year 64 AD there was a fire at the Circus Maximus (where chariot races were performed). For five days the fire burned in Rome. Some eyewitnesses reported seeing people add wood to the fire and hinder the firefighters. According to rumors, Nero had the fires started because he wanted to build Rome again according to his own dreams. Nero accused the Christians of starting the fires, and cruelly punished them. Some were crucified, some were dressed in animal skins and thrown to hungry dogs, and some were smeared with tar and lit like torches. According to strong tradition, the Apostles Paul and Peter were martyred during the persecution that Nero ordered.[15]

Nero died on June 9th in the year 68. For a year between the death of Nero and the coming of Vespasian there was a civil war in Rome where four different men tried to take the throne of the empire. With the coming of Emperor Vespasian the period of political chaos ended and the Flavian dynasty, which would last 28 years, began. It was made up of the reigns of Vespasian (69-79), Titus (79-81), and Domitian (81-96).

According to the date of the writing of Revelation discussed above, Revelation was written at the end of the Flavian dynasty. During those years, the Roman Empire reached to modern day Britain and Germany. The emperor had absolute power.[16] As discussed above, when Revelation was written, worship of the Emperor Domitian was required as a sign of political loyalty.

Religious Background
Jews – As General Titus was defeating a Jewish rebellion against the Roman Empire, his soldiers destroyed the temple in Jerusalem in 70 AD. The people of Israel were dispersed into surrounding countries where they were very often despised. Emperor Vespasian instituted a heavy tax upon the Jews, but they were not required to worship the emperor.

Romans – The Romans worshiped many gods including the Emperor Domitian himself.

Christians – In the year 95 AD Christianity was recognized as a religion distinct from Judaism. Although that might sound like it was positive for the Christians, it was not. Jews were excused from the otherwise mandatory worship of the emperor, but since the Christians were no longer considered a part of Judaism, they were no longer excused from emperor worship. Christians were considered atheists because they would not join in the religious practices of the Romans and did not worship the Roman gods. Some churches and some Christians were persecuted (1:9; 2:10 and 13).

Literary Background

As the Jews witnessed the apparent fulfillment of Daniel's prophecy of "the abomination of desolation" (Daniel 9:27) by Antiochus Epiphanes in 168 BC, they grew more and more desperate. Empire after empire oppressed them, but God was silent. Perhaps Antiochus Epiphanes sparked a renewed interest in the Book of Daniel, because Jewish writers around that time began writing what we now refer to as "pseudepigraphical apocalypses." They were "pseudepigraphical" because although they claimed to have been written by great biblical figures of the past like Enoch, Moses, and Baruch, they were in fact written by now unknown people who longed to see the foreign oppressors thrown off, and the Kingdom of God established in their day.

They were "apocalypses"[17] because they followed the style of Daniel and Zechariah. In a world in which evil seemed to prosper, the apocalypses spoke of the future defeat of the Kingdom of Earth and the establishment of the Kingdom of God.[18] These apocalypses were written between 200 BC and 100 AD. Scholars can only argue now about how popular they were in Jewish society.[19] But even if the popularity of apocalyptic writings in Jewish society is debated, nevertheless they were almost certainly far less popular outside of Jewish circles, in, for instance, the seven churches in the province of Asia! So we might conclude that these apocalyptic visions were almost as strange to many of the early readers as they are to us!

However, the connection with the apocalypse that Daniel wrote, and also Old Testament prophets like Isaiah, Jeremiah, and Ezekiel is everywhere present. Reading the Old Testament prophets along with the Book of Revelation will significantly enrich the reader's insight into the Book of Revelation.

Revelation as Literature

The entire Bible is given to us as literature. It is perfect literature, and at the same time it is literature written in literary forms adopted from the local culture.[20] The Book of Revelation fits into three usually distinct kinds of human literature. It is an apocalypse, it is a letter, and it is a prophecy.

It is certainly apocalyptic literature (1:1), in which John is shown, and relates to his readers, visions of the end times that have profound impact on the readers' lives. He is not shown the future so that he and his readers can escape somehow into it. Rather he is shown the future in which the purpose and plan of the Almighty will prevail and bring about a glorious victory,[21] so that he and his readers can better understand the present, and live in it appropriately.[22]

Although it is apocalyptic literature, the Revelation of John is unique in several ways:
  1. Other apocalyptic literature had nothing like the seven messages to the seven churches.
  2. Other apocalyptic literature did not have nearly as much visual imagery.
  3. Other apocalyptic literature often had long speeches by angels.
  4. Other apocalyptic literature outside the canon was written as if from Moses, Abraham, or some other well-known Old Testament figure.
  5. Other apocalyptic literature considers the present age as meaningless and useless, and reveals a distant, disconnected world.[23]

The Revelation of John is also a letter, as is very clear from 1:4-6 and 1:11. In one sense it is all meant as a single letter "to the seven churches in the province of Asia," and in another sense it also contains seven distinct letters, one each to those seven churches. Letters could be addressed to specific individuals or communities, but sometimes "circular letters" were meant to have a wide audience. In the case of the Revelation of John, there are three sorts of recipients.
  1. Revelation 2:1-7, for instance, was written to the church in Ephesus.
  2. The whole book was written to the seven churches, as is clear from 1:4 and 1:11.
  3. The entire book was written to all believers, as is clear from the repeated expression, "The one who has an ear, let him hear what the Spirit says to the churches."

Letters were a means of communication between people, but they were also used as a means of guidance from wise and learned men.[24]

Besides being an apocalypse and a letter, Revelation is also a book of prophecy. In 1:3 John says, "Blessed is the one who reads and blessed are those who hear the words of this prophecy and keep what is written in it." The distinctive feature of prophecy which demands faith and obedience from the hearers (or the readers) is clearly visible in chapters two and three, which can be compared to the seven messages in Amos chapters one and two.[25]

Interpretation

Because Revelation is so complex, because it deals with controversial eschatological issues, and because it contains many symbols, some of which are explained (1:20) and some are not (3:12), a wide variety of interpretations have been suggested. It is helpful to note the four major approaches to the interpretation of the book.

The "Preterist"[26] view is subdivided into a strict Preterist version and a modified Preterist version. In the strict Preterist view, all the prophecies of the Book of Revelation are fulfilled by the time the Romans destroy the temple in Jerusalem in 70 AD.[27] In the modified Preterist view most of the prophecies of the Book of Revelation are considered fulfilled by the time of the "Cloud Coming" of the Lord in 70 AD, but the Second Coming described in chapters 19-21 is still yet to come. Preterists, in general, support their interpretation by referring to Matthew 24:33-34[28] "In this way you also, when you see all these things, know that it is near, at the door. Amen, I say to you, this generation shall not pass away, until all these things happen." The Lord Jesus must have meant that His return was very near, according to them, and would be experienced by the generation to whom He was speaking. So they say that the Lord Jesus "came in the clouds" when the Temple was destroyed in 70 AD.[29]

Preterists also point to words like "near" and "soon" in Revelation 1:3; 22:7, 10, 12, and 20. They would say that the "cloud coming" to Jerusalem in 70 AD was near, and that the Lord could not have used these words for a coming that was at least 2000 years in the future.[30]

The second view is called the "Historical" view. According to this view Revelation consists of prophecies explaining the history of western Europe until the second coming of Christ. The various interpretations of people following the "Historical" view are not consistent, and it is hard to understand why the Lord would focus on western Europe!

The third view is called the "Futurist" view. According to this view chapters one, two and three tell about a vision that John had of Christ, and about

His seven messages to seven churches in that era. Then chapters 4-22 are prophecies about the end of the age. Morris[31] and Mounce[32] criticize this view because, they say, chapters 4-22 would have no meaning for us, unless we live during the time of the Second Coming. However, this is a weak criticism. News about the coming of the Lord Jesus is relevant for each generation of God's people because that news comforts God's people who are faithful, and brings fear to the unfaithful. Just as people do not go on a picnic as storm clouds are gathering, so also we do not live for ourselves when the Word of God says "Blessed is he who... obeys what is written in it, because the time is already near." The "Futurist" view is the one that is used in this commentary.[33]

The fourth view is called the "Idealist" view. According to that view, Revelation is not about deeds or events. Instead it is meant to yield theological principles.

We can certainly learn something from each view. The "Preterist" and "Historical" views remind us that Revelation was written during a particular historical period, a context that we should understand. The "Idealist" view reminds us that principles presented in the Book of Revelation are useful throughout the history of mankind.

However, it is the perspective of the "Futurist" view that gives us the appropriate framework to understand the book. Revelation 4-22 primarily consists of prophecies that will be fulfilled at the end of the age. As bewildering as the Book of Revelation might seem in some passages, the Futurist view follows the plain and simple approach to the book, as is made clear from 1:19. It is the standard which guards the unity of the book's structure.

Early interpreters of Revelation like Justin Martyr (100-165 AD), Irenaeus (died about 202 AD) and Hippolytus (170-235 AD), wrote that Revelation prophesied about a literal thousand year kingdom, so it seems that they would have preferred the Futurist view. After the literal thousand year kingdom, there would be a general resurrection, judgment, and a New Heaven and a New Earth.[34] This commentary approaches the Book of Revelation with that understanding.

In Alexandria, the church fathers, including Origen (185-254 AD), developed the method of interpretation called "spiritual" or allegorical. This method does not emphasize the literal understanding. It "spiritualizes" passages, finding figurative meanings. Augustine carried this method further. For a thousand years of church history the allegorical method was the preferred method. This view is similar to the fourth view above, the "Idealist" view.

In the 12th century Joachim, a Catholic from Florence, Italy, refused the allegorical interpretation that said that the present age was the thousand year kingdom mentioned in Revelation 20.

Nicolas from Lyra, a theologian from Paris who died in 1340, used the "Historical" interpretation that has been mentioned above to interpret Revelation.

At the end of the 16th century, a Spanish Jesuit named Alcasar used the "Preterist" method. According to Alcasar, chapters 20-22 became prophecy about the victory enjoyed by the church of Christ of that era, a victory that began during the reign of Emperor Constantine.

Even though Revelation contains many symbols, that does not mean that each text has to be interpreted figuratively or allegorically. A "literal interpretation" can acknowledge and even celebrate the use of symbols. So, in this commentary, the author uses the "literal interpretation," meaning that whatever can be interpreted in a literal way should be interpreted in a literal way. And whatever does not make sense to interpret literally has to be given a figurative meaning. For instance, the "seven stars" which the Lord holds in His hand cannot be interpreted as literal stars,[35] and Revelation 12 speaking about a woman clothed with the sun is clearly full of figures of speech.

This writer always seeks to interpret the text literally (as discussed in the previous paragraph) and in accord with the grammar the author employs. The historical and theological setting of the text should also be considered as we interpret a passage. Our interpretation can then be confirmed by the context in the passage and by the structure of the entire book.

Revelation and Systematic Theology

We know of course that the New Testament writers were not writers of systematic theology, but each of them presents truths about theology, expressed in the context of the Gospels or letters they were writing. In the same way, the Book of Revelation presents profound truths about God and His work, expressed in accord with its context, style, and purpose.[36] Bauckham reminds us that "John has no vocabulary equivalent to later trinitarian talk of the divine nature which three persons share. But it is impossible for us to do justice to what he says without speaking somehow of a divine reality in which Jesus Christ and the Holy Spirit... are included."[37] It could be added that even if the Lord Jesus had John write words like "trinity," "nature," and "person," those words did not yet have the theological precision which later trinitarian discussions built into them.

Clearly the Book of Revelation reveals the Trinity, but it does so with its own vocabulary and its own style. Note, for instance, Revelation 1:4b-5a: Grace to you and peace from

> God who is,
> and who was,
> and who is coming,

and from

> the seven spirits before His throne,

and from

> Jesus Christ,
>> the faithful witness,
>> the firstborn from the dead,
>> and
>> the ruler of the kings of the earth.

Using his own style, John gives a greeting of grace and peace from the Triune God. Placing God, the seven spirits, and Jesus Christ all parallel to each other in this blessing of grace and peace could be no less than a reference to the Triune God. The seven spirits will be discussed below.

In 1:8 God the Father describes Himself as

> the Alpha and the Omega,
> who is,
> and who was,
> and who is coming,
> the Almighty

And in 21:6, God the Father is

> the Alpha and the Omega,
> the beginning and the end

These expressions are rooted in Old Testament declarations about the Lord God of Israel.[38] In Isaiah 44:6, the Lord God says of Himself, "I am the first and I am the last; apart from Me there is no God." But in Revelation 1:17; 2:8; and 22:13 it is the Lord Jesus who declares Himself to be "the First and the Last." By using this exact expression about Himself, the Lord Jesus is saying that He is the Lord God of Israel. Note in this case that the idea that Jesus Christ could be some sort of secondary God apart from the Lord God of Israel is strictly excluded: "apart from Me there is no God." Note also Isaiah 48:12. Somehow the Lord Jesus is included in the identity of the Lord God who in Isaiah 44:6 says, "I am the first and I am the last; apart from Me there is no God." Later theologians solved this puzzle with the wonderful doctrine of the Trinity, but in Revelation we are just given these texts, and expected to fully worship and fully obey the Lord Jesus, who is fully and absolutely divine.

This idea is confirmed by the expression, "I am the Alpha and the Omega." It is used by God about Himself in 1:8 and 21:6, and it is used by the Lord Jesus Christ of Himself in 22:13. Somehow both God the Father and the Lord Jesus Christ are "the Alpha and the Omega"! It is the Trinity, put in words before the theologians were able to systematize the idea.

The expression "seven spirits" should also be discussed in this context. It occurs four times, in Revelation 1:4; 3:1; 4:5; and 5:6. This four-fold use of a seven-fold designation suggests a connection with the seven-fold repetition of the four-fold expression, "every nation, tribe, people, and language."[39] Perhaps the connection is that the nations of the earth will only hear the witness of the Gospel by the power of the Spirit. However, some interpreters say that the expression "seven spirits" refers to seven special angels. That interpretation is very unlikely because as noted above, in Revelation 1:4b-5a the "seven spirits" are parallel to God (this refers to God the Father) and Jesus Christ in this text, but it would be hard to imagine a blessing of grace and peace from God the Father, seven special angels, and Jesus Christ.

The expression "the seven spirits" is connected to Zechariah 4:10b, which refers to the Spirit of God saying, "these seven are the eyes of the Lord, they go to and fro in the whole earth."[40] The connection between this expression and Zechariah 4:10 is strengthened in Revelation 5:6, in which the Lamb's seven eyes are called "the seven spirits of God sent out into all the earth." Thus there is a double connection between "the seven spirits" in Revelation and "the seven eyes" in Zechariah.[41] The seven-fold description of the Spirit of God in Isaiah 11:2 also supports the idea that "the seven spirits" in Revelation refers to the Holy Spirit.

God the Father is strangely hidden from us for most of the Book of Revelation. We do see the expression "seated on the throne" eleven times and once there is a similar expression, "...a great white throne, and the One seated upon it" (20:11). Until the Lamb of God completes His work in bringing God's Kingdom to earth, the One who is seated on the throne, that is, God the Father, limits His revealed activity to speaking from His throne in heaven. But once the devil and the beasts are removed, and the New Jerusalem comes down to earth, God the Father makes His dwelling with men. In 21:3 this is made explicit: "God's home is with mankind, and He will live with them, and they will be His people, and God Himself will be with them."[42]

The Interpretation of Numbers and Repetitions

Philosophers in John's era were very interested in numbers and the meanings of numbers. Their writings often discussed in great detail the significance of particular numbers. Pythagoras was considered the foremost thinker in this area. He was born about 570 BC, and lived in southern Italy. His followers considered the numbers 1, 2, 4, and 10 to be the most significant. By the end of the fourth century BC the number 7 also took on special significance, perhaps because of the influence of Babylon. By that time, Pythagorus's influence had declined somewhat, but his writings were still popular even into the second century BC.[43]

At that time a Jew named Aristobulus taught in Alexandria. Probably because of the influence of the Old Testament, he emphasized the significance of the number 7. Philo, a Jewish philosopher that was born about 25 BC, considered 7 to be the most interesting number.[44]

The following observations refer to the Greek text, not a translation.

There are seven spirits-torches-horns-eyes,[45] mentioned seven times (1:4; 3:1; 4:5; and 5:6). The seven angels are always mentioned in connection with the seven trumpets or seven bowls. (Seven angels are not mentioned in connection with the seven seals, which are opened by the Lord rather than by angels.)

There are seven thunders, but what they say is sealed and not to be written down. Those seven thunders are mentioned three times.

The term "woe"[46] is used 14 (that is 7×2) times.

The word spirit/Spirit[47] is used 24 times in Revelation: once for the breath of God (11:11), once for the breath given to the image (13:15), three times of evil spirits (16:13, 14; and 18:2), once for the spirits of the prophets (22:6), four times for the seven spirits of God (1:4; 3:1; 4:5; and 5:6),[48] and 14 times for the Spirit of God.

The expression "I am coming"[49] is used seven times in Revelation, only by the Lord Jesus.[50] Bauckham[51] observes that the term "Lamb" is used of the Lord Jesus 28 times in the original language.[52] Seven times it is used in a way that connects the Lamb with God, as in 5:13, "...To the one seated on the throne and to the Lamb be praise...," or 14:4, "...as firstfruits to God and to the Lamb..."

Given the many allusions to the Old Testament, there is also probably a strong connection between the number seven in the Book of Revelation and the seven days of creation in Genesis.

Collins[53] believes that the twelve signs of the zodiac are the source of the meaning of twelve in Revelation and the seven planets[54] are the source of the number seven, but those are questionable assertions, given that the numbers twelve, twelfth, or one twelfth are used are in Revelation about 135 times, and seven, seventh, or one seventh are used about 436 times![55]

In the Old Testament we get the strong impression that the number seven, whether chosen by man (Genesis 21:28-30, etc.) or by God (Genesis 4:15; 7:2-4, etc.) suggests the idea of completion or perfection, and the same would hold true at the time of the writing of the Book of Revelation. Bauckham[56] notes how the Muratorian Canon "claims that both John (in Revelation) and Paul actually wrote to all churches by writing to seven." According to Philo, the number seven "brings perfection."[57]

In contrast, terms like "devil" and "beast" are repeated a random number of times, without any good numbers of repetitions. For instance, the term "dragon"[58] is repeated 13 times, the Greek word for devil[59] is repeated five times, and the Greek word for Satan[60] is repeated eight times. Bauckham[61] suggests that this gives the impression that meaningful numbers of repetitions are avoided in connection with evil figures in Revelation. Good numbers are only used of evil when the evil imitates the holy, as in for instance 12:3; 13:1; 16:13; and 17:3.

For more information on repetitions like this, see the Appendix.

Turning now to the repetition of phrases, Bauckham[62] explains that these fall into two different categories in Revelation. The first kind consists of the repetition of certain phrases, like "And to the messenger of the church in... write...," or "The one who has an ear, let him hear what the Spirit says to the churches." Those two phrases are both given seven times, with exactly the same wording. These repetitions are used in Revelation to mark the structure of the book. In this way, the repetition of "to show his servants what must soon take place" (these expressions are identical in the Greek, in 1:1 and 22:6) shows that what was begun in 1:1 has been completed in 22:6.

The other kind of repetition of phrases includes some slight variation. This is also very frequent in Revelation. Pairs of phrases that are slightly different from one another become like cross-references (or "hyperlinks" on a website) that tie one passage to another, perhaps in order to emphasize a contrast.

Compare for instance 1:19, which has the expression "what will take place after these things," with 4:1, and its expression "what must take place after these things." This nearly exact repetition says to the careful reader,

"Now we are coming to that third part of 1:19, the "what will take place after these things" part.

Also compare 4:8, which reads, "Each of the four creatures had six wings and was covered with eyes all around, even under his wings. Day and night they never stop saying: 'Holy, holy, holy is the Lord God Almighty, who was, and is, and is to come'" with 14:11, which reads, "And the smoke of their torment rises for ever and ever. There is no rest day or night for those who worship the beast and his image, or for anyone who receives the mark of his name." In 4:8 the phrase is literally "And rest not they have day and night," while in 14:11 the phrase is literally "And not they have rest day and night." This repeated, but slightly changed, phrase surely highlights the utterly contrasting situation of the four creatures worshiping God and the evil people worshiping the beast. The reader should also compare 14:11 with 19:3, or 14:10-11 with 20:10.

Collins[63] says that even though there are some series of sevens in extra-biblical apocalyptic literature, those series are not numbered as they are in Revelation (as in the sixth seal or the fifth trumpet). He also says that the use of numbers in the Book of Revelation is far more significant than in other apocalyptic literature.

The well-ordered and well-numbered design of the Book of Revelation gave early readers comfort and assurance that the world they lived in, as chaotic as it seemed, was actually in the hands of the sovereign God who was working out His good plan through the ages. Early readers were also comforted that God would mark the end of the age with the series of sevens, and that the characteristics of the place reserved for the faithful, the New Jerusalem, were being arranged according to His will complete with His signature, the number twelve.[64]

The above discussion of numbers is not so specific that it becomes speculative. The intended meanings of specific numbers in Revelation are very difficult to identify, but it is informative to observe the intricate numerical design of Revelation.

These repetitions and numbers surely did not happen accidentally. The careful reader who is concerned with such matters – and there were many in those early centuries – would be very impressed with the incredibly intricate structure of the Book of Revelation. These intricate patterns might even have been considered a proof of the book's divine inspiration. Perhaps that is also true in some cultures today where the Gospel has yet to penetrate. If it is, then observations like these could help convince people that this book is indeed from God.

When Bauckham published his study on this in 1993 in *The Climax of Prophecy*, *The Bible Code* had not yet appeared. It should be clearly understood that these observations have nothing to do with the faulty methodology of *The Bible Code*. Neither Bauckham nor the present writer find hidden prophecies, and do not read texts backwards, vertically, or diagonally. (By the way, when you change the number of characters per line of text, that is when you make your columns wider or narrower, you get a whole new set of words that might "show up" vertically and diagonally, so it is not surprising that all sorts of sentences "appear." It is also less surprising that so many words "appear" when you realize that *The Bible Code* only deals with the consonants of the Hebrew text, and excludes the vowel pointing system.) By way of contrast, the observations made in this section about numbers and repetitions in the Book of Revelation are in accord with the interests and culture of its original readers.

The discussion here of numbers and repetitions in Revelation is not yet complete and must be examined more thoroughly. It is sincerely hoped that this and any further discussion of this subject be based on accurate observation in accord with the consistent principles of interpretation.

The Book of Revelation and the Biblical Canon

God not only revealed His Word to His people, He also made sure that only the books that He inspired were included in the Bible. This process is called the forming of the Canon. Guided by the Most High God, His people determined which letters and compositions were inspired and meant to be included in the Bible. Certain books were admitted into the canon sooner than others.

In the era of the church fathers, certain groups did not want to allow Revelation into the canon.[65] Mounce[66] explains that Christian leaders that opposed Montanism (which had many strange teachings, including the idea that the high mountain to which an angel took John in Revelation 21:10 was near the city of Pepuza in Phrygia) were ready to reject Revelation simply because Montanus used Revelation to support his teachings. Even though certain groups did not like Revelation, God did not ask our permission to put Revelation into our Bible. We are not to pick and chose from the Bible so that we only take what agrees with our individual tastes, or is convenient for our particular circumstances!

Key Verse

Revelation 1:3, which says "Blessed is the one who reads and blessed are those who hear the words of this prophecy and keep those things written in it, for the time is near," is the key verse which points to primary theme and purpose of the whole Book of Revelation. The blessing will come to each individual and to each congregation that obeys the Book of Revelation. Those blessings or rewards are described in Revelation 2:7, 10-11, 17, 26-28; 3:5, 11-12, 21; and 6:11, among many other passages.

Overview and Structure

It is important to realize that every book of the Bible has an overall structure. God did not reveal His Word to us in a haphazard way. Knowing as much as we can about how a particular passage fits in that overall structure can be a great help in interpreting and applying the Word. If we desire to experience the blessing promised in Revelation 1:3, then we need to "keep those things written in it." But this is not as simple as it might seem: only commands can be "kept." In the Book of Revelation the commands are almost exclusively in chapters two and three. From chapter four to chapter 22 there are basically no commands for us to keep. This is what Martin Luther was complaining about when he wrote, "Again, they are supposed to be blessed who keep what is written in this book; and yet no one knows what that is, to say nothing of keeping it."[67]

Indeed there is much in this book that we will not understand until it happens, but the things we do not understand are not the most significant problem for us as we read the Book of Revelation. That "problem" for us is instead chapters two and three where there are many commands which are very easy to understand but often hard to obey.

As is the case in several New Testament books, we are helped a great deal by a verse that reveals the structure of the book. Revelation 1:19 does that for us:
"Write, therefore,
      the things you saw,
      and the things that are
      and the things that will be after these things."[68]

It is true that the word "and"[69] is on rare occasion translated as "even" or "that is," but that translation is very hard to defend in this case.[70] The Lord is clearly telling John to write three things, and the book has three parts. That helps us a great deal as we interpret the book!

This diagram shows this overall structure of the book. The most basic structural thing to remember about all this is that the first three chapters are about things in John's lifetime, and chapters 4-22 are about the end times.

According to 1:19 the third section is about the things that "will take place after these things." Clearly 4:1, which speaks of the things that "must take place after these things," is the beginning of that third section.

The first section is the core of the book: it is the revelation of Jesus Christ, the vision of Him. It functions to remind us of the character of Jesus Christ. In order to live for the Lord Jesus we must understand who He is. We need to understand about His character and how it relates to our experiences. The second section is an application of His character to the seven churches in those seven cities of the province of Asia. In it He offers rewards to those who obey His demands. The third section shows many things, including how what has been said in the second section will work itself out in the future. It tells how some believers will be victorious over Satan by the blood of the Lamb and by the word of their testimony, and by not loving their lives unto death, and how Jesus Christ will return to the earth and defeat "those who dwell upon the earth," who have been oppressing the people of God. It functions to encourage the reader that "Jesus Christ is going to win." His coming and His victory will prove the truth of all that is said about Him in the vision of Christ in chapter one. In His victorious return He will bring the rewards promised in the second section, the seven messages.

In summary,
1. chapter 1, The Vision that shows who Jesus Christ is
2. chapters 2-3, Seven Messages that demand obedience and promise rewards
3. chapters 4-22, The Prophecy of the victorious lives of some believers and the victorious return of Jesus Christ

There is a logical flow from one section to the next. Chapter one, the vision of Christ Jesus, is the core and foundation of the Book of Revelation. In the same way, the character of the Lord Jesus becomes the foundation for all our actions and thoughts. Thus the Lord Jesus is to be the center of our existence.

Chapters two and three build on the foundation of section one. Each letter begins with a fact about Jesus Christ that was mentioned in chapter one. But the second section also has a close relationship to the third section, which tells about His coming and victory.

Chapters 4-22 have not happened yet. Even though it is difficult to live for Christ, and difficult to obey the seven messages, obedience is critical because – as the third section so powerfully reveals – the Lord will return with victory, rewards, and joy for those who obey.

Bauckham[71] suggests that the seven messages of chapters two and three are seven different introductions to the rest of the book! For instance, the message to the wealthy and self-satisfied Laodiceans serves as their personalized introduction to the prophetic section of the book, in which they will see what becomes of all their earthly treasures. And the message to the persecuted congregation in Smyrna serves as their introduction to the prophetic section, in which they will see the fate of their oppressors and the great rewards awaiting those that faithfully endure persecution.

Outline

I. "What you have seen" (1:1-20)
    A. Introduction (1:1-8)
        1. Title and Introduction (1:1-3)
        2. Greetings (1:4-8)
    B. The Vision (1:9-20)
        1. Background of the Vision (1:9-11)
        2. The Vision (1:12-20)

II. "What is now" (2:1–3:22)
    A. Message to the church in Ephesus (2:1-7)
    B. Message to the church in Smyrna (2:8-11)
    C. Message to the church in Pergamum (2:12-17)
    D. Message to the church in Thyatira (2:18-29)
    E. Message to the church in Sardis (3:1-6)
    F. Message to the church in Philadelphia (3:7-13)
    G. Message to the church in Laodicea (3:14-22)

The messages to the seven churches follow this basic pattern:
1. The Recipient
2. The Characteristic of Christ
3. Praise for the Church
4. Criticism
5. Demand
6. Warning
7. Promise

III. "What will happen after this" (4-22)
    A. Vision of Throne Room (4:1–5:14)
        1. Transition (4:1-2)
        2. Throne and Surroundings (4:3-11)
        3. Scroll and Lamb (5:1-7)
        4. Praise to Him who takes the Scroll (5:8-14)
    B. Time of Torment (6:1–20:3)
        1. Seven Seals (6:1–8:6)
            a. First Seal (6:1-2)
            b. Second Seal (6:3-4)
            c. Third Seal (6:5-6)
            d. Fourth Seal (6:7-8)
            e. Fifth Seal (6:9-11)
            f. Sixth Seal (6:12-17)

First Insertion: 144,000 People Sealed (7:1-8)
Second Insertion: Many people... out of the great tribulation (7:9-17)
            g. Seventh Seal (8:1-6)

       2. Seven Trumpets (8:7–11:19)
            a. First Four Trumpets (8:7-12)
            b. Last Three Trumpets (8:13–11:19)
                 i. Fifth Trumpet (8:13–9:12)
                 ii. Sixth Trumpet (9:13-21)

Third Insertion: Scroll (10:1-11)
Fourth Insertion: Two Witnesses (11:1-14)
                 iii. Seventh Trumpet (11:15-19)
Fifth Insertion: The Woman, the Child and the Dragon (12:1-17)
Sixth Insertion: First Beast (13:1-10)
Seventh Insertion: Second Beast (13:11-18)
Eighth Insertion: 144,000 People (14:1-5)
Ninth Insertion: Three Angels (14:6-13)
Tenth Insertion: Harvest of the Earth (14:14-16)
Eleventh Insertion: Harvest of Grapes on the Earth (14:17-20)
       3. Seven Bowls (15:1–16:21)
            a. Introduction of the Seven Bowls (15:1–16:1)
            b. Seven Bowls Poured Out (16:2-21)
       4. Babylon as a Prostitute (17:1-18)
       5. City of Babylon Destroyed (18:1-24)
            a. The Fall of Babylon Announced (18:1-8)
            b. Reaction of the World (18:9-19)
            c. Babylon Never Restored (18:20-24)
       6. Rejoicing in Heaven (19:1-10)
       7. Christ Returns (19:11-14)
       8. Christ Defeats the Beast and his Army (19:15-21)
       9. Satan Defeated (20:1-3)
   C. The Millennium and Judgment (20:4-15)
       1. Those who Reign with Christ for 1000 Years (20:4-6)
       2. Final Rebellion (20:7-10)
       3. White Throne Judgment (20:11-15)
   D. The New Jerusalem (21:1–22:5)
       1. Introduction: New Jerusalem (21:1-8)
       2. Walls and Gates of the New Jerusalem (21:9-21)
       3. Glory of the New Jerusalem (21:22-27)
       4. River of Life and Servants of the Lamb in the New Jerusalem (22:1-5)
   E. The Conclusion of the Vision (22:6-17)
   F. The Conclusion of the Book of Revelation (22:18-21)

Purpose

Revelation was written and then sent to the Christians of seven congregations (and to all believers in Jesus Christ) to rebuke or encourage, as needed, so that the readers will live as victors, and so participate in the victory of the Lord Jesus. If believers obey whatever is written in this book, they will be full of joy because of the Lord Jesus and His victory (Rev. 1:3; 2:7, 11, 17, 26-28; 3:5, 12 and 21). Chapters two and three are full of great challenges. In chapters 4-21 the visions about the second coming of the Lord Jesus explain that His victory will bring destruction to "those that dwell upon the earth" and rewards to the faithful. So, in an indirect way those visions support the challenges of chapters two and three. Christ the King will return in victory and will bring rewards for those who overcome the temptations and trials in the way that He overcame them. The careful reader will see that this book is very practical.

Revelation was not given to us for speculation about, for instance, "Who is the Anti-Christ?" or "What is the date of the Lord's return?" That sort of useless speculation distracts us from the true purpose of the book, which is to bring us to repentance if need be, but in any case, to encourage us to stand firm in the heart, character, and deeds that please the Lord.

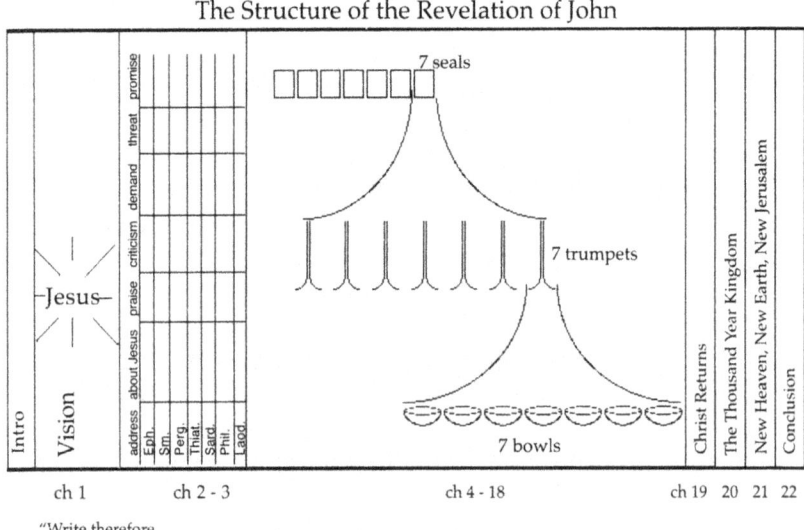

The Structure of the Revelation of John

Exposition of Revelation

I. "What you have seen" (1:1-20)

This section is the core and basis of the whole book, because it is the vision of the Lord Jesus. The other parts of the book connect back to this core. In effect, if you could just respond properly to what this vision shows us concerning the Lord Jesus, you would have no need to read any further. However, we will need help in responding rightly to this section, and that help will be found for us in the remainder of the book.

A. Introduction (1:1-8)

John orients his readers before plunging in to the revelation. This is accomplished in the introduction, verses 1:1-8. The author tells us a little about himself and greets his readers.

1. Title and Introduction (1:1-3)

1:1 The revelation of Jesus Christ, which God gave Him to show to His slaves[72] what things must happen suddenly.[73] He[74] made it known[75] by sending it through His angel to His slave John,

This verse is a serious statement about the authority of the Book of Revelation: it comes from God and is given to His slaves via an entirely reliable process. This verse tells the process of *revelation*: *God gave the revelation to Jesus Christ who made it known by sending it through His angel to His slave John who* is to give it to God's slaves, people who believe and obey Him, either in the seven churches or holy people of other times and places!

The Lord does not want the book to become merely a subject for academic study or debate. He reminds us that all these things must happen suddenly, so we must be ready. In accordance with the primary purpose of Revelation stated above, *what things must happen suddenly* need to be shown to His *slaves* so their lives can be conformed to the truth of His character and coming.

1:2 who testified to the word of God and the testimony of Jesus Christ, which he saw.

This statement serves as a validating signature: John *testified* that this is a valid revelation, so to reject this revelation one must reject John's *testimony*. In John 21:24 he likewise *testified* to the validity of the Gospel of John.

Furthermore, the repetition of the words *testimony* and *word*, usually *the word of God*, throughout the Book of Revelation (note 1:9; 6:9; 12:11; and 20:4) shows the importance and the victory of the preaching of *the word of God*, especially in hostile situations.

1:3   Blessed[76] is the one who reads, and blessed are those who hear the words of this prophecy and keep[77] those things written in it, for the time is near.

This theme of blessing is very important in the Book of Revelation. The blessing is for *the one who reads* the book to the congregation, and for those that obey it. Of course, in that era a congregation would be privileged to have even a single copy of the text, and individual members would not have their own copies. The reading of the Word of God during Christian meetings was therefore all the more important.

The seven blessings of the book refer to special end-of-the-age happiness for obedient people. Those that obey will be *blessed*. This is a key verse for the book. Each of the seven messages that make up chapters two and three includes a blessing for obedience, although the word *blessed* does not appear in chapters two and three. We are to obey this book because soon He that is revealed in its first section, that is, He that speaks in the second section, will return, be victorious, and give out the rewards that He has promised to His obedient ones, as is described in the third section.

If we yearn for this blessing, and continue to read this book in order to obey and be blessed, we may find ourselves very frustrated. So much of this book is about visions of the future, terrible judgments and heavenly events – what are we to obey? This simple question points us to the great importance of chapters two and three, for that is where the commands are found in this book. In obeying those commands we will be *blessed*.

Here are the seven times the word *blessed* appears in the book:
- 1:3 *Blessed* is the one who reads, and *blessed* are those who hear the words of this prophecy and keep those things written in it, for the time is near. (In English the word "blessed" appears twice in this verse, but in the Greek it is there only once.)
- 14:13 Then I heard a voice from heaven saying, "Write: Blessed are the dead that die in the Lord from now on." "Yes," says the Spirit, "so that they can rest from their toil, because their deeds follow them."

- 16:15 "Look, I am coming like a thief! Blessed is he who stays alert and guards his clothing, lest he have to walk about naked and people see his shameful state."
- 19:9 And he said to me, "Write, 'Blessed are those who have been invited to the banquet of the wedding of the Lamb!'"
- 20:6 *Blessed* and holy is he that has a part in the first resurrection. Upon them the second death has no authority, but they shall be priests of God and of Christ and they shall reign with Him for a thousand years.
- 22:7 "And look, I am coming suddenly! Blessed is the one keeping the words of the prophecy of this book."
- 22:14 "Blessed are they that do His commands, so that the right will be theirs to the tree of life, and that they might enter through the gates into the city."

Each of these blessings after 1:3 are explanations and development of the blessedness promised in 1:3. These are for victors. This is the happiness promised if you will do what is written in Revelation.

These blessings are all the more significant because the time is *near*.[78] This does not mean that it must happen within a certain number of years. In Hebrews 1:2 and James 5:3 we learn that we are in the "last days." In 1 John 2:18 it is even said that we are in the "last hour." The Lord could return at any time. In that sense, biblical prophecy speaks of His return as *near*. The theologians would say that His return is "imminent."

The idea that His return is imminent can be illustrated by a person running along the top of a short steep cliff, below which a cool lake offers a refreshing break from the exercise of running. How long will the runner run along the top of the cliff, before suddenly deciding that it is time to cool off in the refreshing water of the lake? A strong and dedicated runner might run for hours, and then suddenly jump into the lake. Another runner might only run for a few minutes, and then suddenly jump. He could jump at any time. And the Lord could return at any time.

As explained in the introduction to this commentary, the Preterist approach to the interpretation of the Book of Revelation claims support for its views from the word here translated *near*.[79] The Preterist would tell us that if the time is *near* in 1:3, then the coming of the Lord, as described in Revelation, must have been soon for those readers. They say that the coming of the Lord described throughout the Book of Revelation could not be a Second Coming that has been delayed nearly 2000 years.

The Preterist says the coming of the Lord was a "cloud coming" which they suppose happened in Jerusalem in the 70 AD when the Romans defeated the rebellious Jewish forces and destroyed the temple. They say that at that point in history the Lord "came in the clouds" to judge Israel. But the Partial Preterist (i.e. the Preterist that says that the "cloud coming" in 70 AD fulfills some of Revelation's prophecies but a still to come Second Coming will fulfill Revelation 19-21) deals with the word *near* inconsistently in 1:3 and 22:10. In both texts it should have the same meaning, since these two passages are clearly functioning as a pair of "bookends" for the entire book. The term *near* in both verses must refer to something that is *near* in the prophetic sense, imminent, something which we all long for and always await with an expectant attitude. Passages like Matthew 24:42, 44; 25:10-13; Mark 13:32-37; and 1 Peter 4:7 all remind us that because the Lord could appear at any time, we should live our lives accordingly. Note especially James 5:8-9, which speaks of the nearness of the coming of the Lord with the image of someone standing at the door. Someone standing at the door can enter the room at any time. His entrance into the room is imminent.

2. Greetings (1:4-8)

Although this is apocalyptic literature, it has elements of both prophetic and epistolary style. These verses look like the greetings of an epistle. Normally, the greetings in Greek letters were concise and plain. However, these greetings are full of meaning and worthy of careful study.

1:4 John, to the seven churches in the province of[80] Asia:[81] Grace to you and peace from God[82] who is, and who was, and who is coming,[83] and from the seven spirits before His throne,

According to these greetings, this book is addressed to the *seven churches* in the Roman *province of Asia*. In effect, the book is like a letter sent to them. They are *seven* literal *churches* whose locations are mentioned in 1:11; there is nothing in the context that suggests that they should be understood as *seven* ages in European or western church history. See the discussion of this issue in the introduction to section II., "What is now" (2:1-3:22).

There were other *churches* in the Roman *province of Asia*, for instance in Colossae, Troas, and Hierapolis, which were not mentioned as recipients of the Book of Revelation. The Lord's reasons for including some and excluding others is not clear. However, we do know that the *seven churches* that were chosen were all located along a Roman postal road. Anyone wanting to communicate with the *churches* of *the province of Asia* would sail into the harbor of Ephesus, and then follow that Roman postal road from Ephesus to Smyrna, and on to each of the other *churches*, in the order given in Revelation 2-3. Furthermore, Ramsay suggests that each of those *seven churches* was most likely well-situated as a distribution hub to further distribute copies that they would have made of the Book of Revelation to *churches* in their own "secondary districts." In that way the *churches* of the entire *province of Asia* would have quickly and easily received copies of the Book of Revelation.[84]

There may have been other reasons the Lord selected those particular *seven churches*. Perhaps *John* had special responsibilities in each of those *seven churches*. Perhaps "by coincidence" representatives of those *seven churches* were on their way to visit *John* on Patmos. As discussed in the Introduction, the number *seven* suggests a perfection or completion.[85] In any case, all through the ages there have been *churches* like those *seven churches*.

Most of Paul's letters[86] also began with greetings that included *grace and peace*. If the greeting *grace* has a Greek sound to it,[87] the greeting *peace* has a Hebrew sound to it, as a translation of the Hebrew "shalom." The blessings of *grace and peace* come from the triune God, much as in 2 Corinthians 13:14.

Concerning the expression *from God who is, and who was, and who is to come*, the Jerusalem Targum[88] translation of the name of God[89] in Exodus 3:14 is "I am He that is and that will be," but in its comment on Deuteronomy 32:29 the Name is translated "I am He who is, and who was, and I am who will be."[90] Note the comments on this verse in the section entitled "Revelation and Systematic Theology."

Because ancient Greek did not have different uppercase and lowercase letters, we cannot be absolutely certain whether *the seven spirits* refers to the seven-fold Spirit of *God* or to *seven* creatures that were before God's throne. However, because *God* the Father was mentioned right before them, and the Lord Jesus is mentioned right after them, it is almost certain that the expression *the seven spirits* refers to the seven-fold Spirit of *God*.

In Revelation, *the seven spirits*[91] are mentioned four times: here and in 3:1; 4:5; and 5:6. Although we often read that the four creatures, the 24 elders, and the many angels all worship the Lord, it is never said that *the seven spirits* worship the Lord. That makes perfect sense if indeed the seven spirits is the Holy Spirit, who does not worship the Lord.

This interpretation is strengthened by the existence of *God* the Father and Jesus in parallel form in the same verse.[92] It also seems appropriate that the

Holy Spirit is meant here, because while angels might be a *channel* of *grace and peace*, they would not be the *source* of *grace and peace*.

1:5   and from Jesus Christ, the faithful witness, the firstborn[93] from the dead, and the ruler of the kings of the earth. To Him who loves us and has washed[94] us from our sins by His blood,

Since this revelation is from Him (as in 1:1-2; 22:16, and 20), and it may demand a great deal from its readers, it is good to know that He is *the faithful witness* who has risen from the *dead*. If the believers in Smyrna have to be *faithful* all the way to death, they will be greatly assured to know that *Jesus Christ* is *the firstborn from the dead*. 1 Corinthians 15:20 would also be a great comfort to the persecuted congregation.

Since it is often *the kings of the earth* that persecute people, it will also be a great comfort to know that, despite all appearances, the Lord *Jesus* is *the ruler of the kings of the earth*. When the name of the Lord *Jesus* is mentioned, praise overflows from John's heart.[95] Further, it is He that *loves us and has washed us from our sins by His blood*. In the original language the word "love" is in the Present Tense, meaning that the Lord *Jesus* continually loves us.

His love was most perfectly proved when He *washed us from our sins by his blood*. This is the Gospel, a Gospel not only of forgiveness, but also of cleansing *from our sins*.

The theme of redemption is frequent in this book. See, for instance 5:9, 12; 7:14; 12:11; 13:8; 14:3-4; and 19:13.

1:6   and has made us to be a kingdom, priests before God, even His Father – to Him be the glory and the power for ever and ever! Amen.

This introductory passage will bring up so many of the things John will describe later. Here John is following the example of the four creatures and the 24 elders in worshiping the Lord Jesus. John's praise here is very similar to the praise in 5:10, which reads, "And for our God You made them kings and priests, and they shall reign upon the earth."

The expression *a kingdom, priests before God* comes from Exodus 19:5-6, "And now if hearing you hear My voice, and you keep My covenant, then you will be My possession out of all the peoples which are Mine in all the earth. And you will be for Me a Kingdom of priests and a holy people."

We know, however, that the nation of Israel did not obey Him fully, and they did not keep His covenant. Now, to a people whose hearts have been transformed from hearts of stone to hearts of flesh, the offer is renewed. See the comments on "You made them kings and priests" in 5:10.

1:7   Look,[96] He is coming with the clouds, and every eye will see Him, even those who pierced Him; and all the tribes[97] of the earth will mourn because of Him. Yes, amen.[98]

This verse draws upon two Old Testament passages, Daniel 7:13 and Zechariah 12:10.[99] In Daniel 7:13 the prophet sees the Messiah coming "with the clouds of heaven." *Clouds* are often associated with the coming of God, as in Deuteronomy 33:26; Psalm 104:3; and Isaiah 19:1.

In Zechariah 12:10 it is written that all the people of Jerusalem "will see Him whom they pierced and mourn for Him…" The mourning limited to the people of Jerusalem in Zechariah 12:10 here extends to *all the tribes of the earth*. It is surely not a coincidence that we will read of Jews and also people from every tribe that will repent and believe in the Lord Jesus.

When the Lord Jesus came the first time, He was seen by thousands of people in an area of the Middle East. But when He comes again, *every eye will see Him*, including *those who pierced Him*.

With a *yes* and an *amen*, John enthusiastically looks forward to the end of evil and the beginning of the Kingdom of God on earth, just as he does in 22:20.

1:8   "I am the Alpha and the Omega,"[100] says the Lord God, "who is, and who was, and who is coming, the Almighty."[101]

The term *God* is not used of the Lord Jesus in the Book of Revelation, though as was discussed in the section "Revelation and Systematic Theology," He is clearly divine, in the highest sense of the word. This is *God* the Father speaking. Likewise in 1:4 the expression *who is, and who was, and who is coming* is used of the Father, and in 4:8 the title *the Lord God Almighty* is used of the Father. However, in 22:13 the Lord Jesus is *the Alpha and the Omega*, and His coming has just been mentioned in 1:7 above. Also, the Lord Jesus is "the Beginning and the End" in 1:17. These ideas are developed more in the section entitled "Revelation and Systematic Theology."

The use of *Alpha and Omega* clarifies that the sovereignty of *God* is for all ages throughout time. Perhaps today He would say "A and Z." *God* already existed before the beginning and will still exist after the end. In 21:6 the same expression is used and is completed with the words "the Beginning and the End." The expressions *the Alpha and the Omega* and "the Beginning and the End" seem to be rooted in the expression "I am the first and I am the last" in Isaiah 44:6; and 48:12 (note also the closely related Isaiah 41:4).

The expression *the Lord God Almighty* is used in the Septuagint to translate the expression "God of the Universe" in the Old Testament. The use of this expression speaks of the sovereignty of *God*. This emphasis on God's sovereignty is closely tied not only to the judgment that will fall upon the earth in the last days, but also to the commands given to us in chapters two and three.

B. The Vision (1:9-20)

1. Background of the Vision (1:9-11)

This event happened when John was on a certain island in the Aegean Sea. This is different from myths and legends, which have vague origins. This vision happened at a specific place, at a specific time.

> 1:9   I, John, your brother and partner in the affliction and kingdom and endurance in Christ Jesus, was on the island called Patmos on account of the word of God and because of the testimony of Jesus Christ.

John introduces himself as their *brother and partner in the affliction and kingdom and endurance in Christ Jesus*. Perhaps theologians and interpreters of Scripture are disappointed that he did not use the more clear expression "John, the Apostle," but perhaps to encourage the original readers, who were already suffering or would soon suffer persecution, John just uses his name, without any reminder of his high prestige as apostle. The Lord *Jesus*, who already suffered and won the victory over death, gives His word to the original readers through the Apostle John, who also suffered.

Although *John* never mentions his own name in the Gospel of John, the situation here is different. He gives us his name. Since we know that he spent many of his last years in Ephesus, his name would have been especially well-known to these seven cities in the province of Asia.

The theme of *affliction* and *endurance* comes up here, and will be a major ongoing theme in the book.

The island of *Patmos* and its harbor are on the sailing routes between Rome and Ephesus. Its harbor is about 105 kilometers (65 miles) from Ephesus.[102] *Patmos* is about 4100 hectares (16 square miles) in area.

John was there *on account of the word of God and because of the testimony of Jesus*. Some might say this means he was there to evangelize, but that is unlikely, given how out of the way the place was. In accord with later traditions,[103] the most natural understanding of this text was that he was exiled there because of his Christian ministry, but actual historical evidence outside the Book of Revelation that people were ever punished by exile to the island of Patmos is lacking.[104]

By using the expression *on account of the word of God and because of the testimony of Jesus*, the Apostle links himself with the martyrs of 6:9; 12:11; and 20:4, all of who are said to have been martyred *on account of*[105] *the word* and also *on account of the testimony*.

1:10   I was in the Spirit[106] on the Lord's Day, and behind me I heard a loud voice like a trumpet,

The expression *the Lord's Day* is very rarely used in the New Testament and thus is hard to interpret. In the Old Testament (for example, Amos 5:18) the expression "The Day of the Lord" is used, referring to the end of the Age. Here it seems to refer to Sunday.[107] Mounce[108] explains that just as the Romans celebrated Caesar's Day, so the Christians celebrated *the Lord's Day*. The only other choice would be the Day of the Lord as in the end of the age, but there is a better way to say that in Greek,[109] and at this point in John's experience he is only an apostle exiled on Patmos, not a time traveler into the Day of the Lord, which he will become!

1:11   saying "That which you see, write[110] on a scroll and send it to the seven churches: to Ephesus, and to Smyrna, and to Pergamum, and to Thyatira, and to Sardis, and to Philadelphia, and to Laodicea."

John is commanded to record the visions that he will see. This book is not the result of John's environment or situation. It is the result of actual visions given to him by the Lord Jesus Christ. Understanding this significantly influences the interpretation of this book.

This is the first place the actual *churches* that were to receive this book are listed. See the comments under 1:4, where we first learned that *the seven churches* are the recipients of this revelation. This command to *write* will be repeated and elaborated upon in 1:19.

2. The Vision (1:12-20)

This is the core of the revelation of Christ, around which the entire book revolves. This vision is the most recent "portrait" of the Lord Jesus Christ, and is worth studying with great care. There are details of this "portrait" that are hard for us to understand, but some of them are clarified in 1:20–3:22.

1:12 And then I turned to see the voice that was speaking to me. And turning I saw seven golden lampstands,

We might find it odd that John writes as though he could *see* a *voice*, but it is a completely understandable expression.[111]

As the Lord Himself explains in 1:20, the *seven golden lampstands* symbolize the *seven* churches mentioned above.

1:13 and in the midst of the seven[112] lampstands, someone like[113] a son of man, wearing a full-length robe with a golden sash wrapped around His chest.

Verses 13-18 are the background for the descriptions that the Lord uses of Himself in the beginning of all but one of the seven messages[114] of chapters two and three, descriptions that are appropriate for the special needs or characteristics of each of the churches.

The interpreter has to be very careful so that his interpretation is not unfounded and random. What is clear and certain in this vision is that Christ is glorious, so glorious that the apostle John himself falls down at His feet. Do not let the discussion of the interpretation of the text take away from the sense of awe apparent in this text.

Verse 13 is interpreted with the help of verse 20 where the Lord Jesus says "the seven lampstands are the seven churches." So this text means that the Lord Jesus is *in the midst* of His churches. He is *in the midst*. How true this is! The Lord walks *in the midst of* the churches, He is present. We must always remember this, or we will grow cold in our hearts, even if we continue to outwardly serve Him well as happened the church in Ephesus (Revelation 2:1) when they left their first love.

The term *son*[115] used here often has a non-literal meaning, as in the following:
- "followers" in Matthew 12:27 (translated "your people" in the NIV, it is more literally "your sons"); and 1 Peter 5:13 (Peter refers to Mark as "my son")
- "members of a large group" as in Mark 3:28 ("all the sins and blasphemies of the sons of men"); Acts 13:26 ("sons of the race of Abraham"); and Ephesians 3:5 (translated "other generations" in the NIV, it is more literally "the sons of men")
- someone that very much resembles someone else can be called the "son" of that person, as in Matthew 13:38 ("The weeds are the sons of the evil one") and Acts 13:10 (Paul calls Elymas the sorcerer a "son of the devil.")

The Lord Jesus is called "the Son of God" 40 times in the New Testament with 23 of those in the Gospels (as in Matthew 26:63), "the Son of Man" 87 times in the New Testament with 83 of those in the Gospels (as in Matthew 8:20), and "the Son of David" 16 times in the New Testament all of which are in the three Synoptic Gospels (as in Matthew 22:42-45).

This expression, *son of man*, is very difficult to interpret. It has various meanings in the Old Testament:
- "mankind" in Psalm 8:4
- the Messiah, Israel, or the King of Israel in Psalm 80:17
- the prophet Ezekiel himself over 90 times in Ezekiel
- the prophet Daniel himself in Daniel 8:17
- "one like a son of man, coming with the clouds of heaven" in Daniel 7:13 (That same Person is mentioned by the Lord Himself in Matthew 24:30, "They will see the Son of Man coming on the clouds of the sky, with power and great glory.")

Clearly, this is the Lord Jesus Himself. Perhaps many of these possible interpretations merge together, because the Lord Jesus is a prophet, He is a *man*,[116] and He is Messiah. There is no contradiction in His three identities.

The expression here, *someone like a son of man*, does not use the same grammar as the expression "the Son of Man" in the Gospels.[117] The expression here in Revelation 1:13 is more like the expression in Daniel 7:13. That connections is further strengthened by Matthew 24:30 where, as noted above, the Lord quotes Daniel 7:13 as a reference to Himself, "the Son of Man."

In Daniel 10:5-9 the prophet sees someone that closely resembles the vision of the Lord Jesus in Revelation 1:12-17. In these two passages the person is wearing *a golden sash* and has eyes like fire, feet like burnished bronze, and a thunderously loud voice.

According to Beasley-Murray,[118] the *full-length robe* is a *robe* that is used by people of high status like the high priest (as in Exodus 28:4), but others besides the high priest might also wear such a *robe*.[119]

In Exodus 39:29, the *sash* of the High Priest was of "finely twisted linen and blue, purple and scarlet yarn," but by the era of Josephus the *sash* of the High Priest was made of gold,[120] so this furthers the impression that the Lord was clothed as High Priest. However, it should also be noted that the angel that appeared to Daniel in Daniel 10:5-21 was dressed in about the same way as the Lord is dressed in this verse.[121]

1:14   Now His head and[122] hair were white as wool, as white as snow, and His eyes were like a flame of fire.

In Daniel 7:9 we read concerning the Ancient of Days, who is God the Father, that "the hair of His head was as pure wool," so this passage seems to connect the Father with the Son. *White hair* calls for respect in Leviticus 19:32 and Proverbs 16:31.

The congregation in Thyatira was warned that His *eyes* are *like a flame of fire*.[123] That was perhaps because the leadership there had tolerated sin, and needed to be told that He tests people's hearts (2:23). So it would seem that *eyes like a flame of fire* emphasizes that He is able to see into people's hearts.

1:15   His feet were like bronze[124] burning in a furnace, and His voice was like the sound of many waters.

Metal that is heated *in a furnace* until it is *burning* or glowing is dangerously hot. The Lord Jesus is able to bring judgment. Just as His eyes can test the hearts of men, in the same way *His feet* can enforce the judgment He makes. For this reason, the congregation in Thyatira was warned concerning *His feet*, which were *like bronze burning in a furnace*. Individuals, leaders, and congregations that do not deal with sin are warned!

The *voice* of the angel in Daniel 10:6 was "like the sound of a multitude," but the idea of a *voice like the sound of many waters* is an allusion to Ezekiel 43:2, where the *voice* of God is "like the roar of many waters." Thus the One who is pictured in Revelation 1 is indeed God and not a mere angel.[125]

1:16   And in His right hand He had[126] seven stars, and coming out of His mouth there was a sharp double-edged sword. And His face was like the sun shining in its power.

The Lord Jesus has the *seven stars* in *His right hand*. In 1:20 we learn that the *seven stars* refer to the *seven* messengers from the *seven* churches. Having them in *His right hand* might mean He has power over them, or that He is protecting them.

The picture of a *sword coming out* of a *mouth* was not strange for the people of God, because in Isaiah 49:2 the prophet says, "He set my mouth like a sharp sword...." Also, in Ephesians 6:17 and Hebrews 4:12 the Word of God is likened to a *sword*.

If the incident with the *double-edged sword* in Joshua 5:13-15 can be used to help interpret this passage, it means the Lord can help, and He can oppose, depending upon the character of the people He is dealing with.

The congregation in Pergamum needed to be reminded about this *double-edged sword* perhaps because they had the idea that the Lord was just their Savior, and would just let them sin now that He had forgiven them. Take care, that *sword* is *double-edged*, so it can be used against enemies or against followers, if there is need! Some among the congregation in Corinth had already died because they ignored this truth, according to 1 Corinthians 11:30.

We read here that *His face*[127] *was like the sun shining in its power.* Apparently His glory was so amazing that *His face* could not be looked upon any more than you might look upon *the sun shining in its power.* Similar things are also said of the Lord in Matthew 17:2[128] and an angel in Revelation 10:1.

Thus the vision of the Lord Jesus has reached its climax. The rest of what will be said in the Book of Revelation has its roots in this vision of Christ. The commands in the Book of Revelation flow from the character and will of the Lord Jesus as revealed in this chapter.

1:17   When I saw Him, I fell at His feet as though dead, and He set His right hand on me saying, "Do not fear. I am the First and the Last.

This is the most appropriate response to the glory of the Lord Jesus. Indeed, others that have experienced something like this also have fallen *at His feet as though dead.*[129]

In the midst of this glorious vision we read, too, of the grace of our Lord. See how *He set His right hand on* John and told him not to *fear.* Here in one verse the glory and mercy of God are powerfully portrayed for us. This is indeed part of the uniqueness of our faith – that we should know such a glorious God, but a God that would approach us and put *His right hand* upon us. The same *hand* that holds the seven stars can be placed upon John's shoulder in an assuring and comforting way. What a God of wonders we know!

The attitude of the Lord Jesus here is the same as His attitude in Matthew 17:7. This is also the attitude of the angel in Daniel 10:10-12.

In this verse He says *I am,*[130] an expression that reminds us of the personal name of the God of the Old Testament, often written LORD in the Old Testament portion of our Bibles. In Exodus 3:14, Moses knew God by this name. The Lord used this expression often in the four Gospels.[131]

The expression *I am the First and the Last*, also used in the Old Testament in Isaiah 44:6 and 48:12, is used of the Lord Jesus. It emphasizes His divinity. He is not merely an exceptional man, and He is not merely one of the many gods of the nations. This expression is like 1:8, "I am the Alpha and the Omega," 2:8 "the First and the Last," 21:6 "I am the Alpha and the Omega, the Beginning and the End," and 22:13, "I am the Alpha and the Omega, the First and the Last, the Beginning and the End." If these four texts are summarized, we see that the Lord Jesus is the eternal God.

> 1:18   I am the Living One; and I was dead, and look, I am alive forever and ever, amen.[132] And I have the keys of death and Hades.

The title "The First and the Last" is expanded in this verse: He is *the Living One*. This title is often found in the Old Testament[133] and New Testament,[134] as well as the writings of the rabbis.[135] He is *the Living God, the Eternal One*.

The Living One has accomplished the incomprehensible: the Eternal One was *dead*, and now He lives, *forever and ever*. Because He accomplished this, He holds *the keys of death and Hades*. He has authority over *death and Hades*, which in the past had authority over us because of our sin. This verse is remarkable. In just a few words, the Lord gives the outline of all His work on the cross and in the now empty grave.

Besides that, this verse emphasizes the deity of Christ because in that era a Jewish leader wrote, "Four keys are delivered into the hand of the Lord of the world which He has given to no ruler: the key of life, the key of the graves, the key of food, the key of rain."[136] This One who *was dead*, and is now *alive forever and ever*, has the *keys* that God never surrenders to any human ruler! Those readers that were threatened by the Roman Empire, fearing its power over their lives, need fear no longer, because their Lord and Savior holds *the keys of death and Hades*. For a few of the seven churches that would receive this Revelation, this would be vitally important.

All of this is glory enough for us to base our lives upon, but it is too hard to understand. In the next section, the Lord will take several of these descriptions about Himself, and use them in His messages to emphasize certain aspects of His character or being. So do not feel like all this is beyond you – it should be beyond you, but the Lord does want you to apply some particular parts of it in your life.

> 1:19   Write therefore what you saw,[137] what is now[138] and what will take place after these things.[139]

As was discussed in the section entitled "Overview and Structure," this verse gives the outline of the entire book. It was a command for John to *write* the vision that he just *saw*, as well as the revelation that was to follow, concerning *what is now and what will take place after these things*. As we shall soon see, that expression fits perfectly with what he will see about the situation of the seven churches in his day (chapters two and three) and the end time prophecies that follow (chapters 4-21). There are hard things to understand about the Book of Revelation, but the broad outline of the book and many specific applications to our lives are not at all hard to understand!

> 1:20 The mystery of the seven stars that you saw in My right hand and the seven golden lampstands: the seven stars are the messengers of the seven churches, and the seven lampstands are the seven churches."

The term *mystery* refers to a truth that was unknowable in the past, but is now made known. The identity of those *seven stars, the messengers of the seven churches*, needs to be considered. The term here translated *messengers*[140] is the Greek word that the English word "angel" comes from. Very often in the Word of God, the messenger that is spoken of is in fact an angel, a heavenly being. However, that is not always the case. In Matthew 11:10 this word is used of John the Baptist.[141] This word does not refer to angels here either. The word here is used of human *messengers*, rather that heavenly ones. This makes sense, because it is more likely that the Lord would have *seven* human *messengers* in His *right hand* than that He would have *seven* angels in His *right hand*. Further, in chapters two and three John is commanded to write to each of these *seven messengers*. If they were heavenly *messengers* (that is, angels), how would John deliver the scroll that he has written to them? If angels were intended here then somehow John, in exile on Patmos, would have had to ask those angels to carry the scrolls he had written to those churches. That does seem very strange. It is much simpler for us to take the basic literal meaning of this word here, and assume that *seven* human *messengers* will become available rather than that *seven* heavenly *messengers* will somehow become available. Perhaps – and this is only speculation – there were *seven* men that had been sent by the *seven* churches to visit John. Perhaps they were pastors or church leaders. John would know what to do with what he had written. If these are indeed human *messengers* visiting John on Patmos, then they would be like Epaphroditus, who was sent from Philippi to serve and encourage Paul under house arrest (Philippians 2:25 and 4:18).[142]

The symbol of the *seven golden lampstands* is a wonderful image, because *lampstands* do not shine, but they provide a place for the lamp[143] that does shine and fill the surrounding space with light. In the same way, Christ shines in the midst of the *churches*.

With this, this vision of the Lord Himself concludes. All that will be said in the remainder of the Book of Revelation has its roots here in this vision. The commands of the book are based on the Lord as He is revealed here. The most appropriate attitude for a follower of the Lord is to respond well to this vision.

II. "What is now" (2:1-3:22)

The function of this section

This section explains and applies the details of the vision we just read about, details that were hard to understand and apply on our own. The commands that must be obeyed in order for us to obtain the blessing promised in 1:3 are only found here in this section. This section is crucial for us to read, understand, and obey, if we are to be blessed, and if the Book of Revelation is to have its purpose fulfilled in our hearts.

The contents of this section

This section contains seven letters to seven churches. These are seven local churches, in seven different cities. In every age somewhere in the world, there have probably been churches very much like each of these seven churches. At any rate, in this era there are certainly churches that resemble each of these seven churches. That is probably why each message contains the exhortation, "The one who has an ear, let him hear what the Spirit says to the churches." The Lord is calling all who have "spiritual ears," that is, all who have hearts open to Him, to listen to the messages to the seven churches; if you want to be blessed, you need to obey the commands of the messages. The same, of course, applies to your church!

The structure of this section

The seven messages of this section are structured according to a careful seven-fold pattern:
  1. The Recipient
  2. The Characteristic of Christ
  3. Praise for the Church
  4. Criticism
  5. Demand

6. Warning

7. Promise

There are, however, exceptions to this seven-fold pattern. Where we would expect to find a note of praise for the congregation in Laodicea, we find none. Where we would expect to find a note of criticism for the congregation in Smyrna, we find none.

Morris[144] observes something like a chiastic[145] structure concerning the spiritual status of the seven churches. He notes that the first and the seventh churches are in grave danger, and the others as follows:

1. grave danger
    2. excellent shape
        3. middling
            4. middling
        5. middling
    6. excellent shape
7. grave danger

Some interpreters say that each church represents a period in church history. For example, the church in Ephesus, with its accurate doctrine, represents the first church at the time of the apostles. This writer rejects this kind of interpretation for the following seven reasons:

1. Western church history does not actually fit well with the flow of these seven messages.
2. We need to understand that there has been a church like each one of these congregations in every generation since Revelation was written.
3. An interpretation like this tends to draw our attention away from the application of these letters in our own lives and in our own churches.
4. Rather than reflecting supposed stages in church history, the order of the cities listed in this text simply reflects the order of those cities along a main road in their province.
5. There is not one indication within this text suggesting that the passage be interpreted allegorically.
6. There is no good answer to the question as to why western church history is prophesied in this passage, but Asian, African, and Latin American church history is ignored.

7. If this were intended, and if it were understood, then the believers in the middle ages, for instance, should have been able to look at the progression and realize that the Lord cannot come until several more "ages" of church history have passed, but we know that the Lord could have returned at any point in church history.[146]

In five of the seven messages,[147] the very first words after the Lord introduces Himself are "I know your deeds." These exact words are used each time.[148] These words probably had a different effect upon the various congregations. For those congregations whose heart and whose deeds were pleasing to the Lord, this would have been an encouragement.

Greek verbs and pronouns have different forms that show whether they are singular or plural, so in the Greek the word "you" clearly refers to one person or to more than one person. In Revelation 2-3 there are plural "yous" in 2:10, 13, 23, 24, and 25.[149] All of the other second person verbs and pronouns are singular. That can be observed with certainty from the text. The reason for this predominant use of the singular can be guessed, but not with certainty. Perhaps it is simply a stylistic matter, or perhaps the Lord is primarily addressing the "messenger" of the church, who is the leader, and He only addresses the congregation a few times. The idea that He is primarily addressing the leader of each of the congregations is appealing because it shows the importance of leadership, but against this idea is the fact that the rewards verses use the singular; would that mean that only the rewards of the leaders are mentioned? That seems unlikely. It seems best to understand that the seven messages are directed to three types of readers. Firstly, and most directly, they are addressed "to the messenger of the church," as the first words of each letter tell us. That is confirmed by the predominate use of the singular as described above. Secondly, according to 1:11, these messages were to be sent "to the seven churches: to Ephesus, and to Smyrna...." Thirdly, these messages were "what the Spirit says to the churches."

A. Message to the church in Ephesus (2:1-7)

1. The Recipient and the local situation (2:1a)

2:1a   "To the messenger of the church in Ephesus write:

As was noted above in the discussion of the previous verse, *the messenger of the church* is a better translation than "the angel of the church."

Of the seven cities mentioned in chapters two and three, *Ephesus* was the wealthiest. It was second only to Rome during this period.[150] Concerning commerce, the city of *Ephesus* was well-situated and prosperous. Transportation is crucial for commerce, and *Ephesus* was located at the mouth of the River Cayster, which made an excellent harbor, except that silt from the river made the harbor more and more shallow as the years passed, even though they deepened the harbor in 150 BC and again in 50 AD, and relocated the city several times. The people of *Ephesus* knew that their harbor, the economic lifeline of their city, was threatened by that silt. Indeed, the buildup of silt continued through the centuries, so that today the present coastline is far away from the ancient ruins of *Ephesus*. In the website dave.hagelb.org click on the "Photos" tab (or go directly to www.flickr.com/photos/davehag/sets/) to view and download many photographs of ancient Ephesus and the other sites of the seven churches of Revelation 2 and 3.

Besides water transportation, three major roads met in *Ephesus*: one from Mesopotamia; another from Galatia; and a third from the Maeander Valley. The markets of *Ephesus* must have been filled with all sorts of local and foreign products.

The first Roman governors would arrive from Rome by ship and use Ephesus' harbor, because there were no other suitable harbors in the new province. This became a point of pride for the Ephesians. When in the second century the harbor was silting up, the city of Smyrna took the opportunity to apply to be the new port of landing for official Roman visits, but their request was denied, and *Ephesus* retained that honor.

Two Roman coins from *Ephesus* express the pride they felt about that honor. The first has a Roman warship on it. Its oars are clearly visible. The writing, "First Landing," indicates that the ship carried the governor to the province of Asia, and his "first landing" was always at *Ephesus*. This particular coin was minted about 245 AD, but the right of "First Landing" was much older than that.[151]

The second coin shows a merchant sailing ship. The writing "Ephesus: First in Asia" expresses Ephesian pride. At that time the only cities of the province of Asia that had harbors were *Ephesus* and Smyrna.[152] Only their coins had ships on them.

Concerning politics, *Ephesus* was foremost in the province. Political life was very stable there, and in appreciation the Roman government allowed them to govern themselves. *Ephesus* was given the status of "free city," and Roman troops were not stationed there. Also, the Roman Emperor honored *Ephesus* on a routine basis because the Roman-appointed governor set up a routine court for the cases that were important to *Ephesus*. The city of *Ephesus* witnessed the luxury and activity of the Greek and Roman cultures.

The theater in *Ephesus* overlooked the harbor. It seated 25,000 people. The photograph shows the theater as seen from the street that goes to the harbor.

Concerning religion, the temple of Artemis[153] was the great pride of *Ephesus*. It was one of the seven wonders of the ancient world. It was built by King Croesus early in his reign. On one of the city's coins it was written "Ephesus, the caretaker of the temple of Artemis." Greeks would say, "As the sun crosses the sky it sees nothing more grand than the temple of Artemis." The temple was burned down by a fame-seeking arsonist on about July 21, 356 BC, at about the same time Alexander the Great was born. In 333 BC, as Alexander came through conquering the region, he offered to pay to complete the rebuilding of the temple, if they would carve his name into the temple. The great conqueror's offer was refused. According to Strabo the careful response of *Ephesus* was, "It is not fitting that one god should build a temple for another god." In about 262 AD the temple was destroyed by the Goths, and rebuilt in the fourth century. Then as Christianity grew stronger, the temple grew weaker. In the year 401 AD St John Chrysostom and some of his followers destroyed the temple, and it was not rebuilt again. In Acts 19:23-40 we can get some idea of the local pride in the temple, especially verse 35, which reads, "But settling them down, the clerk said to the crowd, 'Men of Ephesus, who is the man that does not know that the Ephesian city is the temple-keeper of the great goddess Artemis and of her image that fell from heaven?'"

There is some disagreement among ancient historians but even according to the smaller of the sets of dimensions of the temple it was an impressive 115 meters (377 feet) long by 55 meters (180 feet) wide. Its 127 columns were 20 meters (60 feet) high. In the temple there was a statue of Artemis. This statue was black, short and very coarse. In Acts 19:35 we read of the popular belief that that statue fell from heaven. With a fanatic attitude the citizens of *Ephesus* worshiped and honored an ugly statue.

In the past some people have written about temple prostitutes in the temple of Artemis, but better research indicates that the young women that were priestesses in the temple of Artemis beside the city of *Ephesus* served their brief terms in that role "with piety and decorum."[154]

Some temples in that era had what was called "the right of asylum."[155] People accused of crimes could flee to a temple with this right, and as long as they stayed within the clearly defined area of asylum, they could not be seized or harmed. Through all the centuries of its existence, the temple of Artemis just outside the city of *Ephesus* was a famous asylum. The safety which it offered was called "salvation."[156] Rarely was this right violated, but in 88 BC Mithridates IV ordered the killing of some Romans within the asylum of Artemis. At one point in time the asylum area was defined by the distance of one bowshot from the roof of the temple, but for a time that distance was doubled. That brought some of the city of *Ephesus* into the area of asylum, with the result that leaders in organized crime could live comfortably there. Because of this, the "salvation" that the temple provided actually increased the crime rate for *Ephesus*![157]

The Ephesian enthusiasm for magic was well-known in the ancient world.[158] Acts 19:17-20 tells about how the new converts there burned fifty thousand drachmas worth of magic scrolls, the equivalent of about US$ 10,000. Another way to understand the value given there was that a drachma was the cost of one sheep, so the value of the scrolls burned that day was the same as the value of fifty thousand sheep.

There were also temples in *Ephesus* dedicated to the worship of the Roman emperor.

Concerning the population, there were several different ethnic groups in *Ephesus*. Many years prior to the writing of Revelation the local people were subjugated by some Athenians, whose descendants were still there. There were probably many Jews as well.[159] *Ephesus* was an unusual city. The citizens of *Ephesus* would be tempted to glory in the luxury of their city.

Ephesus, as an excellent transportation hub, would have been strategic for Paul. According to Christian tradition, several years after Paul sent Tychicus to *Ephesus*, John himself moved there, and served there until his banishment to Patmos. We can read about the Gospel ministry in *Ephesus* in Acts 19-20; 1 Corinthians 15:32; 16:8; 1 Timothy 1:3; 2 Timothy 1:18; and 4:12.

Today there are only ruins in *Ephesus*. The Cayster River brought so much silt that what had been a valuable harbor became a field of reeds. The place that was full of activity and wealth has become very quiet today. It is a destination for tourists that have read this message and Paul's letter, and want to see the ruins of the city of *Ephesus*.

2. The Characteristic of Christ (2:1b)

2:1b   ...this is what[160] the One who holds[161] the seven stars in His right hand and who walks in the midst of the seven golden lampstands says:

As was discussed in the comments under 1:20, *the seven stars* were the *seven* messengers of the churches, and *the seven golden lampstands* were the churches themselves.

He *holds the seven stars in His right hand*. This seems to speak of protection and care, in accord with John 10:28-29. If these were church leaders sent as messengers from the churches to visit John, they would be encouraged by the fact that they are held *in His right hand*. If they are church leaders, they will need encouragement as they face the challenges that the Lord brings before them in these *seven* messages, chapters two and three.

The Lord *walks* among *the seven lampstands*, He is personally present. Whether the church is strong or weak, confident or afraid, large or small, He is there. By identifying Himself this way in this letter, He is saying that for some reason the Ephesians, and all other Christians that are like them, need to keep this truth in mind. As we read more of this message we will understand why this is so.

3. Praise for the Church (2:2-3)

2:2-3   I know your deeds, your labor,[162] and your endurance, and that you cannot bear evil men, and that you have tested those who say they are apostles but are not, and you have found them to be liars. And you have steadfastness and have endured for My name, and have not become weary.

The congregation is praised for their *labor* and for their rejection of false *apostles*. They held firmly to sound doctrine, and the Lord praised them for that. What the Lord Jesus says as praise for the Ephesian church is similar to what is said in 1 Thessalonians 1:3, but there is an important difference. The Thessalonian church had work produced by faith, *labor* prompted by love and *endurance* inspired by hope, but the Ephesian church only had their *deeds*, their *labor*, and their *endurance*.

What Paul prophesied in Acts 20:29-31 (that savage wolves would attack the congregation with false teachings) did happen. The false *apostles* realized the importance of the city of Ephesus as well. Some interpreters try to determine the identity of *those who say they are apostles, but are not*, but any certainty concerning their identity was lost many centuries ago. It is not impossible that "followers of Nicolaus" (2:6) are referred to here, but again there is no certainty about their identity or number.

In any case, this church has been steadfast and has *endured* for His *name*. They are active in service and pure in their doctrine. They have rejected false teaching and the teachers that brought it. The teachers in the church in Ephesus taught sound doctrine. The Lord Jesus praised their activity and their *endurance*. But as Mounce notes, "Every virtue carries within itself the seeds of its own destruction."[163]

Sound doctrine is important, and their doctrine was sound. This does not go unnoticed by the Lord. Not only is sound doctrine important, but it is important for the leadership to protect the congregation from so-called *apostles* that bring their lies. The leadership in the church in Ephesus had also done well in this, and is praised accordingly. Many a Christian is looking for a church like this, and many a pastor would be delighted to pastor a church like this! However....

4. Criticism (2:4)

2:4   But I have against you, that[164] you have abandoned your first love. The Lord's words of praise were many and detailed, and His words of criticism were few. Even so, these few words hit hard, if we understand the importance of *love* in the Christian life. They left their *first love*. This was no small issue for the Lord; it was not something He wanted to overlook. They were like Martha, not Mary, in Luke 10:38-42. "Martha, Martha, you are anxious and troubled about many things, but one thing is lacking. Now, Mary has chosen the good part, which will not be taken away from her."

At *first* they doubtless had a deep *love* for the Lord, but as time went on they somehow made a subtle shift – their minds became more and more interested in sound doctrine, and their hearts became less and less interested in the Lord Jesus Himself.

So, the reason the Lord reminds this congregation that He walks in the midst of the seven golden lampstands is so that they will remember that He is a real person in their midst, and not just the primary subject of their sound doctrine.

This *love* is probably especially a *love* for the Lord Jesus, but *love* of God is not easily separated from the *love* of man, as 1 John 4:20 reminds us, "If anyone says, 'I love God,' and hates his brother, he is a liar; for how can the one not loving his brother whom he has seen love God whom he has not seen?" Any congregation or individual like this would do well to carefully read 1 Corinthians 13.

Every Christian that is serious about sound doctrine and serious Bible study should ask, "Have I lost my first love?" Indeed, being a careful student of the Word and of sound doctrine could be spiritually dangerous. In the matter of *love*, do not let yourself become like these Ephesians.

5. Demand (2:5a)

2:5a   Therefore remember from whence you have fallen, and repent and do those first deeds.

The demand or command that the Lord gives to the Ephesians is straightforward and simple. There is nothing here that is intellectually challenging, simply *remember*, *repent*, and *do*. However, this is not an easy thing to do, if you have left your first love. None of the things the seven churches are commanded to do were easy for that particular church.

We do not know *from whence* they had *fallen*, but the Ephesian congregation that Paul wrote to about three decades earlier seemed to be a healthy congregation.

It is clear this is spoken to real believing Christians. If it were spoken to people with a so-called "mere intellectual assent" but without "saving faith,"[165] the Lord would not have called them to *remember from whence you have fallen*, nor would He have spoken of *those first deeds*. The clear meaning here is that these are real born-again believers that have left their devotion to the person of Jesus Christ, and have grown in pure doctrine, and that these people need to go back to what they had in the earlier years. The command to *repent* here is not a call to come to saving faith in Christ, but to turn away from the spiritual coldness that has wrapped up their hearts.

6. Warning (2:5b)

2:5b   But if not, I am coming to you suddenly[166] and will remove your lampstand from its place, if you do not repent.

This text explains what will happen *if* the demand is not met, in other words, it explains what the threat is behind the demand. *If* they *do not repent*, this will happen.

Bauckham[167] observes that the expression *I am coming*, in this form,[168] is used seven times in the Book of Revelation, and each time it is spoken by the Lord Himself, and always in the context of promise or threat.

We know from 1:20 that the *lampstand* symbolizes the congregation. It is a place for the Light of the World. If they do not do as He requires, He *will remove* the church, and Ephesus will go dark. Perhaps the members of the congregation and their descendants will continue to gather on Sundays for generations to come, but in the years to come it will no longer be a *lampstand*; the Light will no longer shine from it.[169] The Lord could do this through persecution, or lack of effective evangelism even towards their own children, so that eventually there would no longer be a Christian congregation in Ephesus. Somehow or other, He will come and see to it that there is no longer a *lampstand* in Ephesus. That is how strongly He desires them to return to their first love!

What had become their pride, that the teaching of the church in Ephesus was so pure, would be taken away by Jesus himself if they did not repent. This is what happens to pure doctrine when it is not accompanied by love!

It is possible that the threat of having the Lord *remove* their *lampstand* was all the more vivid to the Ephesians, who had to move their city several times because their harbor was silting up.[170]

According to Ignatius' letter to Ephesus, they did repent, so that this threat was not realized, or its realization was postponed.[171]

Praise (continued) (2:6)

2:6 But this you have, that you hate the deeds of the Nicolaitans, which I also hate.

Almost as though He does not want to end their assessment on a negative note, the Lord also praises them specifically in the matter of how they handled the *Nicolaitans*.

The Nicolaitans' identity simply cannot be established with any certainty at all. Some say that they were followers of the Nicolas that was chosen for church ministry in Jerusalem (Acts 6:5), who they say later embraced false doctrine. This is in accord with some traditions of the early church, but there were church fathers that did not agree with this. Others say the term *Nicolaitans* is from two Greek words that mean "victory" and "people"[172] because this group defeats the people with false teachings. Both of these possibilities are very speculative. Perhaps the *Nicolaitans* were so named because they were followers of some otherwise unknown man named Nicolas, but we simply do not know,[173] and we do not need to know. The Ephesians knew, and took some comfort in this praise from the Lord, even as they faced His criticism.

7. Promise (2:7)

2:7 The one who has an ear, let him hear what the Spirit says to the churches. To the victor,[174] I will give to eat from the tree of life, which is in the paradise of My[175] God.

At the end of each of the seven messages (prior to the promise in the first three messages, and after the promise in the last four) the exhortation *to the one who has an ear* is given. Perhaps this is just an exhortation to everyone, because everyone has a physical *ear*, but since the content to be heard is *what the Spirit says*, it seems more likely to refer to "spiritual ears," like the ears of Ezekiel 12:2, in which Ezekiel is told, "Son of man, you dwell in the midst of a rebellious house which has eyes to see but they do not see; they have ears to hear, but they do not hear...." This connection is all the more likely because the Lord Jesus used that expression from Ezekiel in Mark 4:9, 23; Luke 8:8; and 14:35. Note also Deuteronomy 29:4; Isaiah 43:8; and Jeremiah 5:21.

If this is the correct understanding, then this is a call to all whose hearts are open to these words in the Book of Revelation, which are not merely written on the page of the Bible before you, they are also being spoken by *the Spirit* to your heart. Furthermore, it is to *hear what the Spirit says to the churches*, not just to the one church that we are in. What is said to the church in Smyrna needs to be heard also by the church in Philadelphia. All believers are to pay close attention to all seven of the messages. Perhaps only one of the seven is particularly applicable to you, but you are to listen to all of them.

In 2:5b there was the warning, "if you do not repent." On the other hand, if they do meet the demand of Christ, if they do remember from how far they have fallen, and repent and do the things they did at first, the Lord Jesus will give them something that is beautiful and pleasing. Once again, this promise is not automatically fulfilled in the lives of everyone who believes in Jesus Christ as their Savior, but only for each believer who obeys the commands of the Lord Jesus in these two chapters.

The reward offered here is *to eat from the tree of life, which is in the paradise of My God*. Nowhere in the whole Bible is there is a single verse that says that every believer, both those who have an unwavering faith and good deeds and those whose faith and deeds are weak, will *eat from the tree of life*. This is a special privilege of the victors. Although according to 22:2 the leaves of this *tree* are meant for the healing of the nations, the fruit is exclusively for those that are victorious (see the discussion of 22:14). This understanding fits with the use of *the tree of life* in Jewish literature outside the Word of God. *The tree of life* is mentioned in Genesis 2:9; 3:22 and 24. Once Adam and Eve fell, *the tree of life* was guarded by cherubim and a flaming sword flashing back and forth. However, when the Lord returns and distributes these gifts according to these promises, the fruit of that *tree* will be given to the victors. Here and throughout chapters two and three, victors are those that will gain the blessing that is promised in Revelation 1:3. They gain that blessing by "keeping those things written in the words of this prophecy."

In the message of the Lord Jesus to the church in Ephesus, we read that He is pleased with the purity of their doctrine, and He also acknowledges their deeds, but those deeds do not spring from a heart full of love, as they ought. To motivate them, He threatens that if they do not return to their first love, He will remove the church from Ephesus, which would make their labor useless. But if they return to their first love, then He will give them the special privilege – which will not be given to every believer – to eat from the tree of life that was long ago forbidden to Adam.

A Major Interpretational Issue:

The issue of rewards is crucial to the overall purpose of the book. We should all be victors. We should all be believers that actually obey Christ. This is required. It is imperative. No Bible teacher would deny this, but the difficulty appears as soon as we discuss what happens if believers do not obey. Some would say that if we do not obey, we are probably showing that we never really had "saving faith," that our faith was "mere intellectual assent." Others would say that if we do not obey, then sooner or later we might lose our salvation.

So many things are offered to victors at the close of each of these seven messages. Are they meant for all truly born-again believers, or are they special rewards for obedient believers?

Those that believe in the Perseverance of the Saints (that all true believers will certainly persevere in good works all their days, as strong Calvinism teaches), will tell us that there is no such thing as a born-again Christian that seriously sins, and does not get back on track and become a faithful Christian. They do not leave room for the idea of a carnal[178] Christian, as discussed by Paul in 1 Corinthians 3:1-3. In 1 Corinthians 11:30 we read "On account of that many among you are weak and sick, and quite a few have fallen asleep." Those were believers that did not properly examine themselves before taking the Lord's Supper, and they died without ever repenting. Those were believers that did not persevere. They were carnal Christians.

Those that hold that serious sin causes loss of salvation tend to believe that if you can finish your life as a saved Christian you are also a faithful Christian, because if not you would have lost your salvation.

As different as those two positions are, neither of them allows very well for three kinds of human beings:
1. solid faithful born-again believers: they will be rewarded with the promises described in the Book of Revelation
2. saved believers not serving God, and full of unconfessed sin: they will be saved but not rewarded
3. unbelievers: they are neither saved nor rewarded

But verses like 3:11 "I am coming suddenly. Hold on to what you have, so that no one takes your crown" (crowns can be taken, so beware, they are not guaranteed), 2:10 "Be faithful until death, and I will give you the crown of life" (death by martyrdom is not required of all Christians, but it is a mark of especially strong faith), 2:26 "To the victor who keeps My deeds to the end, I will give authority over the nations," and 3:4-5 "But you have a few people in Sardis who have not dirtied their clothing and they will walk with Me, clothed in white, because they are worthy," say quite clearly that these rewards are not for all believers, but only for those that faithfully follow the Lord Jesus.

The most difficult verses for this view are 2:11 "The victor will not in any way be harmed by the second death," and 3:5 "The victor, he will be clothed in white clothing. And I will never ever blot out his name from the book of life, but will acknowledge his name before My Father and before His angels." Both of these use the rather uncommon double negative, and 3:5 even provides the contrasting promise that (far from blotting their names out) Jesus will acknowledge their names before His Father and the angels. See those verses for more discussion on this.

So, it is the view of this interpreter that victors here in Revelation are believers that do God's will to the end, are faithful until death, and serve Him obediently. Not all born-again believers will be victors, but those that fulfill these requirements will be richly rewarded. As believers in the Lord Jesus Christ, we cannot lose our salvation, but we can lose these rewards. Although a discussion of this would be beyond the scope of this work, this position is in harmony with the rest of the New Testament teachings on our salvation.

B. Message to the church in Smyrna (2:8-11)

1. The Recipient and the local situation (2:8a)

2:8a   And to the messenger of the church in Smyrna[179] write:

The name *Smyrna*[180] meant "myrrh." Although there were various uses of myrrh, its main use was in embalming the dead.

The city of *Smyrna* is still inhabited today, but its name is "Izmir." *Smyrna* had, and still has, an excellent harbor. In time of war it was easily defended because its opening to the sea was relatively narrow, and thus more easily defended against attackers. *Smyrna* was famous as a wealthy and beautiful city. And like Ephesus, they had good roads. The largest theater in the province of Asia was located there.[181] They had beautiful streets, lined with many trees. The residents of *Smyrna* considered their city to be the most beautiful in the province. Hemer[182] notes that the idea of crowns[183] comes up quite a bit in the study of ancient *Smyrna*. Such crowns or wreaths were presented as awards for civic service, athletic victory, or other honors.

In *Smyrna* there were temples for the worship of Sybil, Apollo, Asklepios, Aphrodite, Zeus, and of course Caesar. In fact, they considered themselves to be the most committed to the worship of Caesar in the whole province. In 195 BC *Smyrna* was the first city to build a temple to the honor of "The Goddess of Rome," and in about 23 BC *Smyrna* outdid ten other cities in the province to gain the permission of Rome to build a temple to the honor of Tiberius.[184] Thus believers in *Smyrna* could see the extravagance of the religions of Greece and Rome all around their city.

The duty to worship Caesar was a serious threat for believers. Even before the worship of Caesar became mandatory, it was already fairly popular. Rome did not want its Caesars worshiped for religious reasons, but for political reasons. The Roman Empire was vast, and included many different nations and people groups. Although many were quite content under Rome (certainly there were benefits like peace, good laws, and good roads to distant markets) among so many there were others that wanted independence, and would fight to gain it. The Roman government took this as a serious problem, and Caesar worship was meant to help. Some people had been worshiping "The Goddess of Rome" spontaneously, and Caesar worship was simply a more concrete expression of the same worship.

As noted in the section titled "Date of Writing" in the Introduction, it seems that emperor worship became mandatory during the reign of Domitian. The Roman government did not require this to test the spirituality of its people, but to test their loyalty to Rome. After doing the required worship, people were free to leave and worship any god or combination of gods they pleased. However, the congregation in *Smyrna* rightly was not willing to use the title "Lord" for anyone but the Lord Jesus. They may have actually been the most loyal subjects of Rome, with whom Rome should have been very pleased, but the law demanded of them the one thing they could not give.

Polycarp was bishop of *Smyrna*, and in his youth he had probably been a disciple of the aged Apostle John. He may have been a young man in the congregation in *Smyrna* when they received the Lord's message. His own letter to the congregation in Philadelphia repeatedly brings up the themes of suffering and resurrection, perhaps reflecting the emphasis of those themes in the Lord's message to *Smyrna*.[185] About sixty years after Revelation was written, he became the twelfth martyr of *Smyrna* and Philadelphia.[186] It was a holiday in *Smyrna*, and a mob was calling upon the authorities to seize Polycarp and require him to worship Caesar. The mob, including Jews (even though it was a Sabbath day), gathered wood for the fire. He was told he must either burn the incense and say "Caesar is Lord," or be burned alive. His response still echoes in the hearts of those that love the Lord Jesus: "Already eighty and six years I have served Christ, and He has never wronged me. How could I possibly blaspheme my King who has saved me?" After he was tied to the firewood, he prayed, "I praise you that You by Your grace consider me worthy to receive such as in this morning and at this hour is happening, so that I may be brought into the group of martyrs, in Your cup."[187] Faithful Christians would die like Polycarp rather than worship Caesar. However there also were those that renounced Christ.

Look again at the words of Polycarp as he was dying, the words of this disciple of John. Did he think that all believers would be given to sit on the thrones of Revelation 20:4, which mentions the souls of those who had been beheaded because of their testimony for Jesus? Or did he understand that only those who were faithful until death would sit on those thrones?

The following two letters were written around 112 AD. The first letter was written to the emperor Trajan by Pliny, the Governor of the province of Bithynia, in the north of Asia Minor.[188]

Pliny's Letter to the Emperor Trajan

> It is my practice, my lord,[189] to refer to you all matters concerning which I am in doubt. For who can better give guidance to my hesitation or inform my ignorance? I have never participated in trials of Christians. I therefore do not know what offenses it is the practice to punish or investigate, and to what extent. And I have been not a little hesitant as to whether there should be any distinction on account of age or no difference between the very young and the more mature; whether pardon is to be granted for repentance, or, if a man has once been a Christian, it does him no good to have ceased to be one; whether the name itself, even without offenses, or only the offenses associated with the name are to be punished.
>
> Meanwhile, in the case of those who were denounced to me as Christians, I have observed the following procedure: I interrogated these as to whether they were Christians; those who confessed I interrogated a second and a third time, threatening them with punishment; those who persisted I ordered executed. For I had no doubt that, whatever the nature of their creed, stubbornness and inflexible obstinacy surely deserve to be punished. There were others possessed

of the same folly; but because they were Roman citizens, I signed an order for them to be transferred to Rome.

Soon accusations spread, as usually happens, because of the proceedings going on, and several incidents occurred. An anonymous document was published containing the names of many persons. Those who denied that they were or had been Christians, when they invoked the gods in words dictated by me, offered prayer with incense and wine to your image, which I had ordered to be brought for this purpose together with statues of the gods, and moreover cursed Christ--none of which those who are really Christians, it is said, can be forced to do--these I thought should be discharged. Others named by the informer declared that they were Christians, but then denied it, asserting that they had been but had ceased to be, some three years before, others many years, some as much as twenty-five years.[190] They all worshiped your image and the statues of the gods, and cursed Christ.

They asserted, however, that the sum and substance of their fault or error had been that they were accustomed to meet on a fixed day before dawn and sing responsively a hymn to Christ as to a god, and to bind themselves by oath, not to some crime, but not to commit fraud, theft, or adultery, not falsify their trust, nor to refuse to return a trust when called upon to do so. When this was over, it was their custom to depart and to assemble again to partake of food--but ordinary and innocent food.[191] Even this, they affirmed, they had ceased to do after my edict by which, in accordance with your instructions, I had forbidden political associations. Accordingly, I judged it all the more necessary to find out what the truth was by torturing two female slaves who were called deaconesses. But I discovered nothing else but depraved, excessive superstition.

I therefore postponed the investigation and hastened to consult you. For the matter seemed to me to warrant consulting you, especially because of the number involved. For many persons of every age, every rank, and also of both sexes are and will be endangered. For the contagion of this superstition has spread not only to the cities but also to the villages and farms. But it seems possible to check and

> cure it. It is certainly quite clear that the temples, which had been almost deserted, have begun to be frequented, that the established religious rites, long neglected, are being resumed, and that from everywhere sacrificial animals are coming, for which until now very few purchasers could be found. Hence it is easy to imagine what a multitude of people can be reformed if an opportunity for repentance is afforded.

Trajan's Letter in Reply to Pliny

> You observed proper procedure, my dear Pliny, in sifting the cases of those who had been denounced to you as Christians. For it is not possible to lay down any general rule to serve as a kind of fixed standard. They are not to be sought out; if they are denounced and proved guilty, they are to be punished, with this reservation, that whoever denies that he is a Christian and really proves it--that is, by worshiping our gods--even though he was under suspicion in the past, shall obtain pardon through repentance. But anonymously posted accusations ought to have no place in any prosecution. For this is both a dangerous kind of precedent and out of keeping with the spirit of our age.

Other passages that emphasize the theme of persecution include 2:2-3, 10, 13; 3:8-10; 6:9, 11; 7:14; chapters 12-13; and 17:6.

Related to the worship of Caesar, the choices of God's people were very limited. They could deny Christ, but many of them knew they would lose their heavenly reward for doing so. Or they could try to flee. Even Polycarp left his home and went to a farm to hide, but he decided to flee no farther and was betrayed by a tortured slave. Or they could become martyrs.

So let us examine the attitude and faithfulness of the church in *Smyrna* at a time when the luxury of idolatry is contrasted with the difficulties of faithfully worshiping Christ.

2. The Characteristic of Christ (2:8b)

2:8b   ...this is what the First and the Last, who was dead and who lives, says:

He *who was dead* and *who lives* is a particularly vital expression to those that are facing martyrdom. This expression is also used in 1:17. Since He is *the first and the Last*, He existed before the world was created and will be there after the earth is destroyed. He will always be there, and He is worthy of their trust, even in the extreme pain of persecution. Their relationship with Him will outlast their pain.

To a person under persecution, it is very important to remember that the Lord Jesus is victorious over death. He is the One *who was dead* and now *lives*. Death is the final earthly result of persecution, a final result which He experienced and overcame.

If a preacher that has never suffered persecution calls upon us to stand firm and suffer for the name of Christ, he does so only with the authority of the Word. However, the Lord Jesus has even more authority than that. He has the authority of the Word, and He has the authority of personal experience. He has been through it, so He is much more able to call others to it.

3. Praise for the Church (2:9)

2:9   I know your deeds[192] and afflictions[193] and poverty[194] – but you are rich! I know the slander of those saying they are Jews and are not, but are a synagogue of Satan.

He knows their *deeds* and their *afflictions*. He knows all about the *Jews* that cause them trouble. These statements assure them that even though He is allowing them to suffer, He has not forgotten them. He knows. Many have asked through the ages, if He knows, why does He not act to relieve the suffering?[195] The answer that is given in the Book of Revelation is simply, "Be patient and faithful in your suffering, and you will receive a crown. You will reign with the King of Kings. Believe and prove your faith with steadfastness." The Book of Revelation shows us all that it is worth it to believe this and act upon it.

Because the city of Smyrna was a rich city it is at first surprising that the congregation would be poor. Perhaps they became poor because of persecution, as in Hebrews 10:34.

According to the Lord Jesus, despite their *poverty* they are actually *rich*. He is referring of course, not to worldly wealth but heavenly wealth. Their being poor and yet *rich* is in stark contrast with the congregation in Laodicea, which was physically wealthy but spiritually poor. This same teaching is often found in the New Testament,[196] but this heavenly perspective is an important aspect of the Book of Revelation, which teaches us the truth hidden by the lies of the world. Despite all that the world teaches us, *poverty* because of Christ means riches; not Caesar, but Christ is Lord; dying for the Lord is victory; and powerlessness because of Him brings authority in the coming age.

The Lord acknowledges *the slander of those saying they are Jews and are not*, and says they actually *are a synagogue of Satan*. Apparently some or all of the Jewish population of Smyrna opposed the Christians. As noted above, years later when Polycarp was martyred, the record shows that *Jews* were involved.[197] Here the Lord rejects their Jewishness as inauthentic. This seems to be like the *Jews* of John 8:31-47 and Romans 2:28-29. Physically they were descendants of Abraham, Isaac, and Jacob, but in a spiritual sense they had abandoned their right to be called *Jews* when they rejected the Jewish Messiah. The Lord's criticism of them is quite strong: they are *a synagogue of Satan*.[198]

4. Criticism

Smyrna and Philadelphia alone go uncriticized by the Lord Jesus Christ. Although this is not the same as saying they had reached some sort of sinless perfection, it is very encouraging to see that the Lord is satisfied with them, and does not see any need to bring up any of their sins.

5. Demand (2:10a)

2:10a Do not fear what you are about to suffer. Look, the devil is about to throw some of you into prison so that you might be tested,[199] and you will have affliction for ten days. Be faithful until death...[200]

This might seem like it is better called a warning, and placed in the next section, but it is not a warning because there is no "If you do not do what I demand, I will do this to you." It is just a fact that they will have to *suffer*. The demand is brief: they are required to *be faithful, even to the point of death*.

The Lord Jesus tells them that they will *suffer* persecution. Some members of their church will be thrown *into prison*. In that era, if someone was put in *prison* normally they would be tortured, or they would be left there awaiting trial or execution.[201] Unlike fines, exile, or execution, imprisonment itself was not a punishment in the Roman world.[202] It is likely this persecution was related to the worship of Caesar in Smyrna. Their condition was difficult, but the Lord Jesus asks that they face it with faithfulness and that they not be afraid. The foundation of this command is the suffering of the Lord Jesus Himself. In other words, "How is Jesus so bold to ask them to be faithful until they are killed?" He is that bold because He Himself was *faithful until death* and He lives again. The Lord Jesus is all the more able to command faithfulness like this because of His death on the cross.

Are we ready to be *faithful until death* if we are persecuted? We can be, if we remember that the Lord Jesus became the foremost example for us by submitting to *death* and then conquering *death*.

Even though there is a real supernatural person named Satan that is behind the persecution, God has a certain purpose in their suffering, that is *so that we might be tested*. The victors, those who will be victorious over their challenges and suffering, will be given great rewards; for instance, they will be seated with Christ on his throne (see 3:21). So it is fitting that they be *tested* to make certain they fulfill the conditions of faithfulness. The victors will be chosen by the Lord Jesus to rule the nations with Him during the Millennium. This is His promise: "To the victor who keeps My deeds to the end, I will give authority over the nations" (2:26).

There are many interpretations of *ten days*,[203] but it is better for the student to stay with the basic normal meaning of an expression unless the context forces the reader into a figure of speech. The words *ten days* may simply mean *ten days*! If so, the Lord was warning them so they will understand that the suffering they will experience will be limited to *ten days*. He motivates them to endure the *ten days*, without being defeated or denying Him.

Anyone who obeys the command to *be faithful until death* is a "victor who keeps My deeds to the end" (2:26). The condition that must be met to receive the reward is faithfulness. This command is very high and very difficult, but the promises that accompany it are glorious and very beautiful.

6. Warning

Smyrna alone receives no warning or threat from the Lord (though the "warning" to Philadelphia is very mildly stated). There was no need to threaten the congregation in Smyrna with the negative consequences of ongoing disobedience, because they were not being disobedient.

7. Promise (2:10b-11)

2:10b-11 ...and I will give you the crown of life.[204] The one who has an ear, let him hear what the Spirit says to the churches. The victor will not in any way be harmed by the second death.

There is irony here, because in exchange for their *death*, they will receive *the crown of life*. Furthermore, physical *death* will be painful for those that are martyred, but *the second death will not* harm them *in any way*. As people threatened with persecution, they were surely thinking about, and perhaps afraid of, the first *death*. The Lord's words here put those concerns into proper perspective.

Just as the church in Smyrna was considered poor by the world but called rich by the Lord, here He says if they are faithful until *death*, He will *give* them *the crown of life*. The city of Smyrna often held athletic competitions, and the victors received temporary crowns. But victors in the Lord receive a *crown* that does not fade. *The crown of life* is prepared specially for the believers that are "faithful until death." The Lord did not promise this reward to believers who backslide because of persecution. He promises eternal life for each one who believes, but the *crown* here is for the believer who is faithful until *death*.

The crown of life is also promised in James 1:12, "Blessed is the one who endures in trials because when he is approved, he will receive a crown of life promised by God to whomever loves Him." Both the Word of God and experience tell us that there are believers that do not "endure in trials" or love God. *The crown of life* is a reward for the believer who endures, who is faithful, who does the work of Christ to the end.

We see in 20:14 and 21:8 that *the second death* is clearly eternal hell. At first this verse seems strange to us, because we know that not a single believer in Jesus Christ will *be harmed by the second death*. However, as we look more closely at this passage, we see that the *not in any way* in Greek is a double negative,[205] so that it is very emphatic.

Loosely translated, this passage says, "The victor will not in any way be harmed by the second death. In fact, rather than being harmed by the second death, I will give him a crown of life!" This is a figure of speech used in the Greek language.[206] The Greek author that wanted to emphasize that something is big might say that it is not small. This figure of speech is used in English as well. When we say, "This meal is not cheap!" what we are really saying is that this meal is very expensive. In the same way, perhaps they will experience the first *death* but they will not at all experience *the second death*. On the contrary, they will receive joy that is beautiful and eternal.

The church in Smyrna, faithful in difficulty, is told that they are going to suffer persecution. The wealth of this world is not promised to them. They are asked to endure suffering. The Lord Jesus promises a beautiful reward, *the crown of life*, if they are faithful in that persecution.

This reward is specially worded for those who are facing persecution and perhaps *death* at the hands of God's enemies. He does not tell them how they might escape that pain. Instead He tells them that in giving up their physical life, they will gain a *crown of life*.

Other verses promising various crowns for special faithfulness would include 1 Corinthians 9:25; James 1:12; 1 Peter 5:2-4; and Revelation 3:11.

C. Message to the church in Pergamum (2:12-17)

1. The Recipient and the local situation (2:12a)

2:12a   And to the messenger of the church in Pergamum[207] write:

In 133 BC King Attalus III died without an heir, and his will gave his kingdom to Rome. It became the province of Asia. His capital, *Pergamum*, competed with Ephesus and Smyrna to be the most important city in the province. In *Pergamum* they valued their place in the Roman Empire, and they worshiped Caesar with special diligence, especially in their huge and famous temple for him.

In the middle of the city there was and still is a steep hill about 300 meters (1000 feet) high, which had temples all along the way up it. The famous temple to Asclepios, "The Savior," was in *Pergamum*. They said that anyone who slept the night in that temple and was touched by one of the snakes that crawled around freely in the temple would be healed.

The city of *Pergamum* was 16 kilometers (10 miles) from the sea. Their harbor was located there at Elaia. *Pergamum* had a huge library of 200,000 scrolls. Now all that remains of the city is ruins, but the city of Bergama is located at the base of the hill.

2. The Characteristic of Christ (2:12b)

2:12b   ...this is what the One who has the sharp double-edged sword says:

The sharp double-edged sword is in 1:16, in the vision of the Lord Jesus. The idea here seems to be that just as a *sharp double-edged sword* can cut in both directions, so the Lord can hurt friend or foe, if needed. This interpretation would be supported by the metaphor "a double-edged sword" in modern speech, but we do not know whether that metaphor was in use in the first century. However, Revelation 2:16, which reads "If you do not repent, I will suddenly come to you, and I will fight against them with the sword of My mouth," might be good support for this interpretation. The relationship between a *sword* and the Word of God also comes out in Hebrews 4:12, which reads, "For the Word of God is living, and active, and sharper than any double-edged sword, penetrating to the division of soul and spirit, joints and marrow, and a discerner of the thoughts and intents of the heart."

If that is the reason *the sharp double-edged sword* is mentioned here, then the congregation in Pergamum should realize that even though they are children of God, He may discipline His children with painful discipline if they need it.[208]

3. Praise for the Church (2:13)

2:13   I know your deeds[209] and where you dwell – where Satan's throne is. And you have held fast to My name. And you did not deny your faith in Me in the days of Antipas, My faithful witness, who was killed among you – where Satan dwells.

The Lord commends this congregation, assuring them that He understands how difficult their situation is, that they *dwell where Satan's throne* is located. Perhaps it is enough to say that the spiritual atmosphere of Pergamum was hard on the congregation. There are several different interpretations concerning just why the Lord would say that about Pergamum. Here are some possible interpretations:

1. Pergamum may have been the capital of the Roman province of Asia.[210]
2. The hill upon which the acropolis was located, with all its pagan temples, might have been Satan's throne.
3. Caesar worship was very strong there.
4. The worship of Asclepios was very strong there.
5. There was also a major temple of Zeus near the top of the acropolis there. Its foundations are shown in the photograph, with the modern city of Bergama in the background.
6. Perhaps it is to be taken literally, and Satan did have his throne there in Pergamum.

When they were commanded to worship Caesar and curse the name of Jesus, they refused. They held fast to His Name. They were faithful, not denying the Lord Jesus even when *Antipas* was martyred. According to tradition that faithful witness was slowly burned alive inside a hollow bronze statue of a bull.[211] Perhaps the expression *killed among you* indicates that the church of Pergamum witnessed the death of *Antipas* with their own eyes. Surely this terrible event tempted them to fear, but they withstood that temptation. This faithfulness under extreme pressure was commended by the Lord, and His statement *I know* must have been a comfort to them. He did not forget their good *deeds*.

4. Criticism (2:14-15)

2:14-15 But I have a few things against you, that you have those there that hold to the teaching of Balaam, who taught Balak to set a trap[212] before the sons of Israel so that they ate meat offered to idols and committed sexual immorality. Further, in the same way you also have those holding to the teaching of the Nicolaitans.

The Word of God is so balanced here. As a whole the congregation and its leaders did well, but there were some serious problems that the Lord must bring to their attention. Unlike the leadership in Ephesus, the leadership of the congregation in Pergamum tolerated false teachers and their teachings. Although the details of the false teachings that the leadership tolerated are not given here, it is referred to metaphorically as *the teaching of Balaam*, and there is a brief explanation that tells that *they ate meat offered to idols and committed sexual immorality*.

Numbers chapters 22-25 and 31:16 give the historical background of *Balaam* and *Balak*. *Balaam* was unable to help *Balak* king of Moab because the Lord made him bless, and not curse, Israel. Then in Numbers 31:16 we see that *Balaam taught Balak to set a trap before the sons of Israel so that they ate meat offered to idols and committed sexual immorality*. In Pergamum some of the congregation was captured by that same *trap*.

Besides this reference to eating food *sacrificed to idols* and committing *sexual immorality*, the Lord rebukes the messenger for allowing people to hold to *the teaching of the Nicolaitans*. The difficulties of identifying this false teaching are discussed under 2:6. But the real difficulty is that the leadership needs to repent for their inaction, and expel the false teachers, as is clear in the next verse!

5. Demand (2:16a)

2:16a Therefore repent!

This call to repentance is made with a singular verb (as were the rebukes in verses 14-15 above), so it appears that the Lord is calling the messenger, who seems to be the leader, to repentance.[213] He should *repent* for not dealing with the members of his congregation that were holding to the teaching of Balaam and to the teaching of the Nicolaitans. This seems to be the reason for the singular verb.

Some readers will feel that this is a simple thing, that the leader just needs to do his job, and crack down on the false teachers, demanding that they leave. However, for the church leader with a deep pastoral heart, this can be a difficult thing. Difficult as it may be, he must do this or else....

6. Warning (2:16b)

2:16b If you do not repent,[214] I will suddenly[215] come[216] to you, and I will fight against them with the sword of My mouth.

Again, the *you* twice in this verse is singular, and of course the *them* is plural. This does seem to mean that if the leader (the *you*) does not take action so that the congregation is rid of *them* (those members of the congregation that have followed the teachings of Balaam), then the Lord Himself will take action against that part of the congregation.

If it seems strange that the Lord *will fight against* His congregation with that *sword*, let this be a reminder that His *sword* is two-edged, and that He very much values the purity of His congregation.

Apparently *the sword of* His *mouth* is a metaphor for His words, which have great power. Note that in 19:15 and 19:21 His enemies are slain by the sharp *sword* that comes out of His *mouth*.

7. Promise (2:17)

2:17 The one who has an ear, let him hear what the Spirit says to the churches. To the victor, I will give to him to eat of the hidden manna, and I will give to him a white stone, and upon that stone a new name is written, which no one knows[217] except the one who receives it.

The previous verse describes the results of disobedience. This verse describes the results of obedience. If they did not obey they would face the Lord Jesus and His sword, but if they repented and did what was commanded, they would enjoy a number of promises. The result of not obeying was not eternal punishment, but the discipline of the Lord. Also, the result of obeying was not entrance to heaven, but special status in the Coming Kingdom.

Manna is the heavenly "bread" described in Exodus 16. The *hidden manna* is perhaps related to Jewish teachings based upon 2 Maccabees 2:4-7[218] that the ark with the jar of *manna* was taken and *hidden* in a cave under Mount Nebo, and that *manna* will be eaten at the Messianic Feast, which we call the Wedding Supper of the Lamb. Here there is some irony because obedient believers that do not eat meat sacrificed to idols will enjoy this far better food, *the hidden manna*.[219]

They will also receive *a white stone*, with a secret *name written* on it. It is not clear what this is, but it is clear that the *stone* is from the Lord Jesus and the *new name* is only known by the one who *receives it*. In that era *white* stones were used as:
1. counters of the judges' verdict
2. counters of things and money
3. a symbol of the day of victory
4. "tickets" for a public entertainment event
5. magical amulets
6. a sign that a popular gladiator would no longer be forced to fight, but that he could retire alive[220]

History records those uses of *white* stones, but it does not identify for us which of those is connected to our text. Thomas[221] prefers the fourth one. The victor will be allowed to attend a special ceremony when the Lord Jesus returns. The sixth one connects well to the theme of the victors who at the end of the age can "retire" from the struggles of this age, but some of the other uses may be related as well.

Ramsay[222] suggests that none of the contemporary uses of *white* stones is intended. Instead, an object from the contemporary culture is given a new meaning. It is not a ticket to a passing event, it is an everlasting symbol of honor and privilege.

Anyone who will receive one of those stones receives it from the Lord Himself, and shares a secret with Him. That *white stone* has a secret *name written on it*. It seems most likely that that *name* is a secret *name* of the victor, a *name* that only he and the Lord know, rather than a *new name* for Christ. This sounds very much like a close friendship.

The church in Pergamum had already suffered deeply and was in the midst of suffering when they received this message from the Lord. He understands their difficulties and He values their determination. But in the same congregation, there is false teaching that must be dealt with in order to avoid the terrifying discipline of God. If the leader of the church does not deal with this, God Himself will surely deal with it in some way. To those that are faithful, He promises rewards that are very pleasing.

D. Message to the church in Thyatira (2:18-29)

1. The Recipient and the local situation (2:18a)

2:18a   To the messenger of the church in Thyatira[223] write:

Little is known about *Thyatira*. It was a small city, but the church there received the longest of the seven letters. The hills near *Thyatira* were not high and rocky enough for a good fortress. Being on the road to Pergamum, every enemy that attacked Pergamum also had to conquer poor *Thyatira* on the way to their target city.[224] Soldiers were first placed in *Thyatira* for the defense of Pergamum in the year 300 BC. *Thyatira* was built, destroyed, and rebuilt many times. It was a good place to be a stonemason, but a bad place to be a soldier! Today *Thyatira* is called Akhisar.

Labor guilds were the ancient world's equivalent of modern day unions, and they were very strong in *Thyatira*.[225] Those guilds' activities included feasts that took place in temples and were in honor of their patron god, Apollo.[226] All of that must have made it hard to work in *Thyatira* as a Christian without compromise. Perhaps the one called Jezebel encouraged them to compromise in that area.

2. The Characteristic of Christ (2:18b)

2:18b   ...this is what the Son of God, who has eyes like a flame of fire and feet like bronze[227] says:

This expression, about the One who speaks to the church in Thyatira, explains that this message is fitting because the Lord Jesus knows the hearts of men and that He is able to fulfill all that He speaks of in this letter, whether promises or warnings. Only here in Revelation is the Lord called *the Son of God*. The background of this expression seems to be in Psalm 2, especially verses 7-8.[228] In the culture of the psalmist, the term *Son* can refer to the king that is set up to rule, and not just the physical descendant of a father. So, the term *Son*, like the term Christ, can refer to the King. This is a strong expression. He is the King appointed by God!

In 19:12, where He comes to the earth to judge and rule, we also read that His *eyes* are *like* flames of *fire*. With *eyes* like that He can see each sin. Those that sin cannot hide from Him.

Also, *feet like bronze* are pure and strong to crush sin. In 2:27 we read likewise that "He will shepherd them with an iron staff; He will break them like clay vessels." The false teachers that the leadership has tolerated in the congregation are not hidden from His *eyes*, and they will not escape the wrath of His *feet*.

3. Praise for the Church (2:19)

2:19   I know your deeds and love and faith and service and your endurance. And your deeds: the recent ones are greater than the early ones.

This congregation was predominantly hardworking and loving. He told them that their *recent deeds* exceed their *early ones*, so in a way they are the opposite of the congregation in Ephesus. The Lord's praise here is effusive. Yet this is a divided congregation.

4. Criticism (2:20-21)

2:20-21 But I have against you that you permit your wife[229] Jezebel, who calls herself a prophetess, to teach and to mislead My servants into committing sexual immorality and eating meat sacrificed to idols.[230] I gave her time to repent, but she is not willing to repent from her immorality.

The congregation, or the leader of the congregation (the words *you* and *your* here are singular), is criticized for tolerating a woman named *Jezebel*. Most likely the name *Jezebel* is a figurative name, taken from 1 Kings 18, 19, 21, and 2 Kings 9.

The important thing to note here is that the Lord strongly rejects permissiveness towards *sexual immorality and eating meat sacrificed to idols*. These activities might be called "victimless crimes" in today's secular society, but the Lord strongly rejects permissiveness towards either. They are not victimless. In both cases there is an unseen spiritual reality that brings real and destructive bondage.

The leadership of any congregation must decide just how narrowly they define allowable doctrines. So much theology has been discussed, and so many interpretations have been put forth, that it is not reasonable or godly for anyone to say that the only teachings that will be allowed in this church are the teachings that I agree with. In that case, each church would have only one teacher, and no member of a congregation would be allowed to read a passage and develop an opinion about what it means. Church leadership must define the boundaries of acceptable doctrine. For whatever reason, the leadership in Thyatira had done this very poorly, and received the rebuke of the Lord.

Those that this *Jezebel* misleads are called *My servants*. They are believers, believers that are making some very bad mistakes. They will not lose their salvation for this serious sin. Neither are they showing that they never had "saving faith." They are born again and eternally saved, but they are sinning badly. Instead of receiving the rewards promised in these two chapters, they will receive the threats. They are saved, but they are not victors, unless they repent!

5. Warning[231] (2:22-23)

2:22-23 Look, I will throw her onto a bed,[232] and those who commit adultery with her into great suffering, unless they repent from her deeds. And her children I will strike dead.[233] And all the churches will know that I am the one who searches minds and hearts, and I will give to each of you according to your deeds.

The Apostle Paul gave a similar threat in 1 Corinthians 3:17, "If anyone defiles the temple of God, God will defile him." The Lord warns that He will take drastic action against this woman and her followers. There is still an opportunity to *repent* (in fact, the expression *unless they repent from her deeds* contains an implied demand for the sinful believers of the congregation) but the threat is very strongly expressed here, with expressions like *great suffering* and *strike dead*. The Lord had already done something similar in Corinth, as Paul explained in 1 Corinthians 11:27-29. He will choose the time and means according to His wisdom, but judgment will fall on them, so they will be cleansed. Christ loves His church.

The expression *I am the one who searches minds and hearts* here confirms the interpretation given above: the reason the description of Christ at the beginning of this letter includes the fact that He has "eyes like a flame of fire" is because He is seeing all the supposedly hidden sin of the congregation.

The idea that He *will give* everyone *according to* their *deeds* is not unique to this passage. It is also stated in 20:12, 13; and 22:12, as well as in Romans 2:6. Only as we consider the doctrine of rewards can we understand how He can do this, and yet forgive all believers of all their sins.

6. Demand (2:24-25)

2:24-25 But upon you, to the rest of you in Thyatira, as many as do not hold to that teaching and have not learned the so-called deep things of Satan's, upon you I do not set another burden. In any case what you have, hold on to it until I come.

There is a demand in this message, but it is not for the false teacher and her followers (except that the words "unless they repent" in 2:22 are an implied demand upon the false teacher's followers). In verse 21 the Lord already explained that He "gave her time to repent, but she is not willing to repent...." His action against her is already decided, as is clear in verse 22. The demand here is specifically *to the rest of you in Thyatira, as many as do not hold to that teaching and have not learned the so-called deep things of Satan's*. The Lord places a solemn expectation upon them.

"Jezebel" and her followers were drawing in the rest of the church to the *deep things* of Satan. There are two ways to understand these words.[234] First, possibly this is satire. According to this understanding, the false teacher here called Jezebel called this teaching or activity "the secret of God" (this agrees with the practices of a several of false teachers during this age, that said that they taught about the secrets of their god). Second, some interpreters say that the false teacher was actually encouraging her followers to investigate the secrets of Satan. There were religions that taught their followers to enter the fortresses of Satan in order to understand the limits of his power. If this interpretation is correct it means that the false teacher encouraged the church in *Thyatira* to join in activities that were pagan, for example, the ceremonies of the labor guilds. She may have taught them that in Christ they will not be defeated, and they will understand better how to oppose Satan. This way of understanding Satan is forbidden by the Lord Jesus. He wants us to guard our holiness.

The demand upon the faithful of the congregation is simply *what you have, hold on to it until I come*. This must have been some comfort to that part of the congregation: they were doing fine, and just needed to continue on as they have been doing. This is not to say that they had achieved a state of sinless perfection. It simply meant that they were doing well, and the Lord was satisfied with their hearts, lives, and ministries.

This demand is very similar to the demand in 3:11, which reads, "I am coming suddenly. Hold on to what you have so that no one takes your crown." It is especially interesting that both of these passages, besides commanding that the readers *hold on to what they have*, also mention the return of the Lord. It is much easier to *hold on* when you know what you are holding on for!

There are also implied demands in the expression "unless they repent of her ways" of verse 22, and in the expression "and does My will to the end" in verse 26. These passages have their various emphases: those that repent will escape the threatened action, and those that do His will to the end will gain the promised reward.

7. Promise (2:26-28)

2:26-28 To the victor who keeps[235] My deeds to the end, I will give authority over the nations. "And He will shepherd[236] them with an iron staff; He will shatter them like clay vessels," as I also have received this authority[237] from My Father. And I will give him the morning star.

Ramsay[238] notes the irony in the fact that the weakest church is offered so startlingly powerful a reward.

These wonderful rewards are not offered to those of the church that have followed Jezebel. They are only promised suffering. However, if the others will just "hold on," or, in other words, if they will keep His *deeds to the end*, they will receive the promised reward.

The close connection between the expression *the victor* and the expression *keeps My deeds to the end* shows quite clearly that victors here in these seven messages are believers that are obedient to Christ all the way to the end of their lives. In 2:25 the Lord gives the command "In any case what you have, hold on to until I come." Verse 26 elaborates and adds the promise: *To the victor who keeps My deeds to the end, I will give authority over the nations.*

The followers of the false teacher in that congregation were not victors, but they were called "My servants" in verse 20. They were believers that had been deceived, and were losing out on the rewards promised to anyone that *keeps* His *deeds to the end*. Whether or not this is in accord with some theologies, the text is clear: some people that are born again will obey and be rewarded, and other people that are born again will be deceived, they will sin, and they will suffer discipline from the hand of their Savior, with no reward.

In Psalm 2:8-9, which is clearly quoted here and in Revelation 19:15, we read that these things will be given by the *Father* to the Son, but now here we read that we are invited to join with the Son, if we *meet this condition*. The explanation *as I also have received from My Father* shows us that the Lord Jesus is extending the promise the *Father* gave Him to us.

This promise of ruling *authority* for obedient believers is taught in other portions of Scripture as well. Note Luke 19:11-27, in which some obedient believers are given "authority over ten cities," and others "over five cities." These promises most resemble the promises to Laodicea.

The last of the promises, almost appearing to have been added as an afterthought, is *the morning star*. Various possibilities have been suggested for the meaning of this expression. Because in 22:16, Jesus is *the morning star*, perhaps the *victor* is given an especially close relationship with Him.[239] Because in the Babylonian and Roman mythologies, *the morning star* symbolizes victory, perhaps the victors' victory is promised here. This interpretation is supported by 2:26-27, near verses which also speak of victory.[240] Because in Daniel 12:3 and Matthew 13:43 this symbol suggests glory in the Kingdom, perhaps that is the intended meaning here.[241] This promise is hard to interpret. It is even possible that a combination of these ideas is intended here.

2:29 The one who has an ear, let him hear what the Spirit says to the churches.

This message closes with the same exhortation that appears in all seven of the messages.

In this message, the Lord Jesus speaks to a congregation that is generally healthy, but is stained with the presence of a false teacher, her followers, and their evil practices. The message of the Lord is so balanced and just. Towards those that do evil, He is strict: He requires real repentance, and He threatens suffering. However, to those that have remained faithful, He brings encouragement, and He promises an extraordinary reward: authority over the nations. The great beauty of the city where they will exercise that authority is described in Revelation 21:9-22:5.

E. Message to the church in Sardis (3:1-6)

1. The Recipient and the local situation (3:1a)

3:1a To the messenger of the church in Sardis[242] write:

Mount Tmolus towered over the city whose church received this letter. Originally, the city was built up on one of its rocky peaks. That old city was on a very narrow mountaintop,[243] high above the surrounding area.

There were cliffs on all sides, except where that high point was connected to the rest of Mount Tmolus by a narrow, rocky, and steep ridge of land. It was extremely well-protected from attack. In fact, it was considered unconquerable. For many many years, even in the years after John heard these words from the Lord, the expression "to capture the acropolis of Sardis" was a proverb that spoke of doing the impossible. (The term "acropolis" means "high city," and would refer in this case to the old city of *Sardis* located high on Mount Tmolus.)[244]

That strong fortress city became capital of the Kingdom of Lydia.[245] The photograph shows what remains of the peak of Mount Tmolus and the remains of a second century AD temple to Artemis. This photograph and others are available for download in dave.hagelb.org under the "Photos" tab.

Gold was discovered in the Pactolus River, which flows along the foot of Mount Tmolus.[246] Around 700 BC King Gyges of *Sardis* produced the first minted coins there, made of an alloy of silver and gold known as electrum.[247]

By the time of this letter, the *Pax Romana* (the peace that the Romans brought about by conquering so vast a territory) meant that a great fortress was no longer needed to be a great city, so the high and narrow little old city was long abandoned and fell into ruin.[248] The new city was built down in the more comfortable valley at the base of the mountain.

There is an interesting event in the history of this city that the Lord does seem to be building upon as He sends this letter to them. The Greek historian Herodotus[249] records that in about 546 BC Cyrus King of Persia (who is mentioned in 2 Chronicles 36:22 and Ezra 1:1-8) was retaliating after a failed attack by King Croesus of Lydia. King Croesus had retreated up into *Sardis*, his "impregnable" fortress. Herodotus' account is an interesting blend of a superstition about a "lion that his concubine bore," a former king, and the ingenuity of a Mardian soldier:

> Now the taking of Sardis came about as follows: When the fourteenth day came after Croesus began to be besieged, Cyrus made proclamation to his army, sending horsemen round to the several parts of it, that he would give gifts to the man who should first scale the wall. After this the army

> made an attempt; and when it failed, then after all the rest had ceased from the attack, a certain Mardian whose name was Hyroiades made an attempt to approach on that side of the citadel where no guard had been set; for they had no fear that it would ever be taken from that side, seeing that here the citadel is precipitous and unassailable. To this part of the wall alone Meles also, who formerly was king of Sardis, did not carry round the lion which his concubine bore to him, the Telmessians having given decision that if the lion should be carried round the wall, Sardis should be safe from capture: and Meles having carried it round the rest of the wall, that is to say those parts of the citadel where the fortress was open to attack, passed over this part as being unassailable and precipitous: now this is a part of the city turned towards Tmolos. So then this Mardian Hyroiades, having seen on the day before how one of the Lydians had descended on that side of the citadel to recover his helmet which had rolled down from above, and had picked it up, took thought and cast the matter about in his own mind. Then he himself ascended first, and after him came up others of the Persians, and many having thus made approach, Sardis was finally taken and the whole city was given up to plunder.

Xenophon[250] gives a slightly different account of that event:

> When day broke Cyrus marched straight for Sardis, and when he came before the citadel he set up his engines as though for the assault and got out his ladders. But the following night he sent a scaling party of Persians and Chaldaeans to climb the fortifications at the steepest point. The guide was a Persian who had served as a slave to one of the garrison in the citadel, and who knew a way down to the river by which one could get up. As soon as it became clear that the heights had been taken, all the Lydians without exception fled from the walls and hid wherever they could.

Regardless of which of these accounts is more historically accurate, the story of the defeat of the unconquerable *Sardis* was told and retold many times.[251] That defeat marked the end of the great Kingdom of Lydia, which at that time covered the western half of what is now the country of Turkey.

In 214 BC the city of *Sardis* was again besieged, and a soldier named Lagoras serving Antiochus the Great was also able to lead soldiers into the "impregnable" *Sardis* using ladders up the steepest part of the cliffs, in an area that the defenders ignored, again thinking it was impregnable.[252]

Even if the actual events leading up to the conquering of *Sardis* were not quite like these ancient historians' accounts, it is clear that *Sardis* was overconfident. *Sardis* had not learned. Both times the conquerors "came like a thief."

Did the church of *Sardis* accept this rebuke from the Lord Jesus so that the Lord did not have to come as a thief? We do not know how this letter was received by the church in *Sardis* at that time. In any case, the lesson of the history of *Sardis* and of this letter still speaks to self-confident and complacent believers. As Paul wrote in 1 Corinthians 10:12, "So, the one that thinks he stands should watch out, lest he fall."

With five roads intersecting in *Sardis*, there was prosperous trade, and the sheep in their fields produced good wool. The people of *Sardis* were known as a lazy people that liked to enjoy life's pleasures, but not to work hard. There was a very large temple of Artemis in the lower city.

The situation of the Christian congregation was apparently as pleasant as the situation of the city. No false teachers threatened the church, and Caesar worship was not emphasized. It was a nice, relaxing place to live.

The village of Sart and many archaeological ruins remain there now. Almost all of those ruins, including the impressive synagogue and gymnasium complex, were built after this letter was written.

2. The Characteristic of Christ (3:1b)

3:1b   ...this is what the One who has the seven spirits of God and the seven stars says:

As was discussed under 1:4 above, *the seven spirits of God* is a reference to the Holy Spirit. Also, *the seven stars* refer to the *seven* messengers from the *seven* churches, as we learned in 1:20. He holds the Holy Spirit and He holds those messengers, perhaps the pastors of those churches, in His hand. They needed the work of the Spirit in their lives, and in the life of their congregations. The Lord had just what they needed.

3. Criticism (3:1c)

3:1c   ...I know your deeds, that you have a name that you are alive, but you are dead.

Although there is clearly a standard order of elements, it is not followed precisely here. They are criticized before any of them are commended. They *have a name*, a reputation among the other churches of the area that they were *alive*, but spiritually they were practically *dead*. This church was like fruit that appears good but inside is actually rotten. They were lethargic and happy to have a good reputation, even if that reputation was undeserved.

In Ephesians 5:14 believers that are not faithful are pictured as people that are sleeping and need to wake up. The same imagery is used here.

4. Demand (3:2a)

3:2a   Wake up[253] and strengthen what remains which you are about to cast off...[254]

If they were "dead" or "about to die," or "asleep," the obvious thing they needed to do was *wake up and strengthen* whatever life they have. This is a call out of lethargy and complacency.

Criticism (continued) (3:2b)

3:2b   ...for I have not found your deeds complete before My God.

None of their *deeds* were perfect, mature, *complete*. He evaluated their works. All their works were colored by their sin. This is a harsh criticism. Even though they have a reputation as a vital congregation, Christ is assessing them from the divine perspective, and from that perspective their *deeds* are incomplete.

Demand (continued) (3:3a)

3:3a   Therefore remember what you have received and heard, and keep it and repent.

There is nothing complicated to understand here about what this means, but it might feel like it is tremendously difficult to actually do this. The Ephesians were also told to *remember* and to *repent*.

5. Warning (3:3b)

3:3b   So if you do not wake up, I will come upon you[255] like a thief, and you will not know at all[256] what time I will come upon you.

They were self-satisfied, self-assured, and suddenly (assuming they did not repent) they were totally surprised. And it would not have been a happy surprise! They had to guard themselves, even though there was no threat of an enemy from outside, and no false prophets on the inside, as was the case with some of the other churches.

If it sounds strange that the Lord would compare Himself to a *thief*, the reader should remember that the point of comparison is that both come unexpectedly. This striking comparison is like the comparison of God and an unjust judge in Luke 18:1-8.

It is ironic that the supposedly "impregnable" fortress city has, through the ages, become a crumbling rock now only visited by tourists.

6. Praise for the Church (3:4a)

3:4a   But you have a few people[257] in Sardis who have not dirtied their clothing...

The Lord gave no commendation for the whole church, but He did acknowledge that there were *a few* there that were righteous. Again, this was a divided congregation. The statement "I know your deeds" was no commendation. He did know about their deeds but the quality of those deeds was shameful.

Nevertheless, in this verse the Lord Jesus says there were *a few people in Sardis who have not dirtied their clothing*. They guarded their holiness just like people who wear white *clothing* need to be careful to keep their clothes clean. They were faithful in a church that was less than faithful.

7. Promise (3:4b-5)

3:4b   ...and they will walk with Me, clothed[258] in white, because they are worthy.

The pronoun *they* here clearly refers to those few *worthy* ones. Is it not clear that these rewards are linked to Christian obedience? *White* clothes can symbolize holiness, joy in festivities, or victory. Roman citizens used their *white* clothing for major celebrations.[259] Is this gift of *white* clothes a special distinction, or will everyone, including the "sleepy" believers in Sardis, receive it? The structure of these verses, as well as clear statements like verse 4, make it clear that these rewards are for *worthy* believers, and that not all believers will be counted *worthy*.

3:5 The victor, he will be clothed in white clothing. And I will never ever blot out his name from the book of life, but will acknowledge his name before My Father and before His angels.

The first promise is *white clothing*, which the Lord mentions both in verse 4 and in verse 5, perhaps for emphasis. Those who have not dirtied their *clothing* with things that are not holy will experience great joy at the marriage supper of the Lamb as those who participate in Christ's victory. Often people think that all believers in the age to come will wear *white clothing*, but that idea is not based on the Word of God.

The second promise concerns *the book of life*. At first glance, this sounds like if someone is not a *victor*, then *his name* will get blotted out of *the book of life*. In other words, you will lose your salvation if you do not perform up to the standards of a *victor*. If that is the case, then it would be logical to say that all the things required of victors here in these two chapters are necessary for us to do to keep our salvation. That might be one way to motivate people to live faithful lives, but is that what this text actually means?

A closer look at this text shows that the Greek translated *never ever* is a double negative,[260] which is incorrect English grammar (as in "not nohow" or "I ain't got no money") but perfectly good and emphatic Greek grammar. It might also be translated "certainly never."

This might be loosely translated "Rather than ever in any way blotting out his name from the book of life, instead I will confess his name before my Father and his angels." This is a figure of speech[261] in which rather than saying something directly, like "I will acknowledge this person's name to My Father because of how well he has done," (as in Matthew 10:32) the speaker denies the opposite, *I will never ever blot out his name*. Note too that the text actually does not say that anyone's *name* will be blotted out.

A Roman master that wanted to free his slave could have that slave's *name* entered into the *book* of citizens of that city. Once that person's *name* was written there, he was no longer a slave; he was a citizen.[262] On the other hand, if a criminal's *name* were erased from the *book* of the citizens, he lost his citizenship.[263]

In the Scriptures *the book of life* is mentioned in Exodus 32:33; Psalm 69:28 (that is verse 28 in English, and verse 29 in Hebrew); 139:16; Isaiah 29:18; Daniel 10:21; Malachi 3:16; Philippians 4:3; Revelation 3:5; 13:8; 17:8; 20:12, 15; and 21:27. In the Old Testament *the book of life* is a *book* containing the names of all living people. When someone physically dies, his *name* is blotted out of the Old Testament *book of life* because he is no longer alive. This is very clear in Psalm 69:28, in which King David prays that his enemies will die, not that they will lose their salvation! However in the New Testament, the expression *book of life*[264] refers to a *book* that has the names of everyone who has or will have eternal *life*.[265] They are citizens of the Kingdom of God.

The third promise is that He will *acknowledge* each victor's *name before* His *Father* and *before* His *angels*. What can compare to this? The Lord Jesus will rise from his throne, stand in front of the *Father*, and say, "Father, this is my servant, faithful and diligent, his name is...." His voice will be heard to the outer reaches of heaven. If we want such words to be spoken about us, we need to be victors. We need to be obedient to Him, even in difficult situations.

The Lord Jesus also gives this promise in Matthew 10:32. There He promises that the believer who courageously acknowledges[266] the Lord Jesus before men will also be acknowledged in front of the *Father* in heaven.

3:6 The one who has an ear, let him hear what the Spirit says to the churches.

Again this exhortation is repeated, reminding us all that we do need to hear this message.

The congregation in Sardis was thought to be spiritually mature, but the Lord had another "opinion." He tells them that most of them are nearly dead spiritually, and He threatens to come as a thief in the night. But to those in the congregation that are spiritually alert, He promises He will give them white clothing and He will confess their names to the Father. The spiritually lethargic there needed to become alert and get refreshed. His threat and His promise have the same intent: that they all have a healthy relationship with Him, so that their character and activities reflect His glory as portrayed in the vision in chapter one.

F. Message to the church in Philadelphia (3:7-13)

1. The Recipient and the local situation (3:7a)

3:7a And to the messenger of the church in Philadelphia[267] write:

In the middle of the second century BC the founder of the city of *Philadelphia* was said to have died in Greece, so his younger brother took the throne. When the rumor turned out to be false, the younger brother gladly restored the throne to his older brother.[268] It was the City of Brotherly Love.

It seems that at one point in time the regions of Mysia, Lydia, and Phrygia all met at one place, and at that place *Philadelphia* was founded to bring Greek civilization to the barbarian Lydia and Phrygia.[269] In that way, it originally had a "missionary" purpose. Goods from the port of Smyrna, as well as Greek culture, were easily taken up the road through *Philadelphia* into those eastern regions.

On the other hand *Philadelphia* was poorly situated, because of volcanoes and earthquakes. In 17 AD the worst of those earthquakes[270] destroyed 12 cities in the region, including *Philadelphia* and Sardis. The aftershocks were so frightening that many preferred to remain in the countryside outside of *Philadelphia*.[271] The promise of the Lord Jesus that those who are faithful will be made into pillars[272] might be connected to such fears.

In *Philadelphia* and in many other areas there was a custom of putting up memorial pillars or statues, dedicated to the memory of faithful civic-minded citizens. *Philadelphia* still exists today, but is known as Alasehir.

2. The Characteristic of Christ (3:7b)

3:7b ...this is what the Holy One, the True One, the One having the key of David, the One who opens and no one will close it except He who opens, and no one opens, says:[273]

The idea of *the key of David* is taken from Isaiah 22:22. *The Holy One* is the Messiah (see John 6:69). The Jews in Philadelphia (mentioned in 3:9) would reject Him as the True Messiah and as the One that holds *the key of David*. Despite their rejection, He *opens* the door of the Kingdom of God.[274] He is the Almighty, who decides who will enter the Kingdom of God, and also what ministry the believers in Philadelphia may and may not have.

3. Praise for the Church (3:8)

3:8 I know your deeds. Look, I have placed before you an open door, which no one is able to shut. Because you have little strength, and you have kept My word and have not denied My name.[275]

Unlike the commendations in the other letters, this commendation emphasizes ministry opportunities. The *open door* that is *placed before* them seems to refer to opportunity for ministry, perhaps among the unreached.[276] Just as Philadelphia was originally built to bring Greek culture to some that were as yet "barbarians," so the church in Philadelphia now has an opportunity to bring the Good News to unreached peoples. The Lord emphasizes that *no one is able to shut* this *door* or take away this opportunity from them. Even though they do not feel equipped to evangelize their area, they can still bear fruit, because the Lord Jesus has *placed before* them *an open door, which no one is able to shut.*

He knows that they have done well for Him, with *little strength.* Surely His comment about their *little strength* was encouraging to that congregation. He knew what it was to be weak, hungry and thirsty. He acknowledges their *little strength,* and that they have remained faithful, and He is giving them even more opportunity to be faithful.

4. Promise (3:9)

The order of the various elements here differs from the standard order. Five different rewards are offered to this faithful congregation.

3:9 look, I will make those who are of the synagogue of Satan, those saying they are Jews, but they are not, instead they are liars, look, I will make them come and prostrate themselves before your feet and acknowledge that I have loved you.

The *Jews* who did not receive the Lord Jesus as their Messiah and Savior are called *the synagogue of Satan,* just like the *Jews* that persecuted the church in Smyrna. This is a powerful condemnation of the *Jews* that have not believed in the Lord.[277] We see a similar attitude in Acts 17:5 and 13, when the *Jews* in Thessalonica were jealous of the success of evangelism in Thessalonica and Berea. Compare this attitude with 1 Thessalonians 2:15-16. If the *Jews* of Philadelphia were persecuting this church, this first promise would comfort and also strengthen those who were suffering.

The first promise is that He will make the *Jews* confess that the True Holy One of Israel loves the Christian congregation. This is a very strongly worded passage, and certainly not in conformity with today's ideas about respecting other religions.

When will this promise be fulfilled? If that *synagogue* repented and believed in Jesus, then that promise has already been fulfilled. If not, then its fulfillment will come at the end of the age.

Praise (continued) (3:10a)

3:10a Because you have kept My command of endurance...

This is another praise from Him. They *kept* His *command* calling them to *endurance.* He does not go into detail here, but His meaning is very clear. This was a good church in His eyes.

Promise (continued) (3:10b)

3:10b ...I will also keep you from the hour of testing that will come upon the whole world to test those who dwell upon the earth.

The second promise is that they will be kept *from the hour of testing that will come upon the whole world to test those who dwell upon the earth*. In one sense this is very clear. Because they have been obedient, they will receive this reward. On the other hand, this is a very difficult passage, because there are several elements that are hard to interpret.

The hour of testing is most likely the Great Tribulation prophesied in Revelation 4-18, that time of sorrow or distress described as the seventieth "week" of Daniel chapter 9[278] and "the coming wrath" in 1 Thessalonians 1:10, rather than one twelfth of a day.

In the Book of Revelation the exact expression *those who dwell upon the earth* is used ten times (in 3:10; 6:10; 8:13; 11:10 (twice); 13:8, 14 (twice); 17:2 and 8), and a slightly different expression is used once in 13:12. It always refers to the people who do not want to believe in the Lamb of God, and instead decide to worship the beast. It is a key expression for the unrepentant of the *earth*, whose hardness of heart is a crucial element in the message of this book.

The expression *the whole world*[279] can refer to the Roman *world* as in Luke 2:1 and Acts 11:28, but can also refer to *the whole* physical *world* as in Matthew 24:14; Luke 4:5; Acts 17:31; Romans 10:18; Hebrews 1:6; 2:5; Revelation 12:9; and 16:14. If it refers only to the Roman Empire, perhaps it refers to some persecution that reaches throughout the Roman Empire, but if it refers to the entire *earth*, then it seems like it would be the persecution at the end of the age.

The expression *keep you from*[280] might somehow possibly mean "protect you during" but the literal meaning is "keep out of."

This promise of protection could refer to:

    1. protection from persecution during the Roman era

The problem with this is that the fulfillment of all the other promises in chapters two and three has to wait for the victorious coming of the Lord Jesus, with the possible exception of 3:9. Is this (and possibly 3:9) the only promise to be fulfilled in their time?

2. protection for the church at the end of the age, on *earth*, during the seven year Tribulation, in line with the Post-Tribulational teachings

The problem with this is that according to Revelation 6:9-11 and 7:9-14, people who believe during the Tribulation will not be protected but will be killed. So the nature of this protection is vague, and this is a weak option.

3. protection only for the faithful, because they will be raptured right before before the Tribulation, in line with "Partial Rapture" teachings

According to this interpretation, the promise will be fulfilled before the Tribulation, only for believers who are faithful during that time period. But support for the "Partial Rapture" view is very weak in Scripture.

4. protection for all believers, including the faithful, because all believers will be raptured before the Tribulation, in line with Pre-Tribulational teachings

This is like the promise to the victors, that they will not be hurt by the second death. See 1 Thessalonians 1:10 and 5:9.

This writer holds that the fourth explanation is to be preferred, but it is a difficult passage. There is also the possibility that this promise has a double fulfillment, so that the first and the fourth are both correct.[281] In any case, in this passage in the original language,[282] it is emphatic that Christ is going to protect them. May this promise comfort each of us in the difficulties we face. He will protect us.

5. Criticism

There is none! This does not mean that the congregation achieved a state of "sinless perfection," it simply means that our gracious Lord was satisfied with their spiritual growth and had no need to criticize them.

6. Demand (3:11a)

3:11a   I am coming[283] suddenly.[284] Hold on to what you have...

This is the closest this letter comes to a demand. They need to keep at it, to maintain the attitudes and ministries that they have. For those in Philadelphia, the coming of Christ would be a comfort, but for those in Ephesus, Pergamum and a portion of the ones in Sardis, words like *I am coming suddenly* should bring about fear. Note that a very similar command was given to part of the congregation in Thyatira in 2:25.

7. Warning (3:11b)

3:11b   ...so that no one takes your crown.

This is the closest that this letter comes to a threat. This brief verse teaches us something crucial about crowns, and by extension about the other rewards in these seven letters. Even assuming we are doing as well as this congregation was, at this point our crowns are not guaranteed to us. Someone might take them from us. The condition for keeping a *crown* is "hold on to what you have." The race is not yet over. If they were tempted and fell, and no longer were living a life pleasing to the Lord, it could be said that whoever tempted them and caused them to fall has already "taken" their *crown*.

Note carefully that this text does not say, "so that no one takes your salvation"! Our salvation is guaranteed by the blood of Christ; our rewards are not.

In 1 Timothy 4:8 Paul speaks very clearly about these crowns: "Finally, there is stored away for me the crown of righteousness, which the Lord, the righteous Judge, shall give to me in that Day, and not only to me, but to all that have loved His appearing." So even though this passage says *so that no one takes your crown*, we understand that those crowns are stored away, to be awarded "in that Day."

This is a good point for serious personal reflection. Who is it that might take *your crown* by drawing you away from obedience? Who threatens your walk with the Lord? Are you on guard against that danger?

Promise (continued) (3:11b-12)

Included in this "threat" is a third promise, their crowns.[285] As long as they hold on to what they have, no one will be able to take their crown. As long as they remain at the level they have reached, as long as they remain obedient, their crown is secure. See the discussion on the message to Smyrna concerning crowns in 2:10. In Smyrna they had to "be faithful, even to the point of death" in order to get their crowns, and this congregation has to hold on to what they have to keep their crowns. These crowns were conditional.

Some would say that all believers persevere in good works (and therefore all believers will be given crowns), but that pushes a great deal of theology into a passage like this, rather than letting it speak for itself.

3:12   The victor[286] I will make a pillar in the temple of My God. Never again will he go out of it. And I will write on him the name of

> My God and the name of the city of My God, the New Jerusalem, which comes down out of heaven from My God; and I will write on him My new name.

Fourth, each faithful member will be made *a pillar in the temple of* our Lord's *God*. This is clearly a metaphor. As noted above, they gave honor to citizens for their service by setting up pillars for them.

In 1 Maccabees 14:25-27 we read of the Israel's gratitude to Simon for his heroic efforts. They said, "'What thanks shall we give to Simon and his sons? For he and his brethren and the house of his father have established Israel, and chased away in fight their enemies from them, and confirmed their liberty.' So then they wrote it in tables of brass, which they set upon pillars in Mount Zion."

Throughout the ages, people have set up various memorials to honor their prestigious citizens. Perhaps the members of this congregation had seen some of those memorials in Philadelphia, and thought, "I will never be honored like those important people." But here the Lord is saying to them that they are important to Him and He will honor them in this way! The details may not be clear, but the intent is to honor His faithful servants in a public way, to be seen by all.

Those that receive the promise that *never again will he go out of it* will have the right to enjoy close fellowship with the Lord forever. This promise is very similar to Psalm 27:4, "One thing I have asked from the LORD, this I seek, that I might dwell in the house of the LORD all the days of my life...." The permanence in this promise can be contrasted with the condition of the buildings of Philadelphia that were ruined from a destructive earthquake.

Fifth, each faithful member of the congregation will somehow be inscribed with *the name of* our Lord's *God, the name of the city of* our Lord's *God, the New Jerusalem,* and the Lord's *new name.*

This reminds us of stone pillars inscribed with people's names. Further, any writing material or any old book that had God's *name* written upon it was honored by the Jews. When it was no longer being used, it could not be thrown away like any common thing. Such materials were held in a special place called a *genizah*, until they could be properly disposed of.[287] But in this case it is not a piece of writing material that will be so honored – it is the victors themselves.

See Isaiah 43:7; Jeremiah 23:6; and Ezekiel 48:35. In about 220 AD Rabbi Jonathan said, "Three are named according to the name of God, that is the righteous, the Messiah, and Jerusalem."[288]

3:13 The one who has an ear, let him hear what the Spirit says to the churches.

With this exhortation this message closes.

Some of these five promises may seem strange to us in the 21st century, but they are beautiful promises, and they are meant to motivate us to the life and ministry the Lord has for us, or to stand firm in that life and ministry. The congregation in Philadelphia did not feel that it was very strong, but it was given unusual opportunities to serve in an unreached area. They were faithful and steadfast in the trouble they experienced, so they were not threatened or told to repent like most of the other congregations.

G. Message to the church in Laodicea (3:14-22)

1. The Recipient and the local situation (3:14a)

3.14a And to the messenger of the church in Laodicea write:

The city of *Laodicea* was founded by Antiochus II, a descendant of one of Alexander the Great's generals who reigned from 261 to 246 BC. He named the new city after his wife, Laodice, whom he divorced in 253 BC.[289] After 133 BC that kingdom became part of Rome's empire, which usually brought many benefits. However, *Laodicea* suffered from unusually heavy taxation[290] and demands to open their homes and provide meals and spending money for government officials and military personnel.[291]

To travel from the west to the area of Phrygia one had to go by way of *Laodicea* and Philadelphia.[292] The city's location, with three main roads meeting there, helped it develop into an important center for trade. Black sheep in the area yielded a valuable soft and shiny black wool for clothing and carpets. The sale of wool, carpets, cloth and clothing was a source of their wealth.[293]

Laodicea became a banking center for the region, and some of its citizens were remarkably wealthy.[294] After the major earthquake in 60 or 61 AD they rebuilt their city with their own funds, refusing the financial assistance that Rome offered![295] They considered themselves wealthy. Although inscriptions describing how various public buildings and facilities were donated by wealthy citizens were common at that time, in *Laodicea* there are a greater number of such inscriptions.[296]

They had a well-developed medical school there that produced the famous "Phrygian powder," used in making eye salve.²⁹⁷

Laodicea's physical location was chosen because of the highway system and trade routes, not for good defense or water resources. Since the nearby Lycus River (less than three kilometers/two miles away) could dry up during the dry season, water for *Laodicea* had to be piped in with a long series of stone water pipes which could easily be broken by enemies, so *Laodicea* knew it was vulnerable in case of attack.²⁹⁸

The neighboring cities of Colossae and Hierapolis had good water at hand. Colossae's was cold and fresh; Hierapolis' water was hot, and valued for its healing properties.²⁹⁹ In contrast, during the summer when the nearby river dried up, the best *Laodicea* could do for water was to use that series of stone pipes to bring in their water. It probably came from the hot springs of what is now called Denizli, about eight kilometers (five miles) to the south, but too many of the stone pipes have been removed to be certain about the source.³⁰⁰ The heavy calcium carbonate deposits that remain to this day in those stone pipes indicate that their water was not pleasant to drink.³⁰¹ The water those pipes delivered was not refreshingly cool, like the water of one particular stream near Colossae, nor was it hot, like the water of the hot springs of Hierapolis. In fact, the water in that region was known to cause people to vomit!³⁰²

Rabbis in Israel complained that other Jews would leave Jerusalem and live in *Laodicea*, with its elaborate public baths and good wine.³⁰³

Now all that remains of *Laodicea* are extensive ruins that silently attest to the physical wealth that once was the pride of this city. The photograph shows some of the excavated and reconstructed ruins of *Laodicea*.

2. The Characteristic of Christ (3:14b)

3:14b This is what the Amen, the faithful and true witness,³⁰⁴ the ruler³⁰⁵ of God's creation says:

Only in this passage is the name *Amen* used as a name of Christ. Basically this word means "It is true," and it is further explained with the expression *the faithful and true witness*. He is the one who can be believed. The emphasis is on His truthfulness, which this lukewarm church needs to believe and act upon in order to repent and eventually receive their reward. The Lord will not deceive them. The words *the faithful witness* are drawn from John's "trinitarian" greeting in 1:4-5.

3. Praise for the Church
This element is, painfully, completely missing!

4. Criticism (3:15)

3:15 I know your deeds, that you are not cold or hot. I wish you were cold[306] or hot!

The Lord Jesus says *I know*, as He says in the other six letters, but in this letter what He knows does not bring a commendation but an extensive criticism.

As noted above, drinking water was certainly an issue for the city. Their water, at least in the summer, tasted bad. The Lord uses the picture of unpleasant drinking water as a shocking rebuke. Just like their unpleasant drinking water, the congregation was neither *cold* nor *hot*.

The words *I wish you were cold or hot* are very emphatic. Being *hot* seems to refer to having great spiritual fervor, as in Acts 18:25 and Romans 12:11.[307]

5. Warning[308] (3:16)

3:16 So, because you are lukewarm, and not hot or cold – I will spit you out of My mouth.

Their hearts were *lukewarm*, and He wants to *spit* them *out of* His *mouth*. Even if we know little about the beverage preferences for people in that region, the Lord's words are shocking and stinging. The Lord Jesus declares that He does not want to fellowship with them in their present state of sin. Their sins greatly disturb Him. This is among the strongest rebukes in the New Testament.

The verb translated *spit*[309] could also be translated "vomit." Even so, the translation *spit* should be preferred, if only because people *spit* out of their mouths, but vomit out of their stomachs.

Criticism (continued) (3:17)

3:17 You say, 'I am rich' and 'I have acquired wealth'[310] and 'I have need of nothing.' And you do not know that you are wretched and miserable and poor and blind and naked.

They considered themselves *rich*, but it was the *wealth* of the world. In the Lord's eyes they were *wretched, poor, and miserable*. How can the Lord Jesus, who is the "true witness," say that they are *poor* when they have so much *wealth*? They had their famous eye salve, but the Lord says they were *blind*. They had their famous black wool, but the Lord says they were *naked*. Note the contrast with the congregation in Smyrna, which was physically *poor*, but spiritually rich.

6. Demand (3:18)

3:18 I advise you to buy from Me gold refined in the fire, so that you may be rich; and white garments to wear, so that you are clothed and your shameful nakedness is not visible; and salve so you can anoint your eyes, so that you can see.

Jesus' demand of the church in Laodicea, alluding to Isaiah 55:1-2, has three parts, in which three things that they were so proud of have been turned around and made into metaphors of their spiritual needs which the Lord Jesus offers to fulfill.

The Lord Jesus may include a hint of irony in the figure of speech He has chosen here. The people of Laodicea were wealthy. They were experts in buying and selling. Perhaps the Lord is hinting to them something like "since you are so good at buying things, let Me tell you what you really should 'buy'!"[311]

They are advised to *buy* from Him three specific things: *gold*, *white garments*, and *salve* for their *eyes*, and each of those three things is followed by a reason for them to buy those things.

They already have *gold*, but their *gold* is not pure. Heavenly *gold* is pure. Heavenly *gold* can be bought with obedience. That which is being offered for sale in this verse is not salvation.[312] In the Book of Revelation, the offer of salvation is quite different. For example, in 22:17 there is an offer which clearly refers to eternal salvation: "...And let the one who thirsts come; let the one who wants receive the water of life freely." What is offered for sale here in 3:18 is not salvation. They have already been saved by grace. What is offered for sale is heavenly wealth, received according to our works. For our works we receive a reward. For our works we receive a crown. For our works we receive the promises offered to the "victors." These must never be confused with what is free, which is eternal life. Eternal life is not based on our works; it is based on the work of Jesus Christ on the cross. Besides that, we should remember that the church in Laodicea is a real congregation of saved people, and one of the seven churches among which Christ walks. It is a church, not a merely human social institution.

They are advised to buy *white garments*. It is clear that these *white* clothes (like those mentioned in 3:4-5; 4:4; and 6:11) are rewards for righteous living, because they already have clothes that are made from their black wool. Also, they are advised to buy the eye *salve so that* they *can see*.

Warning (continued) (3:19a)

3:19a As many as I love, I rebuke and discipline.

Such a statement would not be made to unbelievers. These are beloved believers that are in need of *rebuke and discipline*. Indeed, this verse suggests that the *discipline* and the negative consequences of disobedience mentioned throughout these seven messages are for the good of the believers involved, and do not include any threat of damnation. This verse cannot possibly be understood to mean, "As many as I love, I rebuke and discipline, perhaps even sending them to hell, if their sin is bad enough and too often repeated, so be zealous and repent." Because of His great *love* for the church in Laodicea, He rebukes and disciplines them, as a father disciplines a child so that the child will obey his father. He wants them to draw nearer in fellowship with Him.

This passage and also Hebrews 12:5-7 allude to Proverbs 3:11-12, which reads, "My son, do not reject the discipline of the LORD and do not loathe His rebuke, for whom the LORD loves He corrects, just like a father the son in whom he delights." Such *rebuke and discipline* are signs of His *love*. The term *discipline*[313] normally has the meaning of "training a child," and is closely related to the word for "child."[314] The Lord Jesus is strict with any of His children that will not obey, and He will give beautiful rewards to the ones who will obey. This expression of His *love* reminds us that the members of the church in Laodicea, although lukewarm, have already believed and become children of God.

Demand (continued) (3:19b)

3:19b Be zealous therefore, and repent.

This is another clear demand the Lord makes upon this congregation. He does not want them to be discouraged or think that the God who rebukes them does not love them. He does love them. They were saved, and they had believed in the Lord Jesus, but they were not exercising their faith; they were not living as followers of the Lord.

7. Promise (3:20-21)

There are extensive rewards promised in this message.

3:20   Look! I am standing at the door and knocking. If someone hears My voice and opens the door, I will come in and I will eat[315] with him, and he with Me.

The Lord Jesus is *knocking* on the *door* of their hearts. How far they have fallen! According to this metaphor He is *standing* outside and wants to fellowship again with them. This figure of speech of table fellowship is an expression full of life and warmth.[316]

The idea that the King of Kings and the Lord of Lords would stand outside, knock on their doors, and ask to be invited in must have very deeply touched the Laodiceans, resentful as they were of Roman overlords forcing their way into their homes demanding to be fed.[317]

This verse is often interpreted that the Lord Jesus is *knocking* on the *door* of the hearts of the unsaved, offering salvation. But if we read this verse in its context, we see very clearly that it is simply not an evangelistic verse. There were seven golden lampstands, seven churches, not six churches and one group of unsaved people that called themselves Christians! The church in Laodicea was headed for the discipline the Lord gives disobedient believers, as He warned then when He said, "As many as I love, I rebuke and discipline." The Lord did not urge them to freely receive the gift of the water of life. Instead He urged them to "buy from Me gold which has been refined in the fire." That would be an inappropriate metaphor for the gift of salvation, but a very appropriate metaphor for the hard work of following the Lord as His obedient disciple.

They did not need to be evangelized, but they very much needed to be rebuked and be encouraged to repent. This verse is part of the encouragement their loving Lord gives them to repent from their self-assured attitudes.

3:21   To the victor I will give to sit with Me on My throne, just as I was victorious and sat down with My Father on His throne.

Of all the promises in chapters two and three this one is the most amazing: *to sit with Me on My Throne*. This is the climax of this section. *To sit with* the Lord Jesus Christ on His *throne*! The glory of this promise has no comparison. To serve God year after year faithfully is a challenge, but

His *throne* is promised to the one who serves faithfully. This promise will be realized in 20:4, in the capital city described in 21:9–22:5.

This is very similar to the promise given in Matthew 19:28 to the first followers of the Lord: "Jesus said to them, 'I tell you the truth, at the renewal of all things, when the Son of Man sits on His glorious throne, you who have followed Me will also sit on twelve thrones, judging the twelve tribes of Israel.'" That is basically[318] the same promise with the same condition. In Matthew the condition is to follow Him and in Revelation the condition is to be a *victor*. Likewise in Luke 22:28-30, "You are those who have stood by Me in My trials. And I confer on you a kingdom, just as My Father conferred one on Me, so that you may eat and drink at My table in My kingdom and sit on thrones, judging the twelve tribes of Israel."[319]

The Lord here says the *Father* has given Him *His throne* because the Lord *was victorious*. He was faithful even to the point of death. This is very similar to what we read in Philippians 2:8-9, "And in appearance being found as man, He humbled Himself, becoming obedient to death, even death on a cross. Therefore also God Him exalted, and gave to Him a Name which is above every name...." Because the Lord humbled Himself, God exalted Him. Here the Laodiceans (whose hearts are presently so lukewarm) are invited to join in on that same principle. If they humble themselves and obey Him, they will be given the right *to sit with* the Lord *on* His *throne*!

Because the Lord's purpose is to persuade, not to give a full theological account of things, not much is said about what happens to those who choose not to accept this challenge from Him. At this point He is not interested in saying, "Well, if you are not willing to be a dedicated follower, I can still assure you that anyone that has accepted Me as his or her personal Savior will not go to hell." This is true, but it is not a part of the encouragement that He wanted to bring to the Laodiceans. He did not want to give them the impression that it really did not matter whether they repented or not. We that have accepted Christ as our personal Savior are indeed eternally secure, but it may not be pastorally effective to remind lukewarm believers of that. It is more pastorally effective to tell them how repugnant their sin is, and how great the rewards are that await them if they will dedicate themselves to the Lord.

3:22 The one who has an ear, let him hear what the Spirit says to the churches."

Again, do you have ears to *hear what the Spirit* is saying? He, *the Spirit* of God, is speaking the words of this passage to you.

In the last of the seven messages we are reminded that the witness of Christ is always true and faithful (a very appropriate reminder for those of us that doubt the goodness of His will). Based on the pattern used in all these letters, the reader expects the congregation to be praised for something. But in Laodicea the Lord found nothing for which to praise them. They were harshly rebuked (but reminded that this rebuke was a sign of His love). Like the other churches, the rebuke was accompanied by a demand. They were commanded to face their spiritual poverty, and see the worthlessness of the worldly wealth that they prided themselves on. He threatened that He would spit them out of His mouth. Finally, in a promise that is similar to but more beautiful than the other promises, they were told that if they became faithful they would sit with Him on His throne. God is patient and good, even in dealing with those who have disappointed Him.

In these messages the Lord makes it very clear that He understands the local situation and the heart attitudes of the congregations. As He does that His presence there among them is powerfully illustrated. To each of the congregations He says, "I know...." He knows our hearts and our situations too.

We should imitate the Lord's approach to speaking to the churches. We have seen how He used various elements of their lives and settings to speak effectively to them. Like Him, as we draw near to a certain area or ethnic group, we can also use the elements of their lives as we communicate with them so our ministries can likewise be effective.

In the beginning (Genesis 1:28), God gave Adam and Eve their task: to be fruitful, fill the earth, subdue it, and rule it as His images, His representatives. Adam and Eve did badly, and we his descendants have done badly. Now another, a true son of Adam, is going to fulfill the task God gave so long ago to Adam. And we, redeemed by Christ's sacrifice and given glorified bodies at the resurrection, will be invited to join Him in that task – if we are faithful now! In that way, what has seemed like the dreadful failure of God's plan to create a wonderful world shall, in fact, turn out not to be dreadful at all, but wonderful – and especially wonderful for every believer who decides to reject and turn away from that ancient serpent, and instead follow the Second Adam in obedience and in victory. Will you be there, standing among the victors, enjoying the fulfillment of God's design for this earth? That is the goal and purpose of chapters two and three: be a victor!

However, for our spiritual health it may be helpful to consider for a moment the theological implications of the seven messages. What do they teach us about the idea that our eternal salvation can be lost? Was the congregation in Laodicea, which the Lord scolded so severely, ever threatened with eternal hell? Some Christians speak of "backslidden Christians." What is their situation in these letters? Or, in other words, what is the situation of the carnal Christian? These and other very practical theological questions are spoken of very clearly in the seven letters. They might be called backsliders, carnal Christians, or lazy believers, but they lose their rewards, not their salvation.

The Seven Letters to the Seven Churches

Address	Christ is...	Praise	Criticism	Demand	Warning	Promise
Ephesus	with them	pure doctrine	left first love	remember and repent	remove lampstand	tree of life
Smyrna	alive again	you are rich!		be faithful		no 2nd death
Pergam.	sword	you did not deny	Balaam	repent	sword	hidden manna
Thyatira	eyes, feet	doing more	Jezebel	repent/hold on	she will suffer	authority
Sardis	7 spirits	only a few	you are dead	strengthen	thief	white clothes
Philadel.	holy and true	kept His word		hold on	crown be taken	crown
Laodicea	Amen		lukewarm	buy gold	spit out	throne

III. "What will happen after this" (4-22)

Revelation 1:19 reads, "Write what you saw, what is now, and what will take place after these things." Revelation 4:1 reads, "After these things I looked – and see! – an open door in heaven. And the voice which I first heard like a trumpet was speaking to me saying, 'Come up here, and I will show you what must take place after these things.'" In the Greek the words "after these things" in both verses are the same. The only difference is that 1:19 uses the verb "will," and 4:1 uses the verb "must." Thus we are indirectly told that the third section of the book begins here. We enter now into the long section of the Book of Revelation that tells the story of the end of the age.

The first section, chapter one, was the vision of the Lord Himself. If only we had sufficient spiritual insight, we would understand and apply that vision to our lives, and we would need to read no further. However, we need some help. That vision was too difficult for us to understand and apply in our lives and our ministries. The second section, chapters two and three, helped us apply what was there in chapter one. If only we had sufficient spiritual insight and dedication, we would understand and consistently apply those seven letters appropriately to our lives and the lives of those we serve, and we would need to read no further. However, we still need more help. This third section will help us to see that the promises of chapters two and three were not empty words, but indeed shall be fulfilled. This section will encourage the persecuted among us, as also it encouraged the congregation in Smyrna, to be faithful. It will help those indulging in sexual immorality and idolatry, as in Pergamum and Thyatira, to see that these activities are not "victimless crimes," they are instead a participation in the great prostitute's "abominations and unclean things." It will also help those who are trusting that their wealth will bring them satisfaction, as the Laodiceans trusted, to see that physical wealth is of mere temporary and failing value, and those who love it will certainly be dismayed. In fact, reading and meditating on this section will help each of us who have sensed a spiritual kinship with any of the seven churches to realize that each and every word spoken to each of those churches is to be taken with the utmost seriousness.

We are now living in the time between the third and the fourth chapters of the Book of Revelation. The seven churches are history (although there are many churches like them today), and the visions of the end times are yet to come.

This entire section is given not merely to educate us about the order of events at the end of the age, but more importantly to encourage us to godliness. The insight we gain in reading this section should touch our hearts and encourage us to do what is necessary to be counted among the victors, so we can join the ranks of the victors on those thrones described in 20:4. (Again, we join the redeemed by faith in Christ, but we join the victors by works that come from a vital living faith.) Let there be no doubt that He will make good on His promises to the victors, in a way that on the one hand is well-described here in the Book of Revelation, and on the other hand is more amazing than we can imagine. In this life victors have difficult things they have to do, but the rewards offered are well worth that pain.

Victors are offered thrones and authority to rule. But will they rule this earth, as it is now? In many parts of the world, perhaps in every part of the world, that would be an undesirable reward. Corruption and lawlessness unite with materialism and false religions to make ruling well seem impossible. Are the victors to inherit the world as it is, and have to straighten it out themselves? Certainly not! But what will the Lamb of God do to make this world a wonderful place to rule? That question is answered in this longest section of the Book of Revelation.

This section has the following parts:
    A. The Vision of the Throne Room 4:1–5:14
    B. The Time of Torment 6:1–20:3
    C. The Millennium and Judgment 20:4-15
    D. The New Jerusalem 21:1–22:5
    E. The Conclusion of the Vision 22:6-17

This section is followed by the Conclusion of the Book of Revelation, in 22:18-21.

A. Vision of Throne Room (4:1–5:14)

Right at the beginning of this section, John is transported to heaven. He is not taken to the edge of heaven, or to an intermediate level of heaven, he is taken to the very center of heaven, to the throne room of God. And he describes to us what he sees there.

Just as the seven letters to the churches began with a vision of the Lord Jesus, so also this section begins with a vision of God on His throne, and the Lord Jesus there beside Him. What John experienced, what he wrote about in chapters four and five, is a kind of "hinge" section in the structure of the Book of Revelation, joining the seven letters with the opening of the seven seals of the scroll. On the one hand, these two chapters are strongly connected with the seven letters, especially regarding the rewards that are promised. In both sections, there are thrones, white clothes, and crowns. On the other hand, there are strong connections with the opening of the seals, because in this section the scroll and its seals are introduced.

In chapter four, the One on the throne, who is surrounded by thrones and four creatures, is praised as the Creator. In chapter five the Lamb of God, who comes to the One on the throne, is praised as the Redeemer. The taking of the scroll from the hands of the One on the throne bridges these two chapters. The meaning of the scroll is very important and will be discussed in the following section.

The experiences of the churches of chapters two and three show us that enemies of the church freely threaten and oppress the churches of Christ on the earth. But according to the perspective of the throne room, pictured in chapters four and five, the One who has absolute power is the Lord God, not evil powers on the earth.[320]

All of chapter four tells us about the setting: what the throne room is like, who is there, and the activity there, which is worship.

1. Transition (4:1-2)

4:1 After these things I looked – and see! – an open door in heaven. And[321] the voice which I first heard like a trumpet was speaking to me, saying "Come up here, and I will show you what must take place after these things."

As was noted above, the wording of this verse, especially *what must take place after these things*, clues us in that we have left the second section and are in the third section that was given to us in 1:19. Therefore, this verse moves us into the part of the Book of Revelation that tells about the future.

John is brought to *heaven* to see *what must take place after these things*. The term *must* is important here. Prophecies, which are included in this section, are not just something that *will* happen. These prophecies *must* happen, because the One on the throne has already determined them.[322]

Other apocalyptic writings also tell about doors *open in heaven*.[323] However, as noted in the Introduction, it is far from certain that the early readers in the province of Asia had read or heard very much of Jewish apocalyptic literature.

Some Bible teachers will say that the words *come up here* somehow refer to the Rapture, but the evidence for that interpretation is very weak. It is a command to John in the first century, not to the entire church at the moment of the Rapture.

4:2 And right away I was in the Spirit, and look, a throne in heaven with Someone seated on it,

If we compare this verse with 5:7 we see that the *Someone* sitting on the *throne* is God Himself, but we also observe that very little is said about Him until the New Heavens and the New Earth in chapter 21. Note the comments about the One *seated* upon the *throne* in the section entitled "Revelation and Systematic Theology."

The word *throne*[324] is used 62 times in the Greek New Testament, 47 of which are in the Book of Revelation. God's *throne* is mentioned in many passages of Scripture, including Psalm 45:6; 47:8; Ezekiel 1:26; Matthew 5:34; and Hebrews 12:2.

2. Throne and Surroundings (4:3-11)

4:3   who was like the appearance of jasper[325] and carnelian,[326] and a rainbow was all around the throne, like the appearance of an emerald.

How hard should we try to interpret these things? We read about *jasper, carnelian,* and the emerald-like *rainbow.* As is true in many passages in this book, different interpreters have different levels of boldness in stating their interpretations, but the data available upon which those interpretations are based are very limited. Different teachers express different levels of certainty about an interpretation, but sometimes that level of certainty is tied more to the personality of the teacher than the strength of the evidence of the interpretation. It is truly the student's responsibility to ask, "Why do you hold that interpretation?" He or she should be able to ask "What principle of interpretation supports that view?" A good commentary and a good teacher should have good answers to those questions. It is easy to give very interesting explanations about all these obscure things, if indeed nobody dares ask questions about the facts that provide the basis for such explanations!

Exodus 24:10; 1 Kings 22:19; Isaiah 6:1; Ezekiel 1:26-28; and Daniel 7:9 describe visions with similar elements.

The stone named *jasper* is hard to identify. The stone here called *carnelian* is a red stone which in that era was often engraved.[327] It may be the same as the stone now known as *carnelian.*

There is very little biblical support for giving particular meaning to particular stones. Perhaps they are listed simply to help the reader understand that His *appearance* was glorious. Notice that He simply had the *appearance* of these stones. The stones are not actually present, but the One seated on the throne was *like the appearance of jasper and carnelian.*

4:4 And all around the throne were twenty-four thrones, and upon the thrones were seated twenty-four elders, clothed in white clothes, with golden crowns on their heads.

Very soon in the description of the *throne* room we are told of the *twenty-four elders*. They are on *twenty-four thrones*. They are dressed in *white*. They wear *golden crowns*.

Where else have we recently read of *thrones*, *white clothes*, and *crowns*? The nearer the context, the more important it is for interpreting. These elements are all mentioned in the near context, in chapters two and three! Who are these *elders*? They represent all the victors, who will all be receiving what was promised to them back in chapters two and three. These are the ones who obeyed and were "faithful until death."

There are three problems with this interpretation:
1. There are only *twenty-four elders*, but there should be many more than *twenty-four* victors.
2. They are on separate *thrones* around the one *throne*, but the victors in chapters two and three are said to be seated on the Lord Jesus' *throne*, not their own *thrones*.
3. The *twenty-four elders* appear here in chapter four, but rewards like *crowns*, *thrones*, and *white clothes* are not awarded until much later.

By way of response, it should be noted:
1. It is very reasonable to assume in such a context that these *twenty-four elders* are *representative* of all the victors, perhaps twelve from the Old Testament era, and twelve from the New Testament era, or twelve from Israel, and twelve from the church. Also, since we do hope that there will be many millions of victors amongst more that a billion believers in the Kingdom, it is understandable that all those millions of victors/elders were not shown to John, because if he saw millions of victors he would get the idea that those people were all the redeemed. How could he have been visually shown that those millions are only a part of the billion? The human eye can only see a certain amount of detail, and then things get blurry!
2. It is also very reasonable to minimize the distinction between sitting on the Lord Jesus' own *throne* and sitting on one of the *thrones* that surround His *throne*, since we have not yet seen any of these *thrones*. Perhaps there is a sense in which the many *thrones* are a part of the one *throne*.

3. Although it is true that this interpretation seems to go against the chronology of this section, it is hard to prove that no rewards are given ahead of time. In fact, not all victors receive their rewards at the same time. Note that "the souls of those who had been killed on account of the word of God" were each given *white* robes in 6:9-11. Likewise also the martyrs of 7:9-17 had *white* robes and various other rewards for their faithfulness. It is therefore reasonable that the representative *twenty-four elders* could receive their rewards earlier than other victors.

The *elders* are again mentioned in 4:10. They are also mentioned in passing in 5:5-14; 7:11, 13; 11:16; 14:3; and 19:4. Since they come up so soon in the description of the *throne* room, it is likely that they will be an important part of the book.

Isaiah 24:23 speaks of the Lord Almighty's glorious end-time reign in Jerusalem, "before its elders."[328]

One alternative interpretation is that the *elders* are angels. However, both the designation "elder" and the *thrones* suggest that these are rulers, but angels do not rule over humans. In fact in 1 Corinthians 6:3 Paul says just the opposite: "Do you not know that we will judge angels?" The context indicates that the best understanding is that the *twenty-four elders* represent all the victors that were highlighted in chapters two and three.

4:5 From the throne came lightning, roaring,[329] and thunder. And seven torches of fire were burning before His throne. They are the seven spirits of God.

Such *lightning* and *thunder* is also in Exodus 19:16 when the Lord came down to Mount Sinai. The words of Ezekiel 1:13 are also used in this verse. Psalm 18:14 and Hebrews 12:18-19 also use words that are almost the same about the glory of God in the Old Testament.

The judgments of Revelation are similar to the ten plagues on Egypt before the people of God are freed and the theocratic kingdom of Israel is set up under Moses. Prior to that, when God met Moses at Mount Sinai, there were *thunder, lightning,* and earthquakes according to Exodus 19:16-18 and Psalm 68:8. According to Isaiah 13:13 when the Lord comes to the earth, the sky and the earth will tremble and shake.[330]

As the following chart shows, this is the first of four times this set of terms appears.

Rev. 4:5	Rev. 8:5	Rev. 11:19	Rev. 16:17-21
"came from the throne"	"prayers… went up before God"	"the temple of God in heaven was opened"	"from the temple of heaven from the throne"
in the throne room	the opening of the seventh seal	the blowing of the seventh trumpet	the pouring out of the seventh bowl
lightning	thunder	lightning	lightning
roaring	roaring	roaring	roaring
thunder	lightning	thunder	thunder
	an earthquake	huge hailstones	a great earthquake
			huge hailstones

In 4:5 there are only three of these elements (in the *throne* room).
In 8:5 there are four elements (at the opening of the seventh seal).
In 11:19 there are four elements ds(at the seventh trumpet).[331]

In 16:18-21 all five elements will appear and be developed (at the pouring out of the seventh bowl). According to Bauckham,[332] this suggests that 16:18-21 is the climax of 4:5; 8:5; and 11:19.

Revelation 4:5 tells about the *throne* room of God. All the disasters in the chain of judgments originate from there. In 8:5 we see the results of opening the seventh seal. In 11:19 we see the results of the blowing the seventh trumpet. In 16:18-21 we see the results of the pouring out the seventh bowl. In 16:18-21 all five of the elements are included and expanded upon. These three stages are united by the three elements, then four elements, then four elements, then all five elements in detail. Thus the judgment from God is more clearly seen as one united judgment which originates from God Himself. It is not a random collection of coincidences, but carefully orchestrated judgment by the living God. This is one example that shows the careful structure of this book.

As a side note, this three – four – four – five element development also encourages the telescopic view of these chapters rather than the reiteration view, all of which is discussed in the comments prior to 6:1. If the reiteration view were correct, then the same intensity of judgment should be observed through all these chapters. Instead, we see a carefully designed indicator of increased intensity.[333]

The text tells us that these terrifying things come *from the throne*. This expression, in the context of the Book of Revelation, means "from God." Note the comments about "the One seated on the throne" in the section, "Revelation and Systematic Theology."

The expression *seven spirits of God* refers to the Spirit of God, as is discussed in that same section. Here He is also referred to as *seven torches of fire*.

4:6 And before the throne there was something like[334] a sea of glass, like crystal. And in the center of the throne, and around the throne, were four creatures, and they were covered with eyes, in front and in back.

According to Morris,[335] John could not find words to exactly describe what he saw, so he does the best he can, and uses expressions such as *something like*. The interpreter needs to remember that whatever it was that John saw *before the throne* was not simply a *sea* of crystal-clear *glass*. It is something more awesome than that, but John could not find words to be more precise, so he has to say that it was *something like*....

We do know that the *glass* of John's era was not clear, and it most certainly was not *like crystal*, so this must have been even more amazing to him and to his ancient readers.

The words *something like a sea of glass, like crystal*, along with "lightning, rumblings and thunder" and "seven lamps of fire" give the impression that human beings could not get close to *the throne*,[336] because *the throne* was so very glorious. Compare this passage with Exodus 24:10; Ezekiel 1:22, 26; and Revelation 15:2-3.

The *creatures* are *covered with eyes, in front and in back*. They are *in the center of the throne and around the throne*. Other than the *creatures* only the Lamb of God could stand so close to God (Revelation 5:6 and 7:17). These *creatures*, separately or all *four* together, are mentioned twenty times in the Book of Revelation.[337]

4:7 And the first creature was like a lion, and the second creature like an ox, and the third creature had a face like a man, and the fourth creature was like an eagle flying.

The four creatures are similar to the seraphim of Isaiah 6:1-3 and the cherubim of Ezekiel 10. The creatures in Ezekiel 1:10-11 each have four faces. These in Revelation 4 each have one *face*, but the faces in both texts are the faces of a *man, a lion, an ox*, and *an eagle*. This might somehow symbolize that they are appointed over or represent *man*, all wild animals, all domesticated animals, and all birds, but it is not appropriate to be dogmatic about this interpretation. Some have tried to make parallels with Matthew, Mark, Luke, and John, but there is no biblical support for that connection.

> 4:8 And the four creatures each had six wings. All around and underneath they were full of eyes, and they had no rest day or night, saying:
>
> "Holy Holy Holy, the Lord God, the Almighty,
> Who was and who is, and who is to come!"[338]

In Isaiah 6:2 there are seraphim who also have *six wings*, "with two he covers his face, with two he covers his feet, and with two he flies." According to Thomas,[339] this means that the seraphim are amazed and ready to obey the commands of God. In this text John mentions their *eyes*, which he also mentioned in 4:6.

See the comments under 14:11, where the same expression, *no rest day or night*, is also used of the torment that will be experienced by the unbelievers that worship the beast. This repetition is an intentional contrast. There are those that will have *no rest day or night* in joyful worship, and there are those that will have *no rest day or night* in agonizing punishment.

Concerning the expression, *Who was and who is and who is to come*, see the comments in the section entitled "Revelation and Systematic Theology."

> 4:9 And whenever the creatures give glory, honor, and thanks to the One who is seated on the throne, who lives forever and ever,

This verse reveals that *the creatures* are the leaders of heavenly worship.[340]

> 4:10 the twenty-four elders will throw themselves down before the One who is seated on the throne and worship the One who lives forever and ever, and they throw their crowns before His throne, saying:

The four creatures *worship* God, and in response *the twenty-four elders worship the One who lives forever and ever. As part of their worship they throw their crowns before* Him.

This event is repeated "whenever the creatures give glory... to the One who is seated on the throne," so somehow there are many *crowns* involved. The word here translated *throw*[341] is sometimes better translated "place"[342] or "set," but it more often means throw.[343] On the other hand, the translation "place" may be better because perhaps in the *throne* room of God no one would dare to *throw* anything at all.

4:11   "Worthy You are, the Lord our God, the Holy One,[344]
        to receive glory and honor and power,
        because You created all things,
        and because of Your will they exist and were created!"

The praise here focuses more upon *God* as Creator, but the praise after the scroll is opened will focus more on Him as Redeemer.

The expression *because of Your will they exist and were created* is difficult to translate, but the words *they exist* seem to emphasize the fact that all things *exist*, whereas *and were created* seems to emphasize their coming into existence by the hand of *God*.[345]

The scene of the throne room is awesome, glorious and beyond human understanding. The activity of the throne room is worship. As a part of the continuing worship described here, the twenty-four elders cast (or perhaps "place") their crowns before the throne. This is not a one-time event. They somehow can do it whenever the four creatures praise Him, and those four creatures are doing that continually! Why they do not run out of crowns is not explained to us, but this may help us not to hold too strongly to the idea that there are only a literal twenty-four elders.

Chapter four orients us to the throne room, so that we are ready for chapter five.

3. Scroll and Lamb (5:1-7)

Chapter five is about the Scroll and the Lamb who is in the center of heaven, who is worthy to open the scroll.

In John's era, wills or inheritance documents were written on papyrus scrolls that were sealed with seven seals.[346] Anyone preparing a will would call seven trusted friends, and they would bring their signet rings (rings that each had a stone on it, carved in some special way, perhaps with the owner's portrait, as in the illustration). The signet rings of those seven witnesses were then used to seal the rolled up scroll. Then when the man died, those seven trusted friends were called, and they each testified about whether that seal was truly his own untampered seal or not. Then the scroll could be opened and the inheritance distributed according to the will.[347]

The illustration[348] shows four carved stones that were set in signet rings. The upper left shows a man from the fifth century BC. The upper right is a Greek field marshal of the Hellenistic period. The lower left is a wealthy Hellenistic man. The lower right is a very vigorous man, possibly a Roman. Such rings were used to place a unique mark upon the wax or clay that would become the seal, much like a signature on a legal document today.

Anyone who had ever seen a will or who ever received an inheritance in those days in the Roman empire would surely remember the use of the seven seals to close and seal the scroll. Therefore the meaning of this seven-sealed scroll was very clear to them: someone would soon be given an inheritance.

At first the idea that "victors" will somehow "inherit" the earth seems difficult, because we think that someone has to die for an inheritance to be granted. That is not a problem in the New Testament, where the idea of inheritance is used to describe special promises for those that believe and obey the Lord. In Matthew 5:5 the Lord said, "Blessed are the meek, for they will inherit the earth." Remember that the meek are parallel to the poor in spirit, those who mourn, those who hunger and thirst for righteousness, the merciful, the pure in heart, and the peacemakers. All of that becomes a rather complete picture of the ones that are called "victors" in chapter 2-3. In fact in 21:7 the connection between the victors of chapters two and three and the heirs that will enjoy the inheritance of this inheritance document is made explicit: "The one who conquers will inherit these things, and I will be his God and he will be My son." The victors are also the heirs!

In Galatians 5:21[349] we read, "... envy, murder, drunkenness, carousing, and things like these, of which I say ahead of time to you, just as also I have said ahead of time, that those doing such things shall not inherit the Kingdom of God." 1 Peter 3:9 says "not paying back evil for evil or insult for insult; but instead blessing, knowing that for this you were called, so that you might inherit blessing." These two passages do not say that born-again people that behave that way will not enter the Kingdom, only that they will not inherit it. One can enter a place, a home, for instance, without owning it. Indeed, those that have believed in the Lord Jesus as their personal Savior but have not gone on to follow Him, to be a victor as described in chapters two and three, will enter the Kingdom of God because they are redeemed by the blood of the Lamb, but they will not be seated on any thrones, and will not be given any authority there. The congregation in Laodicea did not need to repent to gain admission into the Kingdom of God, but they needed to repent if they were going to sit with the Lord on His throne.

So, the book centers on the victors and their rewards. In chapters two and three we learned about the demands that had to be met to be a victor, and we learned about the many promises made to victors. There were threats about the loss of rewards to those who would not repent and start living as victors.

Now here in this transition to the opening of the seals, the setting has been described (chapter four). We see the 24 elders (representing all victors) already in possession of some of their rewards (crowns, white clothes, and thrones), but not yet ruling over the earth. And then the inheritance document is taken up by the Lord Jesus, and in chapter six the opening of the seals begins. After the series of seals, trumpets and bowls, we will see the faithful on thrones (20:4).

Since the scroll is an inheritance document, this event has great significance for believers who are truly faithful and who obey what is written in chapters two and three. God has an amazing inheritance planned for the "overcomers," the victors. All that remains is that the scroll of inheritance be opened and that the inheritance be given to the victors. The Roman practice of sealing an inheritance document with seals is used by God as an important element in the structure of the Book of Revelation.

In 5:1-3 the scroll is introduced. It was crucial to find someone that could open that scroll (5:4-5). When the Lamb takes the scroll He is worshiped (5:8), and the opening of the seven seals actually becomes the outline of the Book of Revelation, all the way through chapter 18, as will be explained below.

5:1   And I saw in the right hand of the One who was seated on the throne a scroll written on the front and back, sealed[350] with seven seals.

See the comments in the section entitled "Revelation and Systematic Theology" concerning *the One who was seated on the throne*. Writing was normally only on one side of the papyrus.³⁵¹ It was harder to write on the *back* side of papyrus, because of the "grain" of the material. Perhaps the fact that this *scroll* is *written* on both sides speaks of unusual fullness or abundance.

5:2 And I saw a strong angel proclaiming in a loud voice: "Who is worthy to open the scroll and to break its seals?"³⁵²

It was illegal for unauthorized people to *break* a seal. People would only do that if they wanted to tamper with the will. (Remember that Jesus' tomb was sealed, so that others could not *break* that seal and steal the body in the tomb.) They all understood that not just anyone could *break* those *seals* and *open the scroll*.

5:3 And no one in heaven above or on earth or under the earth was able to open the scroll or look into it.

This highlights the importance of this particular *scroll*. In all of God's creation there was not one person worthy *to open the scroll*. God's creation is here divided into three parts: *heaven*, *earth*, and *under the earth*. This passage proclaims that there is no one in all creation like the Lord Jesus.

5:4 And I was weeping a great deal because no one was found worthy to open the scroll or to look into it.

It was painful for John that there was *no one* that could *open the scroll*. This means that he knew what the *scroll* was, and he very much longed for it to be opened. If indeed it is the inheritance document for all the victors, John's tears are understandable. He longed for the end of the age, when God's Kingdom would at last be established and this inheritance would be made available!

5:5 And one of the elders said to me, "Do not weep; look, the Lion from the tribe of Judah, the Root of David, has conquered. He is the One that can open³⁵³ the scroll and its seven seals."

Somehow John apparently had not understood that the Lord Jesus was in the throne room of God.

The word *conquered* and the word "victor" in Revelation 2-3 are the same Greek word in different grammatical forms. In fact, besides its use seven times in chapters two and three, this same verb, translated "to conquer," "overcome," or "be victorious,"³⁵⁴ is used in the following passages:

- 5:5 And one of the elders said to me, "Do not weep; look, the Lion from the tribe of Judah, the Root of David, has *conquered*. He is the One that can open the scroll and its seven seals."

- 6:2 And look, a white horse, and its rider had a bow, and he was given a crown, and he went away *conquering*, even so that he might *conquer*.
- 11:7 And when they have finished their testimony, the beast that comes up out of the abyss will make war on them and be *victorious* over them and kill them.
- 12:11 And they were *victorious* over him

  by the blood of the Lamb

  and by the word of their testimony,

  and they did not love their lives until death.
- 13:7 And it was given to him to make war against the saints and to be *victorious* over them. And authority was given to him over every tribe, and people, and language, and nation,
- 15:2 And I saw something like a sea of glass mixed with fire, and those who were *victorious* over the beast and his image and the number of his name, standing by the sea of glass, holding zithers from God.
- 17:14 They will make war with the Lamb, but the Lamb will *conquer* them, because he is Lord of lords and King of kings, and those with Him are called, chosen, and faithful.
- 21:7 The one who *conquers* will inherit these things, and I will be his God and he will be My son.

In these verses we see two radically different ideas about victory (or perhaps "success"), and the reader is in effect forced to chose one or the other definition of victory or success in his or her life. On the one hand the Anti-Christ is victorious, 13:7. On the other hand Christ was victorious on His cross, and the saints can be victorious if they follow His example in loving obedience. Do you accept the devil's definition or the saints' definition of victory? Remember, the victory of the saints is by "loving not their lives even until death" (12:11). If you accept that definition, what does it mean about your own values? Are you moving towards victory? According to which definition?

Remember Revelation 3:21, "To the victor I will give to sit with Me on My throne, just as I was victorious and sat down with My Father on His throne." Because Jesus was victorious, He gained His throne, and He can *open* the *seals* of the *scroll* that contains the victors' rewards! The Victorious One is about to *open* those *seals* and give the victors the right to sit on His throne with Him.

The expressions *the Lion from the Tribe of Judah* and *the Root of David* are messianic titles[355] that go back to Genesis 49:9-10 and Isaiah 11:1.

It is the Lord that must *open* each of the *seven seals*, but later we will see that there are *seven* angels that each blow their trumpet, and *seven* angels that each pour out their bowl.

5:6   And I saw, between the throne and the four creatures, and among the elders, a Lamb standing, but looking as if it had been slain.[356] He had seven horns and seven eyes, which are the seven spirits of God sent out into all the earth.

Finally John sees the Lord. John describes Him metaphorically as a *Lamb*,[357] not a Lion. With figures of speech that carry profound Christian truth about Jesus and about our lives and ministries, the Lion triumphed by being a *Lamb*. His death as a *Lamb* is likened to the Old Testament sacrifices made to God. He is *standing*, risen from the dead.

The use of the word "horn" in Deuteronomy 33:17 and 1 Samuel 2:10 tells us that a horn is a symbol of strength, so with *seven horns* He is perfectly powerful.

Likewise the use of the word *eyes* in Genesis 3:5 and Zechariah 4:10 tells us that *eyes* speak of knowledge or wisdom, so with *seven eyes* He is perfectly wise.

The *seven horns and seven eyes* also represent *the seven spirits of God*, or the sevenfold Spirit of *God*. See the section entitled "Revelation and Systematic Theology."

Christ's death and resurrection are metaphorically presented in 5:6. His victory is mentioned in 5:5. Anti-Christ's near death and near resurrection are mentioned in 13:3 and his victory is mentioned in 13:7. Revelation seems to be comparing them, and emphasizing the comparison by highlighting it with these repeated terms. In fact, 5:6 and 13:3 use almost exactly the same exact expression in Greek for *as if slain*. In 5:6 it is used of Christ, and in 13:3, it is used of the Anti-Christ. See the section on "The Interpretation of Numbers and Repetitions." These terms are thus repeated to show an intentional contrast between Christ and Anti-Christ.

5:7   And He came and took[358] the scroll from the right hand of Him who is seated on the throne.

Nobody else can approach God like this! Even the seraphim of Isaiah 6:1-3 have to use two of their wings to cover their feet and two of their wings to cover their faces. This is a very important moment.[359]

When the Lord takes *the scroll*, He is finally doing what the Father invited Him to do in Psalm 2:8.

> 2:7 I tell of the decree of the LORD: He said to Me, "You are My Son; today I have become your Father.
>
> 2:8 *Ask of Me*, and I will make the nations Your inheritance, the ends of the earth Your possession.
>
> 2:9 You will shepherd them with an iron staff; You will shatter them like a potter's vessel."

It is clear that this is an important psalm for Revelation, because verse 9 was already quoted in 2:27. But Psalm 2, written about 1000 BC, was not the only time in the Old Testament that this event was foretold. In about 500 BC, Daniel wrote, in Daniel 7:13-14, "I was seeing in a night vision, and look! – with the clouds of heaven One like a Son of Man was coming even up to the Ancient of Days He reached and before Him He was brought, and to Him was given eternal dominion which shall not pass away, and His Kingdom which shall not be destroyed."

About 600 years later, John saw the vision of the Lamb, looking as if it had been slain, coming and taking *the scroll* from the One *seated on the throne*.

This is the event that godly people throughout the earth have longed for. After so many years, He finally asks, He finally approaches the Ancient of Days, asking for the nations to be made His inheritance.[360]

He takes *the scroll*, and that brings worship and song, expanding out from the Lamb in ever widening circles until all creation is worshiping.

1. in the near circle around the throne 5:8-10
2. in a greater circle around the throne 5:11-12
3. in all creation 5:13

4. Praise to Him who takes the Scroll (5:8-14)

Every person mentioned in this passage worships the Lord because He has taken up the scroll. At the moment He took up the scroll the uncertainty about the timing of His coming and the establishment of His kingdom is gone. The faithful ones are going to be given their inheritance soon. They are going to soon rule over the nations. But first the righteousness of God requires the nations to be purged of evil through terrifying judgments. Then the Kingdom of God will be established on this earth.

5:8   And when He had taken the scroll, the four creatures and the twenty-four elders fell before the Lamb, each with a zither[361] and golden bowls[362] full of incense, which are the prayers of the saints.[363]

As He takes *the scroll*, the ones we have already met in the throne room even more actively worship Him. This dramatic response also indicates how important it is that the seals of *the scroll* be opened.

Though *the prayers of the saints* are considered lowly on earth they are valued in heaven.[364] For years and years, godly men and women have prayed, "Come quickly, Lord." Those *prayers* did not just blow away in the wind, or echo pointlessly against the ceiling. They are being gathered up in *golden bowls* in heaven. In Revelation 8:3-4 *incense* is also offered, and it is also associated with *the prayers of the saints*. As the Lord takes the scroll, those *prayers* are being answered.

5:9   And they sang a new song, "Worthy You are, to take the scroll and to open its seals, because You were slain, and with Your blood You purchased us[365] for God from every tribe and language[366] and people and nation.[367]

The song they sing is not just *new* from the point of view of time.[368] In its essence, it is *new*. Before this there was never a *song* like this *new song*.[369]

God the Father is praised as *worthy*[370] in 4:11 because He created everything. Then in this text, the Lord Jesus is praised as *worthy*,[371] because He has become the Savior. Other than the One who *purchased* mankind from sin, there was no one *worthy* to prepare the inheritance of the victors, no one *worthy* to lift them up to reign with Him.

Their *song* emphasizes that the Lord Jesus is the Redeemer of not only Israel, but of all people *from every tribe and language and people and nation*. This salvation is for all people from all backgrounds.

The four words, *tribe, language, people,* and *nation,* are repeated seven times, never in the same order, never in the reverse of one of the orders. The seven texts that contain those four words are 5:9; 7:9; 10:11; 11:9; 13:7; 14:6; and 17:15. There is slight variation in 10:11 ("kings" instead of *tribe*) and 17:15 ("multitudes" instead of *tribe*). According to Mounce,[372] there is no point in trying to figure out how the four words are different from one another. Used together like this, they point to the totality of mankind, not something in particular. The Lord Jesus is the Savior of all peoples of the earth, not just the Jews.

Because the numeral four suggests the world and the numeral seven suggests completeness, the repetition of four words (*tribe, language, people,* and *nation*) seven times emphasizes that what is said about the tribes in Revelation covers all of mankind.

But there is more to this seven-fold repetition of these four words. Bauckham[373] connects these seven phrases with the victory of the Lamb of God mentioned in 5:5-9, right before the phrase was used the first time in 5:9. We observed in the discussion of 5:6 above that the idea of "victory" and the expression "as though slain" were used in 5:5-6 about the Lamb of God and in 13:3 and 7 about the Anti-Christ. These two passages also include the repeated four words. The relationship between 5:9 and 13:7 emphasizes the contrast between the Christ and the Anti-Christ. The Lamb of God conquers by His own death, so that every "tribe, language, people and nation" will worship Him, and they will become the "kings and priests for God." Similarly, Anti-Christ is almost dead, healed and then is worshiped. Anti-Christ conquers the saints and he becomes a ruler over every "tribe and people and language and nation."

Expressing this in present-day language, one might say that the Christ and the Anti-Christ are in a global competition, one against the other, with very different goals.

5:10   And for our God You made them kings and priests,[374] and they shall reign[375] upon the earth."

At first glance it appears that the word *them* refers to all believers, which would mean that all believers will *reign upon the earth*. However, according to the previous verse, the purchased ones are the twenty-four elders (and the four creatures!), so it is the twenty-four elders, and all the victors that they represent, that shall *reign upon the earth*.

The Anti-Christ intimidates, kills, and gains unworthy worship, but in marked contrast the Christ dies to provide redemption for all people, draws people of "every tribe and language and people and nation" to Himself, and invites them to become *kings and priests*, who will ultimately *reign upon the earth* and worship Him. The Christ is wonderfully worthy of worship!

5:11   And I looked, and I heard something like[376] the voice of many angels, encircling the throne and the creatures and the elders, and they numbered ten thousands of ten thousands, and thousands of thousands,

According to Beasley-Murray[377] the numeral 10,000 is the highest numeral in the Greek language. Literally, John is saying that there were *ten thousands* of *ten thousands* added to *thousands of thousands* of *angels*, but maybe what John means is that the total of *angels* cannot be counted. In Daniel 7:10 and Hebrews 12:22 we read about similarly uncountable numbers of *angels*.

In 5:11-13 the circle of those praising the Lamb gets bigger and bigger, until it includes all creation.

5:12 saying in a loud voice, "Worthy is the slain Lamb, to receive power and wealth and wisdom and might and honor and glory and blessing."

Once again, the word *worthy* is emphasized in the praise of the *Lamb*, and once again He is praised because He became the sacrifice for us. He is praised with seven terms. The first four terms refer to His essence and the last three refer to the attitude of men and angels towards Him.[378]

5:13 And every creature which is in heaven and upon the earth and under the earth, and upon the sea, and those in them, I heard them all saying "To the One seated on the throne and to the Lamb, blessing and honor and glory and power into the ages of ages. Amen!"

In 5:6 John's vision is expanded to see the Lord Jesus. In 5:11 his vision is expanded further to see an uncountable number of angels in heaven. In this verse, John is able to hear *every creature*. In mentioning *heaven, upon the earth, under the earth, upon the sea, and those in them*, John is emphasizing that God is praised by the whole creation. We should meditate on this verse. These are not merely details far removed from the purpose of John. This verse is the climax of the praise that is like the ripples in a pond, going out wider and wider until it reaches all creation. Because His redemption reaches all of His creation, praise to Him will come from all of His creation.[379]

In chapter four, God (*the One seated on the throne*) is praised. In 5:1-12, the Lord Jesus (*the Lamb*) is praised. In 5:13-14, both *the One seated on the Throne* and *the Lamb* are praised. There may be students of the Bible and theologians on earth these days that are unsure of the relationship between God the Father and the One who is here called *the Lamb*, and some of them may wonder whether *the Lamb* is really deity, and whether He should be worshiped, but in the Book of Revelation there is no doubt about these things! Praise and worship are offered both to *the One seated upon the throne* and *to the Lamb*. In this passage there is no hesitation in giving jubilant worship to the Lord Jesus Christ.

5:14   And the four creatures were saying "Amen!" And the elders fell and worshiped.

In 4:8-10 all the praise that is pictured in the throne room of God begins with the *four creatures* and the twenty-four *elders*. Now in this verse that praise is closed by them.

From chapters two and three readers understand that they will possess the wonderful rewards that were promised to them if they do the will of God until the end of their days. In chapters four and five readers come to understand that the day will come when our Redeemer and King will ask of God the Father that the world be prepared as an inheritance for them through terrifying cleansings, so that our King can establish His kingdom and His faithful ones can rule with Him.

B. Time of Torment (6:1–20:3)

The Structure of this section

The opening of the seven seals of the scroll, the blowing of the seven trumpets, and the pouring of the seven bowls provide the outline or backbone of the events of the seven year Tribulation. Eleven other events are told, but they are inserted into this "backbone."

There are two ways to look at that backbone. One is that the events of the Tribulation are told three times. The seals, the trumpets, and the bowls are all talking about the same time periods, three times over. This "Reiteration" view is possible, and is held by many. The angel's words in 10:5-7 that there will be no more delay would be good support of this view. However, it is hard to explain the change in attitude of 6:9-10, the fifth seal, and 16:4-7, the third bowl, if the same time period is "reiterated," or told three times. Why do the souls under the altar go from a "How much longer until we are avenged?" attitude in 6:10 to a "Yes, You are just for giving those people blood to drink" attitude in 16:6. That would be hard to explain according to this threefold retelling idea.

Also, if the Reiteration view were correct, one would think that in 8:1-2 when the seven trumpets are introduced, there would be a clue to the reader that we are now going back in time to the time that was first described in 6:1-2, but there is no such clue for us.

The following interpretation seems to be the simplest and the most natural:

The seventh seal contains all seven of the trumpets,[380] and also the seventh trumpet contains all seven of the bowls.[381] This might be called the "Telescoping View." See the chart just before the discussion of Revelation 1:1.

This "Telescoping View" emphasizes the severity of the judgments. When "those who live on the earth" experience the dreadful judgments of the first through the sixth seals, maybe they will think, "Since there are only seven seals, there is only one more judgment left." But they will be surprised because the "one more judgment" includes seven judgments (the seven trumpets). Then after the sixth trumpet, maybe they will think, "Finally, only one more judgment," but they will again be surprised because the "one more" includes seven more judgments, the seven bowls.

Here are six good arguments in support of this "telescoping" view of the seals, trumpets, and bowls:

1. The trumpet judgments are not as severe as the bowl ones (in the trumpet judgments only part of humanity is affected, but all are affected in the bowl judgments).
2. The order and the content is different in each of the three series of seven.
3. In 7:3, during the seal judgments, we learn of the sealing of the servants of God, and then later during the fifth trumpet (9:1-11) we learn of "the people who do not have the seal of God on their foreheads," so the trumpets seem to be after the seals.
4. In 8:1-2 it certainly sounds like the seventh seal's judgment is the seven trumpets: "And when He opened the seventh seal there was silence in heaven for about half an hour. And I saw the seven angels who stand before God, and seven trumpets were given to them."
5. The bowl judgments are explicitly called "the last plagues," and by them God's wrath is "completed."
6. The words "It is done" are only spoken after the seventh bowl is poured out, 16:17.[382]

The seals, trumpets, and bowls become a narrative chain through the book. Into this narrative chain a few other things have been inserted. Each "insertion" becomes another motivation for the seven churches of chapters two and three to be victorious.

This section tells of the "Tribulation", the 70th "week in Daniel 9, a period that covers seven years.[383] Other texts, such as Amos 5:18-20 and Isaiah 2-3, tell of the suffering which will be experienced by the people of Israel during that time.

By content (not structure) these chapters are quite similar to Mark 13, Matthew 24, and Luke 21 where the Lord Jesus prophesies about the end times. Beasley-Murray[384] lists the similarities as follows:

Mark 13	Revelation 6
1. Wars	1. Wars
2. International Strife	2. International Strife
3. Earthquake	3. Famine
4. Famine	4. Plague
5. Persecution	5. Persecution
6. Eclipse, falling stars	6. Earthquake, eclipse, falling stars

Psalm 79 may serve as a background to this sevenfold judgment upon the earth:

> 10 Why are the nations saying, "Where is their God?" Make known before our eyes among the nations that You avenge the outpoured blood of Your servants.
>
> 11 May the groaning of the prisoner come before You; according to the greatness of Your arm preserve the sons of death.
>
> 12 Return into the chests of our neighbors seven times the reproach they have reproached You with, O Lord.
>
> 13 And we Your people, the sheep of Your pasture, will praise You forever; from generation to generation we will tell of Your praise.

1. Seven Seals (6:1–8:6)

As each seal is opened, there is judgment upon those who live on the earth. This judgment originates in heaven, not from Satan or from the beast. God judges the earth. The scroll, which is the last will and testament for "the victors", is opened by the Lord, not by Satan.

a. First Seal (6:1-2)

6:1 And I saw that the Lamb opened the first of the seven seals, and I heard one of the four creatures saying, with a thunderous voice,[385] "Come and see!"[386]

It is *the Lamb*, the One who was slain, the One who was worthy, the Lord Jesus, that opens the *first* seal. This is in line with what was already explained by John in chapter five. Only the Lord Jesus can open the *seals*.

One of the four creatures around the throne responds by calling out, apparently to the rider of the white horse, for him to *come* forth.

6:2 And look, a white horse, and its rider had a bow, and he was given[387] a crown,[388] and he went away conquering, even so that he might conquer.

It seems that these four horses are related to the four chariots which are prophesied in Zechariah 6:1-8. The four colors of the horses in Zechariah 6:1-8 represent the various directions the four chariots there will go, but here in Revelation the four colors of the horses relate more to the kind of disasters their riders bring.[389]

It is difficult to identify the *rider* on the *white horse*. He might be Christ, Anti-Christ, an unidentified agent of judgment, or terrible warfare in general. In Revelation 19:11-12 Christ Himself rides *a white horse*, so some would say that it must be Christ on this *white horse*. However, the other riders are not divine, so it would be difficult to have Christ be parallel to those other riders. Also, it is difficult to see how one of the four creatures could command the Lord to come forth. The *rider* on the *white horse* is probably not Christ, but it is unclear whether it is Anti-Christ, an unidentified agent of judgment, or terrible warfare in general.

b. Second Seal (6:3-4)

6:3-4 When He opened the second seal, I heard the second creature say, "Come!" And another horse came out, a fiery red one,[390] and to its rider was given to take peace from the earth, so that they might slay one another. And a large sword was given to him.

The *rider* on the *fiery red horse* has power to take peace from the earth. This is in line with Matthew 24:6-7 where there are "wars" and "rumors of wars" and "nation will rise against nation." For the first *rider* the emphasis was that he was conquering, but the emphasis here is the state of warfare among men.

c. Third Seal (6:5-6)

6:5 And when He opened the third seal, I heard the third creature saying, "Come and see!" And look, a black horse! Its rider had a pair of scales[391] in his hand.

One of the results of war is famine. This *black horse* and *its rider* bring famine on the earth. The *pair of scales* is a symbol of famine, as is clear from the next verse.

6:6 And I heard a voice among the four creatures, saying, "A quart of wheat for a denarius,[392] and three quarts of barley for a denarius, and do not harm the oil and the wine!"

In times of famine, there is less food to buy, so prices go up. The price of these ingredients for bread given in this verse is about twelve times the normal price.[393] A *denarius* was a normal daily wage, and the bread an adult would eat each day would be made from *a quart of wheat*. Thus the wage of an adult would only buy enough bread for him to eat, and he would have nothing left over for other needs, or for his family. In that culture the poor would mix *wheat* and *barley* for cheaper bread of lower quality, because pure *wheat* would be too expensive for them. This is in accord with Matthew 24:7, in which the Lord prophesied war, famine, and earthquakes.

There are two possible interpretations of the expression *do not harm the oil and the wine*. Perhaps it means that the rich are still comfortable, enjoying plenty of food, with *oil and wine*. Or perhaps it means that the drought which damages the *wheat* and *barley* harvests is not severe enough at this point to damage the more hardy olive trees and grape vines.[394]

There are interpreters who look for a spiritual meaning for the words *oil* and *wine* (for instance, the *wine* represents the Lord's Supper so somehow this verse promises that believers will not suffer persecution at this time) but there is no indication in these verses that *oil* and *wine* have a symbolic meaning. Beasley-Murray[395] wisely writes, "The commentators' lust for identification must be resisted."

d. Fourth Seal (6:7-8)

6:7-8 And when He opened the fourth seal I heard the voice[396] of the fourth creature saying, "Come and see!" And look, a green[397] horse! And the one who rode it was named Death, and Hades was following it. And authority over a fourth of the earth was given to him, to kill with the sword, and with famine, and with plague,[398] and by the beasts of the field.

With *the fourth seal*, out rides *Death*. Besides those who died of *famine* and warfare as mentioned above, a *fourth* of humanity dies here. They die from *the sword, famine, plague,* and wild *beasts*.

These four types of suffering, *the sword, famine, plague,* and *the beasts of the field,* are also prophesied in Ezekiel 14:13-21.

If this judgment happened now, 1.75 billion people would be killed. In 9:18 it says one-third of mankind will be killed, but it is not clarified whether that is one-third of the original population, or one-third of the survivors.

e. Fifth Seal (6:9-11)

6:9 And when He opened the fifth seal, I saw under the altar the souls of those who had been killed on account of the word of God and on account of the testimony[399] of the Lamb[400] which they were holding on to.[401]

This *seal* is different from the others because the opening of this *seal* does not bring judgment. With *the fifth seal* our attention is turned to the martyrs, who are very important in the Book of Revelation, as was already suggested in the letter to Smyrna, where the suffering church is asked to be faithful until death and thus receive a crown of life.

Though they are strange to us, some of the elements from this text were familiar in Jewish literature at that time. For example, having the *souls* of the martyrs *under the altar* would not be foreign to the Jews.[402] Mounce[403] explains that from the viewpoint of those of us on the earth martyrdom is an accident, but from the viewpoint of heaven martyrdom is worship offered in ministry. Note Philippians 2:17, where faithful service to God is metaphorically described as a sacrifice.

In Matthew 24:9 the Lord told His disciples about persecution and martyrdom in the end times, telling them "Then they will deliver you into tribulation, and they will kill you; and you will be hated by all the nations on account of My name."

6:10 And they cried out with a loud voice, saying "How long, Master,[404] holy and true, will You not judge and avenge our blood against those who dwell upon the earth?"

When Stephen was killed (Acts 7:54-8:1) he prayed, "Lord, do not hold this sin against them." When the Lord Jesus was crucified (Luke 23:34) He prayed, "Father, forgive them, for they do not know what they are doing." But these martyrs under the altar are not asking that their persecutors be forgiven. They ask instead, *How long, Master, holy and true, will You not judge and avenge our blood against those who dwell upon the earth?* Perhaps this striking difference is a matter of the heart motivation. When we on earth reject forgiveness for those that persecute us, and instead seek to be avenged, it is most likely motivated by our self-interest. But these martyrs in Revelation 6:9-11 left all selfishness behind the moment they died. They are instead purely concerned with the glory of the *holy and true* One, and they long for His holiness and righteousness to be displayed to the whole earth. As long as He has not yet judged evil on the earth, there are people who can say that the Almighty One is not *holy and true*. These martyrs long for the Kingdom of God to be established on the earth so that the earth is full of God's holiness and righteousness like the water covers the sea. In 19:2 their prayer is answered.[405]

In Jewish literature like 1 Enoch 47[406] we often see that:
1. The martyrs demand vengeance.
2. God has already chosen the number of martyrs.
3. The prayers of the martyrs will be answered when the Kingdom of God is revealed.[407]

Isaiah 61:2-3 contains several similar themes.

See the comments on the expression *those who dwell upon the earth* in the discussion of 3:10.

6:11 And to each was given a white robe,[408] and it was said to them to rest yet a while, until the number is completed of their fellow slaves and their brothers[409] and those that are about to be killed, as also they were killed.[410]

The reader will remember where he has read about *white* clothing already, and who it was that will be wearing it. It was given to the 24 elders and the "victors." These are the ones that were "faithful until death" which are mentioned in 2:10. Death is not the end of man, and believers that are faithful until death are given something special to show their faithfulness. When reading this, surely the members of the church in Smyrna were encouraged. When we understand the importance of rewards in this book, we are assured that they are very satisfied with what they have received from the Lord, because it is a token of their status as victors.

The total *number* of martyrs has been determined by God. That total *number* needs to be *completed* first and then the Lord will come to earth to establish His Kingdom. The Lord is not interested in lowering the *number* of those that will *be killed* for Him. He gives the high privilege of this victory to a certain *number* of people whom He values, and whom He will reward. Note Philippians 2:17 and 2 Timothy 4:6.[411]

Even though the events of the fifth seal might seem to be far from the experience of the majority of readers, we all have seen things that do not appear fair (if not martyrdom, some lighter form of suffering) but we do not yet see the judgment of the "Master, who is holy and true." Through

His word He reminds us that He is arranging everything according to His glorious plan, and He asks that we be patient in faith.

f. Sixth Seal (6:12-17)

This judgment is truly terrifying. It seems like the earth is about to be utterly destroyed. At any rate, that would be the impression of those who dwell upon the earth. Earthquakes, the sun, stars, the sky and mountains are related to Judgment Day in the Old Testament (Joel 2:31; 3:15; Haggai 2:6; Isaiah 13:10; 34:4; and Jeremiah 4:23-28). The ones that must experience the disasters prophesied in these verses surely will think that the final judgment has already come. According to some commentators, this text, 11:15-19 which is about the seventh trumpet, and also 16:17-21 which is about the seventh bowl, tell about the end of the disasters prophesied in the Book of Revelation.[412] But the earthquake prophesied in 6:12 is also recorded in Matthew 24:7-8. There the earthquake is said to be "just the beginning of birth pangs."

As was explained earlier, the seventh seal contains the seven trumpets and the seventh trumpet contains the seven bowls. The earthquake in 6:12 is less terrifying than the earthquake that is prophesied in 16:18 in connection with the seventh bowl.

6:12 And I saw when He opened the sixth seal, a huge earthquake happened, and the sun became as black as sackcloth made of hair,[413] and the whole moon became as blood,

We need to be careful in interpreting symbols, figures of speech, and literal words in the judgment of *the sixth seal*. There are some commentators that say that the elements of this judgment are only symbols. According to them, there is no literal *earthquake*. Some say that the *earthquake* is a symbol meaning the powerful on the earth will be overthrown. This kind of symbolic approach is very subjective. Even though there are no indicators in the context, the interpreter says, "this is a symbol" or "that has a spiritual meaning." If the context does not tell the interpreter that something is not to be taken literally, how does he know? It is better to interpret things as literally as possible. If the context requires a symbolic meaning, then we take it as symbolic, but otherwise we should try to leave it literal.

So, it is better that we understand the judgments connected with *the sixth seal*, including the *huge earthquake*, to be literal. So it is also with *the sun* becoming *black*, and *the moon as red as blood*. A literal interpretation does not mean that all figures of speech are rejected. However, in 6:14 John wrote that "the sky was separated like a scroll rolling up" which is a figure of speech that pictures the terror of the disasters in the sky. This is clear because there is still a sky in 20:11. So also with "the mountains and islands." There are still mountains in 6:15.

Events such as *the sun became as black as sackcloth made of hair* were already prophesied in texts about Judgment Day. Note for instance Isaiah 13:10; Ezekiel 32:7-8; Joel 2:10, 31; Amos 8:9; and Matthew 24:29.

6:13   and the stars of heaven fell upon the earth like a fig tree dropping its summer figs when shaken by a strong wind.

We know that *stars* are actually far larger than *the earth*, and that if a planet like *the earth* were to get too near a star, the star's stronger gravity would pull that planet into a fiery destruction. So a possible way of understanding this verse is that the term star[414] has a wider meaning than the usual meaning of this word today. Perhaps the word can refer to what we now call meteors or "falling stars," meaning that there will be terrible meteor showers, likened to *a fig tree dropping its summer figs when shaken by a strong wind.*

This and the next verse are from Isaiah 34:4 which says that all the *stars* will fall "like withered leaves from a vine, and like withered fruit from a fig tree," and that the sky "will be rolled up like a scroll."

6:14   And the sky was separated like a scroll rolling up, and every mountain and island was moved from its place.

Ancient scrolls were made of sheets of papyrus or properly treated animal skins. Those sheets were glued together to form a *scroll*, which would be rolled up at both ends. If the glue holding any two of the sheets of an open *scroll* came undone, then the *scroll* would suddenly roll up to the right and left, and it would have to be repaired.

Those interpreters that hold to the Reiteration View described above say that these verses here describe the end of the Tribulation, and that these events will be retold as the trumpets are sounded and the bowls are poured out. That interpretation does seem strong, because these verses do sound like the end of the world. However, as has been described above, that view does not really work very well.

Certainly these are terrible calamities in *the sky* and on the earth, and they may even appear to be the end of all things. They only make God's judgment all the more severe, when the reader realizes that no, this is not all that God will do, He still has more judgment to pour out upon those that dwell upon the earth.

There were terrible meteor showers, and there were earthquakes so terrible that *every mountain and island* was shifted *from its place*. The cosmic calamities were so terrible that it seemed like even *the sky* was destroyed. We know, however, that more judgment remains to be poured out. We also know that at the very end of the age, in 20:11, there is still a *sky* that will flee from the presence of the One seated on that Great White Throne.

6:15   And the kings of the earth, and the nobles, and the commanders, and the rich, and the powerful, and everyone – slave and free – hid themselves in the caves and among the rocks of the mountains.

The seven types of people listed here reach all levels of mankind with an emphasis on the upper levels of society who resist the work of God on the earth. The list of people is repeated in 19:18 where the judgment that they fear actually befalls them. See also Isaiah 2:10, 19, 21 about hiding from God's judgment.

Earlier, members of the church of Smyrna had reason to be afraid of *kings, nobles, commanders, the rich, and the powerful*. They were persecuting them, and seemed to have great authority over them. Now, reading about this punishment, that congregation and congregations like them today, need fear no more. When the Lord opens those seals and sends His judgments upon the earth, these "important" people will no more terrorize the people of God. They will hide themselves *in the caves and among the rocks of the mountains*.

6:16-17 And they said to the mountains and to the rocks, "Fall upon us, and hide us from the face of the One seated on the throne and from the wrath of the Lamb, because the great day of His[415] wrath has come, and who is able to stand against it?"[416]

Again, imagine how the congregation in Smyrna, and the faithful members of the congregation in Pergamum, might have reacted to this prophecy. Their persecutors seemed so bold and powerful, but here in their desperation they are begging *the mountains and to the rocks* to fall upon them!

It is ironic that such powerful people should be so afraid, and it is ironic that they would be afraid of *the wrath of the Lamb*, since lambs are normally such gentle animals. These words are only here and in 14:10.

The Eleven "Insertions"

In all of the Book of Revelation there are about eleven "insertions" that the Lord placed into the framework of the book, that is, the series of seals, trumpets, and bowls. Do not understand the term "insertion" to mean that these passages were inserted by a later author. John is writing down what he was being shown. There is a series of seals, trumpets, and bowls, but he also saw events that seem to be independent from the seals, trumpets, and bowls.

These first two "insertions" are very relevant to the judgments that are being described, and also very relevant to the seven churches of chapters two and three.

First Insertion: 144,000 People Sealed (7:1-8)

This text, 7:1-8, is the first of those insertions. It is about the 144,000 Jews that will be sealed. There is a wide diversity of interpretation concerning this passage, partly because some interpreters hold that the church is the "New Israel," a view this writer does not accept.

> 7:1 And after this I saw four angels standing at the four corners of the earth, holding back the four winds of the earth so that no wind would blow upon the earth, nor upon the sea, nor upon any tree.

According to Bauckham,[417] in the Book of Revelation the numeral *four* refers to the natural world. Note Revelation 20:8, "...to deceive the nations in the four corners of the earth." The praise expressed in 5:13 (when *four* different parts of *the earth* will praise God) has *four* parts, but all the other praise in the Book of Revelation has seven parts (5:12 and 7:12) or three parts (4:9, 11; and 19:1).

The expression *the four corners of the earth* suggests that this will be a world-wide disaster. Comparing this text with Jeremiah 49:36-38 suggests that *the four winds of the earth* speak of an inescapable and complete judgment.

However, for the moment that judgment is withheld. *EBC* notes that we do not read anywhere else in the Book of Revelation concerning these *winds*, so perhaps they represent the on-going judgment of God, which is withheld for the moment.

> 7:2-3 And I saw another angel ascending from the east, having the seal of the living God. And he shouted out with a loud voice to the four

angels who had been given permission to harm the earth and the sea, saying "Do not harm the earth or the sea or the trees until we have sealed the slaves of our God upon their foreheads."

In Ezekiel 9:3-6 there is a similar judgment. People that grieve over the sins of Jerusalem are marked with a "tau," the last letter in the Hebrew alphabet, on their forehead, and all that do not have that mark are to be killed.

The nature of this sealing in chapter seven is debated. Some say that this sealing in Revelation 7 is a spiritual sealing and thus spiritual protection, so that all the *sealed* will certainly have eternal life, much like the sealing of Ephesians 1:13. In Revelation 14:1 they are standing on Mount Zion with the Lamb. In 14:3 and 4 they are said to be redeemed from the earth. In Revelation 14:1 and 22:4 it seems like the mark of these seals is the Lamb of God's name and the name of the Father. But more likely the sealing provides physical protection for those believers, because in this context it is physical disasters that threaten them and are held back so they can be *sealed*. It seems best to say that this *seal* protected them from the coming trumpet judgments. In Revelation 9:4 we read that the "locusts" that appear out of the smoke that came out of the abyss are given power to torture people with terrible agonies, but they are only allowed to harm "the people who do not have the seal of God on their foreheads." So, again, we see from that passage that the seals in this passage provide protection from God's judgment that will fall upon those that dwell upon the earth.

7:4 And I heard the number of the sealed, a hundred and forty four thousand, sealed from all the tribes of the sons of Israel.

Some commentators[418] say that the 144,000 represent all of God's people or church, despite the mention of each of the twelve *tribes of Israel* by name. They make several objections to the interpretation that this text is about the physical descendants of Abraham, Isaac, and Jacob, the literal Old Testament *tribes of Israel*:[419]

1. The New Testament, especially Ephesians 2:11-19, teaches that there is now no difference between Jews and gentiles. The answer to that objection is that Ephesians 2:11-19 is about the relationship between believing Jews and believing gentiles during this age, in the church, not during the age to come. But Revelation 4-21 is about the age to come, not the church age. This long section of the Book of Revelation is about the era in which the promises that were made long ago to Abraham, Isaac, and Jacob and their descendants will finally be fulfilled. Again, see Romans 11:11-32.

2. Since the Captivity, many or most Jews have not known to which tribe they belong. This is actually an odd objection, because in Revelation 7 those Jews do not seal themselves, so they do not have to know their tribal ancestry. That is a problem the angels will be able to sort out!
3. The number 144,000 is twelve times twelve times 1000, and that is sometimes given as proof that the number is exclusively symbolic. Certainly 144,000 is a highly symbolic number, but it would be odd to say that if the Lord were sealing literal descendants of Abraham, Isaac, and Jacob, the number of them that He would have chosen would have no symbolic importance.
4. The order of *the tribes* in this list is different from the order of *the tribes* in the Old Testament, but that is really not a problem, because in the Old Testament there is no particular order for the listing of *the tribes*. According to Mounce[420] there are actually 18 different orders for the listings of *the tribes* in the Old Testament.

7:5-8   From the tribe of Judah, twelve thousand sealed,

from the tribe of Reuben, twelve thousand sealed,

from the tribe of Gad, twelve thousand,

from the tribe of Asher, twelve thousand,

from the tribe of Naphtali, twelve thousand,

from the tribe of Manasseh, twelve thousand,

from the tribe of Simeon, twelve thousand,

from the tribe of Levi, twelve thousand,

from the tribe of Issachar, twelve thousand,

from the tribe of Zebulun, twelve thousand,

from the tribe of Joseph, twelve thousand,

from the tribe of Benjamin, twelve thousand sealed.

In the entire New Testament this is the only list of the tribes of Israel. This list does bring up a fundamental interpretational and theological problem. Does the church the *permanently* replace the people of Israel? Is the church then the New Israel? If so, then the promises given to Israel concerning the future Kingdom of God, the Messianic Age, as in Isaiah 4:2-6, must already be, or shall be, fulfilled in the Church. And so this verse must also be interpreted in that way. Those that hold this view would say then that this is about the church. They would use Revelation 2:9 and 3:9 as support for this approach. However, those verses only say that the physical descendants of Abraham, Isaac, and Jacob that do not believe in Jesus Christ are not true Jews. That is different from saying that anyone that believes in Jesus becomes the only kind of true Jew that the Lord is interested in. Those interpreters would also turn to James 1:1 and Matthew 19:28. But those verses only prove that there are twelve tribes of Israel, and a part of them have believed in Jesus. Galatians 3:28 might be offered in support of their idea, but it only says that in this age there is no spiritual difference between Jew and gentile; it does not say that there will be no difference after the church age closes. In fact the best and the most complete discussion of this issue in the New Testament is Romans 9-11, and particularly 11:11-32.[421] These verses clearly say that there is a future full of hope in which the Old Testament messianic kingdom promises will be fulfilled for an entire generation of the physical descendants of Abraham, Isaac, and Jacob, all of whom will believe in the Lord Jesus. Part of that is described in Revelation 7.

In Numbers 1:21-43 and 26:4-51 the numbers of the tribes of Israel are irregular numbers, but when the Lord fulfills His promise to redeem all of Israel the numbers of each *tribe* will be uniform and perfect.

The *tribe* of Dan is not listed, apparently because of their idolatry (Judges 18:30) and also because they built an unauthorized place of worship (1 Kings 12:29).[422] Even though Dan is not listed, there are still twelve tribes, because *Joseph* and *Manasseh*, his son, are both listed.

Second Insertion: Many people... who come out of the great tribulation (7:9-17)

This great multitude is not the same as the 144,000 Jews in 7:1-8. This is clear because they are specifically "from every nation, tribe, people, and language," and this group cannot be numbered, but the 144,000 are numbered.

7:9   After these things – and look![423] – a great multitude that no one was able to count, from every nation, tribe, people, and language, standing before the throne and before the Lamb clothed in white robes, and with palm branches in their hands.

To show that this vision is distinct from the one in 7:1-8, John begins this section with the words *after these things*.

This group was so large that *no one was able to count* them. They were *from every nation, tribe, people and language*. This does not mean that *everyone* from every nation is gathered there. In fact standing in stark contrast, 11:9-10 tells us that people from "every people, tribe, nation and language" celebrate the death of God's two witnesses.[424]

Here in 7:9 their *white robes* remind us of the *white robes* given to victors in chapters two and three. The *palm branches* they hold are connected to victory and purification in 1 Maccabees 13:51 and 2 Maccabees 10:7. See also John 12:13.

7:10 And they are shouting out in a loud voice, saying "Victory to our God, seated on the throne, and to the Lamb!"

Their cry is often translated "salvation to our God," but a better translation would be *victory to our God....* This is for three reasons: firstly, because *our God* simply does not need salvation; secondly, because *victory* is implied in the palm branches of 7:9; and thirdly, because it is appropriate for them to yearn for and call out for the *victory* of *our God*. This term[425] means *victory* or "deliverance" in Luke 1:71; Acts 7:25; Hebrews 9:28; Revelation 12:10; and 19:1.

7:11-12 And all the angels were standing around the throne and the elders and the four creatures, and they fell on their faces before the throne and they worshiped God saying, "Amen! Blessing and glory and wisdom and thanksgiving and honor and power and strength to our God forever and ever! Amen."

The praise that is given to *God* in these verses is similar to 4:8-11. The *angels*, the *elders* and the *four creatures* agree with and continue the praise of the unnumbered multitude.

7:13 And one of the elders responded saying to me, "These clothed in white robes – who are they and where did they come from?"

Among the twenty-four *elders*, there is *one* who speaks to John and shifts his focus back to the huge group from every nation. This verse is similar to some passages in the prophets (Jeremiah 1:11, 13; 24:3; Amos 7:8; 8:2; and Zechariah 4:5) in which a heavenly person asks questions of the prophet.[426]

7:14 And I said to him, "My lord,[427] you know." And he said to me, "These are the ones coming out of the Great Tribulation, and they have washed their robes and made them white in the blood of the Lamb!

The expression, *the Great Tribulation*,[428] could also be translated "the great suffering." The use of the article (the word *the*) shows us that the meaning is not suffering in general which God's people experience from age to age, but *the Great Tribulation* that will happen at the end of the age. It is the time that is covered by Revelation 4-19, the seven year period that (as we learn from other books in the New Testament) begins with the Rapture of the church, and ends with the coming of the Lord Jesus to establish His Messianic Kingdom.

It is worth considering the relationship between those *coming out of the Great Tribulation* and those who are killed "on account of the word of God and on account of the testimony of the Lamb" that are "under the altar" and given *white robes* in 6:9-11. They must be the same people, martyrs that were killed in the *Tribulation*,[429] especially since martyrs do play a large role in the Book of Revelation.

If indeed these are *Tribulation* martyrs, then their attitude in 7:10 is very interesting: they are not crying out about their own sufferings, but about the victory of the *Lamb* of God.

The statement *they have washed their robes and made them white in the blood of the Lamb* is very rich and powerful. If indeed these are martyrs, then their clothes were not stained with sin.[430] Rather they were stained red with their own blood when they were, like Antipas mentioned in Revelation 2:13, killed for their testimony. From a human perspective they appeared horrific. But by being *washed in the blood of the Lamb* who Himself was slain, and was victorious, those horrific-looking clothes become *white*. With the *white robes* of the victors of chapters two and three, they can stand "before the throne and before the Lamb." Here we see them standing in front of the throne upon which God the Father is seated, and in front of Jesus Christ, but later in Revelation 20:4 we will see them seated upon thrones, to rule and reign with Christ for a thousand years.

In chapter six, especially verse 16, the wrath of the *Lamb* of God is stressed, but in these verses His grace is emphasized.

7:15   Therefore they are before the throne of God, and they are serving Him day and night in His temple, and the One seated upon the throne will dwell with them.

Their right to be in the *temple* of *God* reminds us of the right of the victors in 3:12, who "never again… go out of" the *temple*. In chapters two and three we read promises given to the believers who are faithful to death, and in these verses we read of some of the fulfillment of those promises.

As was discussed in the section entitled "Revelation and Systematic Theology," we are told little about *the One seated upon the throne* until the end of the Book of Revelation. It is as if His face is turned away from us. But here, for these Tribulation martyrs, He is more personal. He *will dwell with them*. He does not hide His face from them. In fact, in verse 17 it is

He that wipes away every tear from their eyes. Note also that in the New Jerusalem, in Revelation 21:3 His "home is with mankind, and He will live with them." The closeness that these martyrs enjoy with *God* during the remainder of the Tribulation will be enjoyed by all the victors, living in the New Jerusalem, as described in Revelation 21:3.[431]

In the Old Testament, God's tent or dwelling was closely related to His *throne* and His protection. This can be seen in Exodus 40:34; Leviticus 26:11-12; and Isaiah 4:5-6.[432]

7:16   They will hunger no longer, neither will they thirst any longer, nor will the heat[433] of the sun fall upon them, nor will any burning heat,

During the persecutions they suffered in the Great Tribulation they had to flee their homes, and were subject to *hunger, thirst*, and *the heat of the sun*. All that is now past for them. These words surely comforted those of the seven churches enduring persecution, and should be a comfort today to all persecuted believers.[434]

7:17   because the Lamb in the middle of the throne shepherds them and leads them to springs of living water, and God will wipe away every tear from their eyes."

This is a well-known reversal of roles. Normally a shepherd would lead a lamb, but in this case *the Lamb shepherds*[435] the people. He *shepherds them* with so much goodness and kindness. Despite His exalted position *in the middle of the throne*,[436] He *leads them to springs of living water*.

The idea that the LORD *God* or the Messiah will be like a shepherd for His people is not limited to the well-known Psalm 23. In Isaiah 40:10-11 the prophet says of the LORD *God*, "like a shepherd He shepherds His flock." Likewise in Ezekiel 34:23 the LORD says, "Over them I will make one shepherd stand, and he will shepherd them, My servant David; he will shepherd them, and he will be for them a shepherd." In Ezekiel 37:24 the LORD *God* promised about Israel, "And My servant David will be king over them, and there will be one shepherd for all of them, and they will walk in My judgments, and they will keep My statutes, and they will do them." Note also Psalm 78:52.

Isaiah 49:9-10 not only describes the people of Israel as well-tended sheep, but also mentions the promises of Revelation 7:16, and the idea that He will lead them to *springs of water*.

In John 10 it is very clear that the Lord Jesus is the One who was promised in all those Old Testament promises. He is the Good Shepherd. He fulfills the promises made about "My Servant David."

In 2:7 there is a special promise for the victors, that they will be given "to eat from the tree of life, which is in the paradise of My God." Most likely these *springs of living water*, offered to those who come "out of the Great Tribulation," are also located in that paradise.

Mounce[437] writes that the tears that will be *wiped away* by *God* from their eyes are not tears of repentance for a life wasted on what was fleeting. Rather, these are like the tears that are on the face of a child who was sad and then suddenly joyful. The tears are still on their faces but the sadness has been forgotten and replaced with joy. The ones who come out of the Great Tribulation are like that. On their faces there are still tears from the heavy suffering that they experienced in the world before they were killed because of their witness. As noted above, *God* Himself will *wipe* these tears *away*. He is not distant and removed from those heroes, the martyrs from the Tribulation.

If indeed these are martyrs, then this statement is significant. Two things are strongly implied in these words: one, the special blessings offered to victors are really worth pursuing at any and all cost, and two, failure to gain those special blessings, while certainly not like eternal hell, is very much to be avoided. See especially Luke 19:11-27, and the difference between the ashamed servant that just buried the mina, and the enemies of the king that are killed in front of him. That servant who is ashamed represents believers who will be ashamed at His coming – they receive a rebuke rather than a reward; the enemies of the king represent those that never believed in Jesus – they will be thrown into eternal punishment.

See also 1 John 2:28, which strongly implies that some of the readers, addressed as "dear children," will be ashamed before Him at His coming. See 1 John 2:12-14 for proof that those "dear children," and all the readers that John is addressing in 1 John, are believers.

See also 1 Corinthians 3:10-15, and note that in verse 15 the believer that has "built upon the foundation" using "wood, grass, and straw" will indeed "suffer loss, but he himself will be saved, but as through fire." He will be in the Kingdom of God, but not with the high status there that the victors will enjoy.

Chapter seven tells about two of John's visions, called "insertions" because they are not a part of the chain of judgments that accompany the opening of the seven seals. The first vision is of the 144,000 Jews who were sealed, and the second is of the great multitude too great to count. They are related to the judgment of opening the seventh seal. They also have a close relationship to the seven churches of chapters two and three.

g. Seventh Seal (8:1-6)

The judgments of the seventh seal are the seven trumpets and their "contents." This seventh seal is opened and seven angels receive and prepare the seven trumpets.[438] If somehow those that dwell upon the earth could see these heavenly scenes, they might have thought that there is just one more seal to open, so maybe they could survive, but once the seven angels and their seven trumpets appear, those hopes are dashed. The judgments falling on those who dwell upon the earth are still heavy, with many to come.

8:1 And when He opened the seventh seal there was silence in heaven for about half an hour.

Finally, after the two insertions that tell about God's people, our attention is turned again to the last *seal* that must be opened.

There will probably be a great feeling of suspense during that *half an hour*, and no one will dare to say a thing. What will the Lamb do now? Are these judgments upon those that dwell upon the earth complete? Is the Kingdom of Earth (as the rabbis used to call it) ready to be "invaded" by the Kingdom of Heaven?

This is the first of the "telescopic extensions" mentioned just before the discussion of 6:1.

8:2 And I saw the[439] seven angels who stand before God, and seven trumpets were given to them.

Once they see that *the seven angels* standing *before God* are *given seven trumpets*, *trumpets* that will each have to be sounded, those that will be watching when these things unfold will know the answer to the question, "What is the Lamb going to do now that the seven seals have been opened?" In the previous verses each judgment began with the opening of a seal, but here each judgment begins with the sounding of a trumpet.

In Numbers 10:1-10 the LORD instructs Moses on the crafting and use of *trumpets* for Israel. They sound to signal to the community the time to depart, to get the community to gather before the Tent of Meeting, to get the heads of the community to come to Moses, and to go into battle.[440] *Trumpets* are also sounded during the feasts for certain sacrifices. In other Bible passages we learn that *trumpets* are sounded to celebrate the ascension of a king of Israel to his throne (1 Kings 1:34,

39; and 2 Kings 9:13). They are also used in the context of the Judgment Day (see Zephaniah 1:14-16; Matthew 24:31; 1 Corinthians 15:52; and 1 Thessalonians 4:16), because the coming of the Messiah to establish the Kingdom of God on the earth brings difficulties such as war for some (see Amos 5:16-20) and joy for others (see Isaiah 40). Departure, gathering before God, joy, warfare, and the ascension of a king are certainly relevant themes in this setting, so it is no wonder *trumpets* are prominent in the Book of Revelation![441]

Those *seven angels* are said to *stand before God*. This means they are ready to serve Him.[442]

8:3 And another angel came and stood beside the altar holding a golden censer. And a great deal of incense was given to him so that he might offer it up, with the prayers of all the saints, on the golden altar before the throne.

Exodus 30:1-10 tells about *the altar of incense* where the priests serve in the Old Testament. In the Tabernacle, the censers were made of bronze[443] (Exodus 27:3), whereas those used in the Temple were made of gold (1 Kings 7:50). Note also Revelation 5:8 where *incense* and *the prayers of the saints* are also mentioned.

8:4 And the smoke of the incense, with the prayers of the saints, went up before God from the hand of the angel.

So often we pray against evil, and we pray that righteousness will prevail, but we wonder if our *prayers* are even heard. Probably the church in Smyrna felt that way too. Some of our *prayers* seem to be stored up in heaven waiting for the day described here, because they are mixed with *incense*, and those *prayers* also mix with the *smoke* of that *incense*, and they rise up to *God*. This is a powerful image of how *God* experiences our *prayers*. Our *prayers* are like the powerful smell of *incense* rising up, which cannot be ignored.

8:5 And the angel took the censer, and filled it from the fire from the altar, and threw it to the earth, and there were thunder, roaring, lightning, and an earthquake.

Apparently as an answer to the prayers of the saints, God has that *angel* take *the censer* of incense, which is somehow metaphorically related to our prayers, and that *angel* sends that fiery *censer* crashing down on *the earth*. It is as though God has gathered the prayers of His people, prayers against wickedness, into a great fiery ball, and finally sends that blazing ball down upon the wicked! Your prayers, oh suffering congregation, will be answered. And you in Laodicea (or in other places...), make sure that nobody needs to pray against you for lack of kindness to the poor, or lack of Christlike tenderness to those less fortunate!

Our prayers are not just being heard; our prayers are being answered. In 6:10 those whose souls were under the altar asked "How long, Master, holy and true, will You not judge and avenge our blood against those who dwell upon the earth?" In this verse their prayers come before *God* and their prayers are answered. Apparently in response to the prayers of the saints, *God* who sits on the throne judges and avenges their blood with *thunder, roaring, lightning, and an earthquake.*

Just as the seal judgments were preceded by incense and prayer in Revelation 5:8, so the trumpet judgments are preceded by incense and prayer. This text is similar to Exodus 19:16-18 and Ezekiel 10:2.[444]

8:6   And the seven angels having the seven trumpets prepared themselves so that they might blow them.

Of course we do not know what sort of preparations these *seven angels* might need to make before sounding their *trumpets*, but this verse adds a feeling of suspense as our attention is focused again on *the seven angels* who are about to bring judgment upon the earth.

2. Seven Trumpets (8:7–11:19)

These Trumpet Judgments are somewhat parallel to the ten plagues on Egypt in Exodus 7-11,[445] but the Bowl Judgments are even more closely parallel. Just as God judged those that oppressed His people before He inaugurated a new age, the age of Israel, so He will judge those that have oppressed His people before He inaugurates the age of the Messianic Kingdom.

These judgments are full of strange elements. But once again, we will assume that an interpretation should be as literal as possible, just as we would interpret any written material. For example, in 8:10 there is a "huge star" which strikes the earth. As noted in the discussion on Revelation 6:13, it could not be a taken literally because stars are thousands of times larger than the earth. This is a figure of speech showing a terrifying event; perhaps "huge star" can refer to a very large meteor.

a. First Four Trumpets (8:7-12)

Just as the first four seals were grouped together, so also the first four trumpets form one group.

8:7 And the first[446] blew his trumpet, and there was hail and fire mixed with blood, and it was thrown to the earth, and a third of the earth was burned up, and a third of the trees were burned up, and all green grass was burned up.

Part of the judgment of the *first trumpet* is that *a third of the earth was burned up*. This dividing of *the earth* for judgment is similar to what is prophesied in Ezekiel 5:12 and Zechariah 13:8-9. This *first trumpet* judgment is like the seventh plague on Egypt, in Exodus 9, with its *hail* and lightning.

For some reason, the judgments that come forth as a result of all the trumpets (except the fifth and the seventh) include the destruction of a *third* of something.

8:8-9 And the second angel blew his trumpet, and something like a huge burning mountain[447] was thrown into the sea. And a third of the sea became blood, and a third of the living creatures[448] in the sea died, and a third of the ships were destroyed.

If the first *trumpet* brought disaster to the earth, the *second* brings disaster to *the sea*. John can only use the expression *something like* because human language, or specifically the Koine Greek language, just did not have terms for what he saw. The result of *a third of the sea* becoming *blood* is similar to the first plague on the Egyptians in Exodus.

8:10-11 And the third angel blew his trumpet, and a huge star burning like a torch fell from the sky; and it fell upon a third of the rivers and on the springs of water. (And the name of the star is Wormwood.) And a third of the waters became wormwood,[449] and many of the people died from the waters because they were made bitter.

As noted under 6:13, a *star* falling to earth is probably a meteor. In Jewish writings, meteors were a sign of the suffering of the last days.[450] This *third* trumpet's judgment is also like the first of the ten plagues in Egypt recorded in Exodus 7, where the waters of the Nile River became blood.

The first three trumpets brought judgment using fire, in accord with the censer full of fire from the altar which was thrown down in 8:5.

8:12 And the fourth angel blew his trumpet, and a third of the sun was struck, and a third of the moon, and a third of the stars, so that a third of them were darkened. And a third of the day did not shine and likewise a third of the night.[451]

This *fourth* trumpet's judgment of darkness is like the ninth plague of three days of darkness mentioned in Exodus 10. It is probably not a coincidence that there were three days of darkness then, and here we see one *third of the sun darkened*, one *third of the moon darkened*, and one *third of the stars, a third of the day*, and *a third of the night*.

In Amos 5:18 the prophet says, "Woe to those that long for the Day of the Lord! Why is it so for you, the Day of the Lord? It will be darkness, and not light!" In that text, as here, darkness is related to the judgment coming at the end of the age.

b. Last Three Trumpets (8:13–11:19)

i. Fifth Trumpet (8:13–9:12)

8:13 And I saw and I heard one eagle[452] flying high in the sky, saying with a loud voice, "Woe! Woe! Woe to those who dwell upon the earth[453] because of the remaining sounds of the trumpets of the three angels who are about to blow them!"

The eagle's announcement of *woe to those who dwell upon the earth* signals a difference between the first four trumpet judgments, which were upon earth, sea, waters, sun, moon, and stars, and the last three trumpet judgments, that are against mankind.

The first four *trumpets* are covered in just six verses, but the fifth and sixth *trumpets* are so serious that takes 21 verses to tell about them. The *eagle* says *woe* three times, which corresponds to the *three trumpets* still to be blown.

9:1 And the fifth angel blew his trumpet, and I saw a star, fallen from the sky to the earth, and the key to the pit of the abyss[454] was given to him.

How strange that *a star* be *given* a *key*. We think of stars as physical objects in outer space, but apparently they have personality in the Book of Revelation. This seems to be a figure of speech, *star* being a metaphor for "angel." In Isaiah 14:12; Judges 5:20; Job 38:7; and Revelation 12:4 the word *star* seems to be used in a similar way.

9:2 And he opened the pit of the abyss, and smoke rose out of the pit like smoke from a burning furnace.[455] And the sun and the air were darkened by the smoke of the pit.

Just as *the sun* and moon became dark because of locusts in Joel 2:10, here in Revelation 9:2 *the sun and the air were darkened by the smoke of the pit*.

9:3 And out of the smoke came locusts onto the earth, and to them was given power like the power of the scorpions of the earth.[456]

This judgment is related to the plague of *locusts* in Exodus 10:1-20, but it is even more closely related to Joel 2:4-10. *Locusts* come from the wilderness, sometimes in a huge mass, looking for farmland where they can strip fields of their crops, devastating the livelihood of the farmers. In 1866, 200,000 people in the area of Algiers died of famine because their crops were eaten by *locusts*.[457]

9:4 And it was said to them that they must not harm the grass of the earth, nor any greenery, nor any tree, but only the people who do not have the seal of God on their foreheads.[458]

As noted in the discussion under 7:2-3, those who *have the seal of God on their foreheads* are protected from the judgments of God.

The passive expressions "was given to him," in 9:1, "was given power," in 9:3 and *it was said to them* are more examples of "the Divine Passive" discussed in an endnote under Revelation 6:2. Here these expressions remind us that these judgments are arranged by the Lord *God*.[459]

Usually locusts ruin crops but do not *harm* people; not so these "locusts."

9:5 And it was given to them so that they do not kill them, but that they torment them for five months; and their torment is like the torment of a scorpion, whenever they strike a person.

This disaster is indeed horrific. An adult stung by a *scorpion* experiences unusually strong pain, but he will not die. But if the scorpions can fly like locusts and they are as numerous as locusts, and if the tormenting sting lasts for *five months*, this is far more horrific than natural locust plagues.

9:6 And in those days people will seek death, and they will certainly not[460] find it; and they will desire to die, and death will flee from them.

The description of their terrible suffering continues in this verse.

9:7 And the locusts looked like[461] horses equipped for battle. And on their heads were something like gold crowns, and their faces were like the faces of men.

These are not ordinary *locusts*! The rest of the "woe" pictures the form of their terror. This verse suggests that these are not just unusual *locusts* but actual demons.

As in Joel 2:4, the *locusts* are compared to *horses*, perhaps because the shape of the head of the *locusts* is similar to that of *horses* and because an attack from the ranks of war *horses* is similar to an attack of these *locusts*.

There is an Arab saying that *locusts* have *heads* like *horses*, breasts like lions, feet like camels, bodies like snakes, and antennae like the hair of a maiden.[462] Normal *locusts* have nothing resembling *gold crowns*, and *their faces* are not *like the faces of men*. Such *faces* leave the impression that these "locusts" have intellect and are not like normal insects. Verse 11 also suggests that they are demons, but it is not possible to be certain about this.

9:8   And they had hair like the hair of women, and their teeth were like lions' teeth.

Their long *hair* makes some commentators think of the long-haired Parthian horseback-riding soldiers.⁴⁶³ At any rate, these are terrifying and overwhelming enemies. In Joel 1:6 the locusts' *teeth* were also *like lions' teeth*.

9:9   And they had breastplates like breastplates of iron, and the sound of their wings was like the noise of many chariots and horses running into battle.

Those "locusts" could not be resisted, not just because there were so many of them but also because of their *breastplates of iron*. All of this is made worse by their *noise*, perhaps the most frightening sound in all the ancient world, that of *chariots and horses running into battle*.

9:10   And they have tails like scorpions, and stingers. And in their tails they have the power to harm people for five months.

Here we learn some more about the "locusts," as John repeats the explanation about the strength of their sting and tell us that their *stinger* is in the *tail*, just *like scorpions*.

9:11   They have a king over them, the angel of the abyss, whose name in Hebrew is Abaddon, and in Greek he has the name Apollyon.

These "locusts" are not like normal locusts. The have *a king* whose name is *Abaddon*⁴⁶⁴ and *Apollyon*.⁴⁶⁵

9:12   The first woe has passed. Look! Two woes are still coming after these things!

This verse marks our progress through the three *woes* announced by the eagle in 8:13. The next *woe*, the one connected to the sixth trumpet, is the second *woe*. The third *woe* is not the same as the seventh trumpet because that trumpet is not followed by punishment, but by the seven bowls. So the seven bowls are the third *woe*.

ii. Sixth Trumpet (9:13-21)

In the disasters brought by the fifth trumpet no one died because the "locusts" were only given power to torture. In the next disaster, one-third of mankind will die!

9:13 And the sixth angel blew his trumpet, and I heard a voice from the four horns of the golden altar that is before God,

In 6:9 John "saw under the altar the souls of those who had been killed on account of the word of God and on account of the testimony of the Lamb." In 6:10 they cry out: "How long, Master, holy and true, will You not judge and avenge our blood against those who dwell upon the earth?" In 8:3-5 the prayers of the righteous before the *altar* begin to be answered. Apparently in this passage, those prayers continue to be answered. Again here the seven churches in Asia are reminded of the power of prayer, and again the source of the *voice* is not clearly explained.

9:14 saying to the sixth angel who had the trumpet, "Release the four angels binding the great River Euphrates."

The identity of these *four angels* is not revealed to us. In 7:1-3 there are *four angels* who are forbidden to act before the 144,000 servants of God are sealed. These may be different *angels, binding the great River Euphrates*.

In any case, the location of these *four angels* is a foreboding place. In the Old Testament era, this was the area of the Assyrian Empire (Isaiah 7:20; 8:7; and Jeremiah 46:10),[466] and in the New Testament era the *Euphrates River* was the eastern boundary of the Roman Empire. Beyond it were the Parthians. They were a terrifying enemy. The worst defeat Rome had experienced was at their hands in 53 BC at Carrhae, in northern Mesopotamia, in which General Crassus was defeated by the Parthians.

During the battle, the legions of Rome formed squares with twelve men on a side, standing so close their shields overlapped, and protected by nearby cavalry. But the Parthians were all mounted on horses, with tremendously powerful composite bows and long arrows. The Parthians covered their impressive armor, but when they drew near to the Roman legions they threw off the covers and showed steel helmets and breastplates. Even their horses were armored. Their composite recurve bows, a technological development that Rome did not have, were so powerful that their strong arrows went further than the Roman arrows, and pierced Roman defensive shields.[467] Their arrows literally nailed the Romans soldiers' hands to their shields, and their feet to the ground. Sometimes, two Roman soldiers were pierced by a single Parthian arrow. Furthermore, at the height of the battle, at noon, with their drums sounding, the Parthians unfurled their unbelievable banners. The colors of those banners were intense, shining and shimmering in the sun, and the weakened Romans fled in terror. In the years to come Rome would fight and win great battles for that shimmering fabric, but on that day none of them had ever seen silk before!

Of those 40,000 Roman soldiers, 20,000 died, and another 10,000 were taken prisoner. This was a horrific loss to Roman pride. General Surena of the Parthians had won such a great victory over the huge Roman army that the Parthian emperor had him murdered for fear that the victorious general would usurp his throne.

So it is easy to understand that any reference to the *Euphrates*, to long-haired mounted warriors with iron breastplates and frightening sounds, would certainly frighten people in the Roman Empire that had heard of Crassus' defeat not too many years past.[468] All of that does not mean that these prophecies are mere historical allusions to Crassus. They are about a future judgment upon those that inhabit the earth, and they are terribly frightening to any reader, but especially to the Romans!

9:15   And the four angels that were prepared for that hour and for that day and month and year were released, so that they would kill a third of mankind.

God had already *prepared* this punishment. The sovereignty of God is emphasized again.

As in 8:7-12 the term *a third* appears again. Note the comment about *a third* under the discussion of 8:7. This sixth trumpet brings the worst of all the judgments involving *a third* of something.

9:16   And the number of soldiers mounted on horses was ten thousands of ten thousands; I heard their number.

The *ten thousands of ten thousands* surprises the reader. Where do they come from? That question is not answered in Revelation. Although the *soldiers* were so numerous, this number given by John is not an estimate; he *heard their number.*

These seem to be different from the locusts/scorpions of Revelation 9:3-11. These are from the sixth trumpet, those are from the fifth trumpet. These have colorful breastplates, those have iron breastplates.

9:17   And this is how I saw the horses in the vision: those seated on them had breastplates the color of fire, hyacinth, and sulfur,[469] and the heads of the horses were like the heads of lions, and out of their mouths came fire and smoke and sulfur.

What we have here is all we know about those who rode *the horses*. In the terrifying cavalry of the Parthians, *the horses* and the riders would both be wearing *breastplates*.[470]

Some say that these *horses* are modern tanks, maybe because *out of their mouths came fire and smoke and sulfur*, but some other elements of the description do not fit well with the tanks of modern warfare.

These *horses* and their riders, like the locusts/scorpions in 9:3-11, most likely are demons that are assigned to bring the punishment of God to those who dwell upon the earth.[471]

There are some prophecies in the major prophets (see Isaiah 5:26-30; Jeremiah 6:22-26; and Ezekiel 38:14-17) where soldiers from unbelieving nations will attack Israel, but this passage seems to prophesy that demonic soldiers will attack the enemies of God.

9:18 From these three plagues a third of mankind was killed, from the fire and the smoke and the sulfur that was coming out of their mouths.

The first woe brought torture, and the second woe brought death.[472] As in 9:15, the term *a third* appears again. Perhaps only *a third* are *killed* because the intent of all these judgments is that those who dwell upon the earth repent, so it is not yet the time that all will die. *A third of mankind* is *killed* as a reminder to those who still live,[473] but according to 9:20 they are not willing to repent.

9:19 For the power of the horses is in their mouths and in their tails, for their tails were like snakes, having heads, and with them they harmed people.[474]

The demons that are described in this passage are horrifying. Not only are *their mouths* dangerous, but *their tails*, which are *like snakes*, also have power to harm *people*.

9:20-21 And the rest of humanity, who were not killed by these plagues, did not repent[475] of the deeds of their hands; they would not stop worshiping[476] demons and idols made of gold, and silver, and bronze, and stone, and wood, which are not able to see or hear or walk. And they did not repent of their murders, or their sorcery, or their sexual immorality, or their thievery.

Here their deep sin and their lack of repentance is emphasized. This reminds us of Pharaoh's hardness of heart in Egypt. This lack of repentance becomes a key theme in the judgments upon those that dwell upon the earth.

In this passage we learn something about effective evangelism today. Experiencing the miraculous may help some people to believe the Gospel (note Revelation 11:11-13), but some that even experience amazing miracles do not *repent*, as is emphasized in this passage.

We read in the Old Testament (for example, in Deuteronomy 4:28 and Psalm 115:5-7) that *idols* cannot *see or hear or walk*. God's Word also emphasizes (Deuteronomy 32:17 and 1 Corinthians 10:20) that what is offered to *idols* is given to *demons*. So in fact those who are not killed by those demonic horses and their riders will *not stop worshiping demons!*[477]

Those in the congregations of Pergamum and Thyatira that ate meat sacrificed to *idols* would be reminded of the evil involved in any participation with *idols*.

The sixth trumpet has already sounded, but there are two insertions before we hear the seventh trumpet.

Third Insertion: Scroll (10:1-11)

This passage emphasizes the Apostle John's role as a prophet who has to proclaim what must be proclaimed and be silent about what must not be proclaimed. This role brings joy, but it also brings grief.

> 10:1 And I saw a mighty angel descending from heaven, encompassed by a cloud, and a rainbow was on his head, and his face was like the sun, and his legs were like pillars of fire.

Although the elements of *cloud, rainbow, sun,* and *pillars of fire* remind us of the Son of God,[478] the expression *a mighty angel* is hardly something one would use to describe the Son of God, though there are commentators that take that view. Also, the Lord Jesus returns to the earth in chapter 19. It seems unlikely that He would come temporarily in chapter ten but come again in chapter 19. It is better to understand this as an *angel*, not as the Lord Jesus.

In any case, this is an unusual *angel*. This seems to be the only *angel* in the book with such a detailed description about his appearance. Even though he is so well-described, the things this *angel* does are hard to interpret.

> 10:2 And he had in his hand a scroll[479] that was open, and he put his right foot on the sea and his left on the land.

The meaning of the *scroll* and the placement of his feet *on land* and *sea* are not explained to us. Maybe the placement of the angel's feet *on land and sea* means that his message is for all of mankind, for those *on land* and those *on the sea*.[480]

This *scroll* is *open*[481] unlike the *scroll* in 10:4 that John is told to seal up. It is also different from the *scroll* in chapter five which was closed and sealed. Apparently this *open scroll* symbolizes John's role as a prophet of God.

10:3 And he shouted in a loud voice like a lion roars, and when he shouted, the seven thunders spoke with their own voices.[482]

His *loud* shout seems to be an invitation to *the seven thunders*, who then speak. Just as the *seven* seals were opened, and the *seven* trumpets were sounded, so here *the seven thunders spoke.*

Readers having read about the *seven* seals and the *seven* trumpets might be thinking that the *thunders* will also be accompanied by disasters.

10:4 And when the seven thunders spoke I was about to write, and I heard a voice from heaven saying, "Seal up what the seven thunders spoke and do not write it."[483]

Once *the seven thunders spoke,* John expected that there would be judgments upon the earth, but instead he is told *not to write* what he heard. Although it might seem strange to *seal up* something that was not even written down, the expression *seal up* here clearly has the figurative meaning of "keep secret."

Commentators give various opinions regarding the idea that the *thunders* are not included in what John wrote for us. Leon Morris suggests that this is like 2 Corinthians 12:4, a personal message for John alone.[484] Ladd says that message is kept secret, but will be revealed at the right time in the future.[485] Bauckham says that there should only be three in the chain (seals, trumpets, and bowls), so the *thunders* are excluded.[486] Mounce agrees, and adds that there is no need for another series of judgments like the trumpets, because men have shown that they will not repent under judgments like that.[487] One remembers Jesus' words, in Matthew 24:22, "And if those days were not shortened, no flesh would be saved, but because of the elect those days will be shortened." Any one of those explanations might be the correct one, but it is not possible to be certain. Perhaps the lesson for us is simply that there are some things that we are not told.

10:5 And the angel which I saw standing on the sea and on the land raised his right hand to heaven,

In the Old Testament the raising of one's *right hand to heaven* was a customary expression for making an oath, as in Genesis 14:22[488] and Deuteronomy 32:40. The next verse makes it clear that that is what is happening here. Further, this passage is related to Daniel 12:6-7, which tells of an *angel* who took an oath that the plans of God would be accomplished in an orderly predetermined time.

10:6   and swore by the One who lives forever and ever, who created heaven and what is in it, and the earth and what is in it, and the sea and what is in it, "There will be no more delay!

Speaking for God, who orders all of time, the angel swears that the end of the ages will not be postponed any more. This is very different from "yet awhile" in 6:11.

10:7   But in the days of the sound[489] of the seventh angel, when he shall blow his trumpet, the mystery of God is completed, as He has proclaimed to His slaves the prophets."

At the time of the events in this verse, *the days* of the blowing of the *seventh trumpet*, the *trumpet* must be blown and the seven bowls must be poured out because the seven bowls are "contained within" the *seventh trumpet*.[490] The completion of those days is described in 11:15, where we are told there is joy in heaven as the *seventh trumpet* is blown.

In the New Testament the term *mystery*[491] means truth which is not known except by revelation from *God*. This does not mean there is a new *mystery* in this passage, because the *mystery* meant here *He has proclaimed to His slaves the prophets*. In all of time, *God* has had one purpose, to see that "The kingdom of the world has become the kingdom of our Lord and of his Christ, and he will reign for ever and ever" (Revelation 11:15). Perhaps the expression *mystery of God* in this passage refers to God's purpose that the Kingdom of *God* will fill the earth.[492]

10:8   And the voice which I heard from heaven was again speaking to me and saying, "Go, take the little scroll that is open in the hand of the angel who is standing on the sea and on the land."

After the seven thunders are sealed up, our attention is drawn again to *the little scroll that is open in the hand of the angel*, which John must *take*.

10:9-10 And I went to the angel, asking him to give me the little scroll. And he said to me, "Take and eat it up, and it will make your stomach bitter, but it will be as sweet as honey in your mouth."[493] And I took the scroll from the hand of the angel and ate it up, and in my mouth it was as honey, sweet, and when I ate it, my stomach was made bitter.

This is one of the few times where John becomes involved in the narration. It is hard to be certain, but it appears *the little scroll* represents the Word of God John must pass on, and this experience is a confirmation of John's own call as a prophet of God. This passage is very similar to Ezekiel 2:8–3:3, where the prophet Ezekiel is told to *eat a scroll* that is *sweet* in his *mouth*. The expression *sweet as honey in your mouth* is also similar to what is written in Psalm 19:10 and 119:103.

The bitterness in John's *stomach* is more difficult to understand, and various commentators make various suggestions. Morris and Ladd[494] say the *bitter stomach* means that God's Word will concern His judgment on those who refuse to believe in the Lord Jesus, and telling about that judgment will be a *bitter* task for John. According to Beasley-Murray[495] the *sweet* taste represents the joy the Word of God conveys, and the *bitter* taste represents the pain that the Word of God conveys. According to Mounce,[496] the *sweet* and *bitter* tastes represent the final triumph of the church along with the difficulties the church of Christ will face in the final days.

10:11 And they said to me: "You must prophesy again about many peoples and nations and languages and kings."

Because this statement follows directly after John's experience with the angel and that little scroll, it seems like it must be related to it. Somehow eating the scroll relates to John's prophetic ministry *about many peoples and nations and languages and kings*.[497] This is a command to *prophesy*, with a warning that this ministry will be both bitter and sweet for him.

Fourth Insertion: Two Witnesses (11:1-14)

We have already noticed in the insertions in chapter seven that there were elements of witness and martyrdom. Then, the insertion in chapter ten told about a prophet's proclamation with its bitterness. In this next insertion also, there are elements of witness and martyrdom. This passage describes the two witnesses' empowerment, as well as their ministry, their martyrdom, and their resurrection.

11:1 And a reed[498] like a staff was given to me, and I was told, "Arise and measure the temple of God and the altar and those worshiping there.

Again John is invited to actually participate in the revelation. He is given *a reed* for a measuring rod. These reeds grew along the Jordan River, and could be as long as 6 meters or 20 feet. Because they were straight and light, they were often cut to the appropriate length and used as measuring rods. John is told to *measure the temple and the altar and those worshiping there*.[499] It is unusual to *measure* people with a measuring rod.

One important issue here is whether indeed there will be a *temple* in Jerusalem when these things happen. Unless this passage has an extended metaphorical meaning, verses like this, as well as Daniel 9:26; 11:31; 12:11; and 2 Thessalonians 2:4 would suggest that the Jewish *temple* will be rebuilt in Jerusalem before these things happen.

In Zechariah 2 Jerusalem is measured. In Ezekiel 40-41 the wall around the *temple*, and the *temple* itself, are measured in great detail. In Revelation 21:15-17 the walls of the New Jerusalem are measured, but there is no *temple* to *measure* there.

In Ezekiel 40-42 the prophet saw a man who was bronze-looking that measured the *temple* and its surrounding courts and gates. That seems to lead up to Ezekiel 43:4-5, where the glory of the Lord entered and filled the *temple*.

There are various interpretations of the meaning of the measuring of the *temple*. Ryrie[500] says it means that *God* knows what will happen to His people, and He sets limits to what will happen to them. Ladd[501] says it refers to God's protection of His people. That interpretation would be supported by Revelation 11:2, because there John is told not to *measure* the outer courtyard, which somehow is not protected, and is given over to the gentiles. Perhaps measuring something with *a reed* is a way to emphasize that it is real, but that explanation would not help us understand why the outer court, because it has been given to the gentiles, was not to be measured.

11:2   And disregard the outer courtyard of the temple; and do not measure it, because it has been given to the gentiles, and they will trample on the holy city for forty-two months.

The *outer courtyard*, which he is told *not to measure*, was the Court of the Gentiles, which consisted of about 26 acres or 10 hectares. Literally he is told, "and the courtyard that is outside the temple itself, exclude it...." The reason given is that it has been *given over to the gentiles*, who *will trample on the holy city for forty-two months*.

This time period, *forty-two months*, is the same as the "1,260 days" mentioned in 11:3 (assuming a month is 30 days) and the "times, time, and half a time" mentioned in 12:6 (assuming "times" is two years and a "time" is one year). A comparison of 12:6 and 12:14 proves this. Both clearly refer to the same three and a half year period, but 12:6 uses the expression "1,260 days," and 12:14 uses the expression "a time, times and half a time."

This is the second half the 70th seven year period of Daniel 9:27. Comparing Revelation 12:14 with Daniel 7:25 and 12:7 shows that there is a strong connection between Daniel and Revelation in this area. Those familiar with the angel Gabriel's statements to Daniel in Daniel 9:22-27 will see that these verses in Revelation fit right into what Daniel was told. In Daniel 9:24 the angel Gabriel tells Daniel that "seventy sevens have been decreed upon your people and upon your holy city." The term "sevens" there might possibly refer to seven days (as in one week), but given the context of Israel's punishment by exile into Babylon for seventy years, in connection with Jeremiah 25:11-12 and 29:10, and given that whenever in Daniel 10:2 Daniel uses the term "sevens" to speak of seven days, he makes it clear by saying "sevens of days," Gabriel in Daniel 9:24 means "seventy periods of seven years each," or 490 years. In Daniel 9:24 Gabriel give six things that will be accomplished during those 490 years. Not all of those things have been accomplished. In 9:25 Gabriel explains that the time from the proclamation to rebuild Jerusalem to the coming of Messiah will be 69 of those seventy sevens (since 69 times 7 is 483, he means 483 years). The "clock will run" for 483 years. The Messiah will come to Israel 483 years after the proclamation to rebuild Jerusalem. But Gabriel explains something quite strange in Daniel 9:26. After the sixty-two sevens, that is, after 434 years, the Messiah will be "cut off." Gabriel tells us the Messiah will "have nothing." The angel Gabriel does not explain, but we know that He was rejected and crucified. And "the clock stops." Then after an unexplained period of time, "the clock starts running again." The final seven, the last seven years, then begins. In Daniel 9:26 there is someone called "the leader who will come." In 9:27 that man makes a covenant strong "for one seven," for seven years, the last of the seventy sevens mentioned in 9:24. In 9:27, right in the middle of those last seven years, that man sets up "the abomination of desolation." How long will it be from the middle of that seven years until the end? Yes, it will be *forty-two months*, as it is written in Revelation 11:2. It will also be 1,260 days, as it is written in Revelation 11:3. It will also be three and a half years, as the "times, time, and half a time" of Daniel 7:25; 12:7; and also Revelation 12:6 suggest! And then, as Daniel 9:25 tells us, "the Messiah, the ruler, comes." See also Psalm 79:1; Isaiah 63:18; and Luke 21:24.

11:3   And I will give My two witnesses even that they will prophesy for 1,260 days, dressed in sackcloth."

In the midst of Jerusalem being trampled by the gentiles, God empowers *two witnesses* to *prophesy* for Him three and a half years. Jerusalem is being trampled by the gentiles, but the Lord is doing His great work through these two men. In fact, the end of 11:13 describes great fruit from their ministry, in contrast to the lack of repentance from all the judgments that are poured out on those that inhabit the earth (note 16:9). Here we see the important idea that judgment does not bring people to faith, but Gospel witness does.

The identity of the *two witnesses* is often debated. In Malachi 4:5 there is the promise of the return of Elijah, the prophet, before the great and terrible day of the Lord, so it is very possible that one of these miracle-working *witnesses* is Elijah. The other might be Enoch or Moses. Neither Enoch nor Elijah has died yet! It is also possible that they are ordinary people called and given a special assignment in that era. Their ministry follows the pattern of Moses and Elijah, especially in 11:6, when they do things that Moses and Elijah did. However, since the Lord did not clarify their identity, discussions concerning the identity of the *two witnesses* are speculative Their clothing emphasizes their roles as prophets (Zechariah 13:4) calling people to repent (Jeremiah 4:8 and Matthew 11:21).

Bauckham[502] gives an interesting idea. He suggests that the *two witnesses* are spoken of as a parable to encourage the people of God to do the ministry of prophecy and witness, calling the nations to repentance. In the Book of Revelation, witness is powerfully effective in combination with the judgments of God. Without any witness, judgments have brought about little repentance throughout the book. Bauckham may be saying that there never will be *two* physical human *witnesses*, but that they have a purely symbolic meaning. But it would be better for us to say that there will be *two* physical human *witnesses*, and that they will also have that symbolic meaning. Those *two* physical human *witnesses* will come, they will serve as described here, and they will also be symbols of effective evangelistic witness; these prophecies about them encourage the people of God to witness, to share the Gospel. Witness and martyrdom are certainly major themes in this book. See 7:9-17 and 10:11 as well.

11:4   These are the two olive trees and the two lampstands that are standing before the Lord of the earth.

They are called *olive trees* and *lampstands*, terms also used in Zechariah 4. In the same way as Joshua and Zerubbabel in Zechariah were reminded of God's resources as they completed their tasks, so we are reminded that the two witnesses will have God's resources as well.[503] Just as *olive* oil makes the lamp produce light, so also the two witnesses of God can serve "not by strength, and not by might, but by My Spirit" (Zechariah 4:6). This verse seems to emphasize that the *two* witnesses serve in the power of the Spirit.

> 11:5   And if anyone wants to harm them, fire comes out of their mouths and devours their enemies. And if anyone wants to harm them, they must be killed in this way.

No one can stop God's servants until He decides that their ministry is completed. Their ability to call *fire* down upon any who would *harm them* is like Elijah's power in 2 Kings 1:10-14, though the *fire* did not come out of Elijah's mouth.

> 11:6   These men have the power to close the sky so that rain does not fall during the days of their prophecies. And they have power over the waters to turn them into blood, and to strike the earth with every kind of plague as often as they might want.

Their *power* to cause a drought reminds us of Elijah in 1 Kings 17:1. Their *power to turn the waters into blood* reminds us of Moses in Exodus 7. Whatever these men of God do to confirm their witness to the nations may be even more terrible than what was done by Moses or Elijah in the Old Testament, but Moses and Elijah become good models for the ministry of the witnesses of God in the final days.

Bauckham[504] observes that the plagues or judgments by themselves will not bring repentance, as emphasized in 9:20-21. In the ministry of the two witnesses there are two distinct elements that are not in the chain of judgments of the seals and the trumpets: the death of the witnesses, and the news that they tell. Plagues from God, if not accompanied by the witness of people ready to die, will not bring unbelievers to repentance.

> 11:7   And when they have finished their testimony, the beast that comes up out of the abyss will make war on them and be victorious over them and kill them.

Without a lot of explanation, John introduces *the beast that comes up out of the abyss*. It seems that this person is the same as *the beast* which is "coming up out of the sea" in 13:1, known in other parts of the New Testament as the Anti-Christ.

The two witnesses will not be killed until they have *finished* their ministry. In fact, as the Lord explained in John 11:7-10, they could not be killed until they *finished* their ministry. This is comforting! We too will not be killed a moment before our ministry from God is completed. This was especially important for the congregation in Smyrna, and is today especially important for all persecuted churches. But witnesses like this, who according to 11:13 will be very fruitful, must be willing to die, just as the church in Smyrna was encouraged to "be faithful until death...."

11:8   And their corpses will be in the street[505] of the great city that is spiritually called "Sodom" and "Egypt," where their Lord was also crucified.

To not bury a corpse is a terrible offense, both in the Greek culture (as the stories of the death of Patroclus and of Hector in *The Iliad* make very clear) and in the Hebrew culture (as is clear in 1 Kings 21:23-24; Jeremiah 8:1-2; and 14:16.) The *city* where their bodies lie exposed and unburied is called "Sodom" and "Egypt" because it is the unrepentant Jerusalem, *where their Lord was also crucified*. If they are not two individual human beings, and if the text is parabolic, then this verse must also be interpreted figuratively. Perhaps the idea would be that any city that martyrs God's witnesses is figuratively *called "Sodom" and "Egypt."*

Note that this city is *spiritually called "Sodom" and "Egypt."* The use of allegory here is clearly indicated by the expression *spiritually called*. The reader should not generate his or her own allegories, but we clearly understand the use of allegory here.

11:9   For three and a half days those from every people, tribe, language, and nation[506] will look at their corpses, and it will not be permitted to place their corpses in a tomb.

If the two witnesses are two actual individuals, then this verse could be an indirect prophecy of television or the internet. However if the activity of the two witnesses is intended solely as a parable, then the many witnessing martyrs will be seen laying in streets all over the world, and people all over the world would see them in their own streets without any need for television or the internet.

Perhaps the *three and a half days* that their bodies are exposed to public and worldwide view is parallel to the *three and a half years* of their ministry, but this is not clear from the text.

11:10   And those who dwell upon the earth[507] will rejoice over them and be delighted, and they will give gifts to one another, because these two prophets had tormented those who dwell upon the earth.

Bauckham[508] notes that this text is reminiscent of Esther 9:19 and 22, even though in that text it is the Jews rejoicing over a victory against evil, but in Revelation 11:10 it is Jew and gentile rejoicing over an apparent victory over God's two witnesses.

11:11 And after three and a half days a breath of life from God entered into them, and they stood on their feet, and great fear fell upon those who were watching them.

If Bauckham's idea is correct, and this passage is solely a parable, it is hard to understand what this verse might mean. Because of that, this verse might be the best support for the idea that there really will be two witnesses, and the passage is not solely a parable, as Bauckham suggests. However, it is also possible that there will be two witnesses, and besides that there is a parable in this future event for us to understand: the witness that is ready to die for his or her faith is a very powerful instrument in God's hands!

This event is similar to that written in Ezekiel 37. Surely this verse would impress those in Smyrna to whom the One "Who was dead and Who lives" said "be faithful until death and I will give you the crown of life."

11:12 And they heard a loud voice from heaven saying to them: "Come up here!"[509] And they went up into heaven in a cloud and their enemies watched them.

Note that just as the Lord Jesus ascended into a *cloud* while others looked on, so the two witnesses went up into *heaven in a cloud* while their *enemies watched them*. It might also be significant that "Elijah went up in a windstorm to the heavens" while Elisha *watched* (2 Kings 2:11).

11:13 And in that day[510] there was a major earthquake and a tenth of the city fell; seven thousand people were killed in the earthquake, and the rest became afraid and gave glory to the God of heaven.

Note that just as the resurrection of Jesus was accompanied by an *earthquake*, so the resurrection of His witnesses is accompanied by an *earthquake*.

The *earthquake* causes a *tenth*[511] of the city of Jerusalem to fall and *seven thousand* to die. Other disasters were more destructive, as in chapters eight and nine where one third of everything was destroyed.

To give *glory to the God of heaven* is to truly repent and believe. See Revelation 4:9; 14:7; 16:9; and 19:7. It often means that in the Old Testament. See Joshua 7:19 and Jeremiah 13:16. See also Psalm 96:7-8; Isaiah 24:15-16; and 42:12. Never in the Book of Revelation is *glory* given to *God* in any superficial sense. These were people that really repented, really believed, and really worshiped *God* in Christ.

To properly understand this passage we must understand that it is as though 1 Kings 19:18 were rewritten! In that passage only *seven thousand* are righteous, but here all *except seven thousand* are righteous. Having only *seven thousand* die, and the rest repent, is really wonderful when it is compared with the corresponding events in 1 Kings 19:14-18. In that passage, during Elijah's ministry, *seven thousand* believed, and all the rest were idolaters. Besides that, a *tenth* is also used in the Old Testament (note Amos 5:3 and Isaiah 6:13) about the remnant of the people of Israel who did not experience judgment. But now *seven thousand* die, and all the rest repent. That is much more wonderful! This is the climax of the witness theme in the book, and highlights the importance of being a witness who is willing to die.[512]

In summary, as opposed to the lack of results when judgments fall upon those who dwell upon the earth, when there is a witness that is willing to die and the power of God is present, the Old Testament pattern is turned upside down: rather than a few believing but most perishing, we see many believe and only a minority die. This is a great encouragement to Smyrna and Philadelphia – and us – to witness in the power of God, and see great results. It is also part of the on-going theme of martyrdom in this book.

11:14   The second woe has passed; the third – look! – it is coming.

This announcement is a continuation of 9:12. This verse marks 11:1-13 (the fruit of repentance from the witness and martyrdom of God's people) as an insertion of the Book of Revelation.

With this announcement about the *third woe*, we return to the chain of plagues that are the backbone of this section. Because the seventh trumpet is not followed by a special disaster but instead is followed by the seven bowls, it may be said that the *third woe is* the seventh trumpet, and it *contains* the seven bowls.

iii. Seventh Trumpet (11:15-19)

Now the seventh trumpet is blown. The sound of the trumpet brings unidentified voices from heaven and also from the twenty-four elders. Both of these responses to the blowing of the seventh trumpet emphasize a very important theme in Revelation, which is a transfer of authority. The Kingdom of God is coming. After this there is a description of the Temple in heaven.

11:15   And the seventh angel blew his trumpet, and there were loud voices in heaven saying:

"The kingdom of the world
has become the kingdom of our Lord
and of His Christ,

and He will reign for ever and ever."

The *seventh trumpet* is blown, followed by *voices* celebrating the transfer of authority⁵¹³ from the *world* to the *Lord*. Their joy seems to come too soon, because there are still seven bowls to be poured out. But because there are no more trumpets and because the final *trumpet* contains the seven bowls,⁵¹⁴ they celebrate the completion of the judgments here. They are right to rejoice because with the sound of the final *trumpet*, the final events will follow immediately.

Normally in the New Testament the term *Lord* refers to Jesus Christ, but in this passage the term is referring to God the Father.

When the *seventh* seal was opened, there were no judgments; there was silence for half an hour. The blowing of the *seventh trumpet* is similar. There are no judgments, only joyful news. The *seventh* seal contained the seven trumpets; so also the *seventh trumpet* contains the seven bowls.

11:16   And the twenty-four elders who are seated on their thrones before the throne of⁵¹⁵ God fell upon their faces and worshiped God

Since chapter seven *the twenty-four elders* have not been mentioned, but in this section they are praising *God*. Revelation 7:11 and 11:16 are very similar, but in 7:11 it was the angels that *fell upon their faces and worshiped God*, while here in this verse the *elders fell upon their faces and worshiped God*.

11:17   saying,
"We give thanks to You, O Lord, God All-powerful,⁵¹⁶
the One who is and who was,
because You have received⁵¹⁷ Your great power
and begun to reign.⁵¹⁸

Perhaps *You have received Your great power* refers to how He *received* the scroll from the One seated upon His throne in 5:7.

From what we have seen in chapters four, five, and seven, when the elders or angels speak together, they are praising *God* the Father or His Son.

In 1:4 and 1:8 we read about "God who is, and who was, and who is coming," but in 11:17 and 16:5 the expression "and is to come" is not used, because it is as if He has already come.⁵¹⁹

11:18   And the nations were enraged,⁵²⁰
but Your wrath⁵²¹ has come,
and the time for the dead to be judged,

> and the time[522] to give wages to Your slaves, the prophets,
>
>> and to the saints and to those who fear Your name, small and great,
>
> and to destroy those who destroy the earth."

In a short but packed verse, their song explains the meaning of the coming of Christ, a coming full of joy.[523]

The Lord comes with his own *wrath*.[524] If the expression *the dead* means those who died without Christ, then this verse has a structure that is beautiful and balanced: first, judgment for those who oppose God; second, rewards for all those who lived for Christ; and third, the destruction of those who opposed God.

God's judgment is not random. He left *the earth* in the care of mankind (Genesis 1:26-28), but man destroyed what was given to him. Because of this, unrepentant man will be destroyed.[525]

11:19 And the temple of God in heaven was opened, and the ark of the covenant of the Lord[526] was visible in His temple. And there were lightning, roaring, thunder,[527] and huge hailstones.

The blowing of the seventh trumpet is not followed by a judgment upon the earth. Instead, it seems that the end is at hand. But in 15:7 we see that there are still seven bowls of judgment to be poured out. All that hoped that 11:15-19 was the end are disappointed to hear that the "telescope" is to be extended out again, just as they were disappointed when it turned out that the seventh seal's judgment consisted of the seven trumpets. They will learn soon enough that the seventh trumpet's judgment consists of the seven bowls.

This short vision closes this section. In this verse *the ark of the covenant is visible*. In the Old Testament *the ark of the covenant* symbolized the presence of God among the people of Israel,[528] but only the High Priest could see it and then only once a year. According to Jewish tradition (2 Maccabees 2:7), *the ark* will be found among the people of Israel when the Messiah comes.[529] In Revelation once the Lord Jesus returns to the earth, *God* dwells visibly in the midst of His people. What is said by symbols here in this verse later will become clear in Revelation 21-22, especially in 21:3.

The *lightning, roaring, thunder and huge hailstones* here point to the presence of the Lord *God*. At Mount Sinai there was "roaring, lightning and thick clouds" (Exodus 19:16), and the Psalmist says "the earth shook" (Psalm 68:8). In the Book of Revelation, the day of the Lord's coming is often spoken of in terms that remind the reader of the freeing of God's people from Egypt. As noted above, the plagues that strike the earth are similar to the plagues of Exodus. According to Isaiah 13:13, at the time of the coming of the Lord *God* to the earth, the sky and earth will tremble and shake with very destructive earthquakes.[530]

In this verse there are *lightning, roaring, thunder and huge hailstones*. Note the discussion under 4:5 in which this verse is described as the climax of a carefully constructed series of passages. The Book of Revelation stresses that the chain of plagues are connected: they are one judgment which originates from *God* Himself. The coming of the Lord is already very near! The seven trumpets have been sounded, and the corresponding judgments have struck those who dwell upon the earth.

Comments Closing this Volume

We have read Revelation chapter one, the words John recorded about the vision that he saw of the Lord Jesus while he was on the island of Patmos. We know that if we could make those words the cornerstone of our lives, our attitudes, our words, and our deeds, then our lives would be pleasing to the Lord, and He would give us His blessing. But we ourselves experienced some bewilderment as we wondered how to understand those words, and how to live them. What are we to do with the fact that His eyes were like a flame of fire, and a sharp double-edged sword came out of His mouth? It was too much for us, we did not understand, or were afraid to understand.

As we read chapters two and three, we saw that some of us did not need to apply the fact that a sharp double-edged sword came out of His mouth, but we need to apply the truth that He walks among the seven golden lampstands. This was not to ensure our salvation – He has already done that on the Cross – but to ensure our rewards. Others of us realized that we need to act upon the fact that He was dead, but He was victorious over death, and is now alive. As we continued to read those seven amazing messages, we perhaps saw that one of them gave us more insight into our own deepest heart than we had ever dared to ask. And we saw that He did not ask a great many things of us, but what He did ask us was very difficult. We dared to wonder what it would be like to be a victor with Him, to overcome the all too real temptations and challenges we face, as He overcame death. But we were still disturbed, even frightened, and we needed more help.

We read on into the visions that began in chapter four, and learned that the Day will come when He will open the seven seals of an inheritance document, so that the victors will inherit the earth. We read of how high and how wide His praise will be on that great Day. We read of such terrible judgments that will fall on those that have never trusted Him as their Savior, once He begins to open the seven seals. Those judgments continued relentlessly as one by one the seven angels blew the seven trumpets, and the Lord God showed His great power and perfect justice by judging those that have hated and opposed Him. We read of "the wrath of the Lamb," and of the victory of those that died faithfully serving Him. We read about how our prayers are to Him like sweet-smelling incense that rises up to Him, and how He does answer those prayers. And in all this we were strengthened to make our stand as victors, to give up those sins that have distracted us, and to stand firm as victors in the same victory that He earned so many years ago.

What is written in Revelation 12-22 will also strengthen our resolve to live as victors, so that we can participate in the great joys of the victorious day of the Lord's return.

Appendix: Repetition in Revelation

This appendix presents more examples of the repetition of words, as discussed in the Introduction. Again, all of these word counts are based on the Greek text.

The number four is used in connection with God's creation and with angels that are given authority over nature: 7:1, 2; 9:14, 15; and 20:8. Clearly, nature stands out in the use of the number four, all the more if we remember that the four creatures have the form of animals or man as part of nature, that is, a lion, a calf, a man, and a flying eagle.[532]

Remembering that the number four is often connected to nature (which is ultimately restored through the sacrifice of the Lamb of God), it is appropriate that the Lord Jesus is called "the Lamb of God" 28 times (4x7) in Revelation.

The number seven is also used of evil. In 12:3 the dragon has seven heads and seven crowns, and in 13:1 the Anti-Christ has seven heads (also in 17:3, 7, and 9). In 17:10 and 11 the seven heads stand for seven kings, the allies of the Anti-Christ. It is hard to be certain of the significance of this use of the number seven. Perhaps it means that the Anti-Christ is completely evil, or that he imitates Christ's perfection.

These words are used seven times: Abyss,[533] worthy,[534] to reign,[535] to be full,[536] sickle,[537] adultery,[538] and the expression "the Lord God Almighty,"[539] assuming the expression "'I am the Alpha and the Omega,' says the Lord God, 'who is, and who was, and who is to come, the Almighty,'" found in 1:8, is included in the count.

The word "star"[540] is used 14 times.

The numbers ten or tenth are used ten times in Revelation. The number one tenth is used once. In 2:10 there is tribulation for ten days. In 21:20 the tenth stone is chrysoprase. Except for those two passages, the numbers ten and tenth are used to tell about the horns, crowns, and kings that oppose the Lord God and His people, so it seems like the number ten refers to evil and suffering.

The words "true,"[541] "number,"[542] "thunder,"[543] and "image"[544] are used ten times.

The numbers twelve and twelfth are used 24 times in Revelation. Twelve is only used in connection with the people of Israel (7:5-8, 12 times; and 12:1) and the New Jerusalem (21:12–22:2).

Eleven times the expression "One seated upon the throne" is used. Then the use of that expression climaxes with Revelation 20:11, which says "And I saw a great white throne, and the One seated upon it – from before whose presence the earth and the heaven fled, and no place was found for them." Thus God is referred to twelve times as being seated upon a throne.

In the final vision of the book, that is 21:9–22:5, the word "twelve"[545] appears twelve times. This is not clear in the English translation, but this is correct in the Greek Majority Text.[546] Within that same vision, the term "Lamb" and the term "God" are both used seven times! This simply did not happen by accident.

The expression "the Lord God" appears ten times in Revelation (4:11 is not counted, because there the expression is not "the Lord God," but "the Lord and the God"). The term "Christ" appears ten times. As mentioned above, the word "Spirit"[547] is used 14 times for the Spirit of God.

Endnotes

1   Despite his prominence in the Gospels and in Acts 1-8, surprisingly little is recorded in the rest of the NT about the Apostle John. All we know from the NT outside of the Gospels and Acts is that he was "recognized as a pillar" of the church in Jerusalem (Gal. 2:9), he wrote his three NT epistles, and on Patmos he received the Revelation.

2   Mounce, p. 29. Robert M. Mounce, Ph.D., dean of Potter College of Arts and Humanities at Western Kentucky University, wrote a commentary on Revelation that is balanced, complete, and detailed.

3   Mounce (p. 30) notes a few such differences. For instance "believe" is used 98 times in the Gospel of John but is not used at all in Revelation. In fact, one-eighth of the words that are used in Revelation are not used anywhere else in the NT.

4   Morris, pp. 29-30. This commentary by Leon Morris, M. Sc., M.Th., Ph.D., is short and concise.

5   Mounce, p. 27.

6   The statement by Irenaeus that Revelation was written by "John, the disciple of the Lord" is weighty evidence because as a young man, Irenaeus knew Polycarp who knew the Apostle John (Mounce, p. 27).

7   If the newspaper says that Obama did something in the United States, we do not ask "Which Obama?" There may be several other people in Washington, DC named "Obama," but clearly President Obama is being referred to.

8   See also Rom. 16:22 (which notes that Tertius actually wrote the letter); 1 Cor. 16:21; Gal. 6:11; Col. 4:18; 2 Thess. 3:17; and Philem. 1:19.

9   P. 8. Dr. George Eldon Ladd, who taught New Testament at Fuller Theological Seminary, held to post-tribulation theology. The commentary of Dr. Ladd is brief, but he mentions and evaluates the opinions of other scholars.

10   Hemer, p. 9, cites chapter 13 of Suetonius' work on Domitian. Concerning Domitian Suetonius wrote, "With equal arrogance, when he dictated the form of a letter to be used by his procurators, he began it thus: 'Our lord and god commands so and so;' whence it became a rule that no one should style him otherwise either in writing or speaking" (translation by Alexander Thomson).

11   Mounce, p. 33. Eusebius, *Church History*, Book III, Chapter 17, reads, "Domitian, having shown great cruelty toward many, and having unjustly put to death no small number of well-born and notable men at Rome, and having without cause exiled and confiscated the property of a great many other illustrious men, finally became a successor of Nero in his hatred and enmity toward God. He was in fact the second that stirred up a persecution against us, although his father Vespasian had undertaken nothing prejudicial to us." (Translated by Arthur Cushman McGiffert. From *Nicene and Post-Nicene Fathers*, Second Series, Vol. 1. Edited by Philip Schaff and Henry Wace, Buffalo, NY: Christian Literature Publishing Co., 1890.) Eusebius died in about AD 340. Some modern historians reject Eusebius' comments on this persecution, saying he is biased. But perhaps

they are also biased! Although Suetonius does not mention persecution against Christians, his descriptions of Domitian's cruelty indicate that persecution of Christians was well within the pattern of his actions.

12   The Acts of John, 106-115, tells of John's death. However, there is no certainty at all that The Acts of John is historically accurate.

13   Mounce, p. 76.

14   These distances are the actual distances between those cities. Since the road was not at all straight, the distances for the traveler would have been quite a bit longer.

15   Bruce, pp. 399-402.

16   Bruce (p. 413) gives an example of two events that showed the absolute power of the emperor. First, according to Eusebius, Emperor Domitian called in two of the grandchildren of James, the brother of Jesus, to see if they, as descendants of King David, would struggle to regain the kingdom. Evidently as two low-paid workers, they were not interested in politics, so Emperor Domitian freed them. In the second example, the nephew of Emperor Domitian, called Flavius Clemens, was accused of "atheism" and put to death by Domitian. In those days, Christians were called "atheists" because they would not bow to the gods of Rome. Many scholars think that Flavius Clemens was a Christian. With a similar accusation Flavius Clemens' wife was exiled to the island of Pandateria. According to church tradition, Clemens and his wife believed in the Lord Jesus. Long before this happened, their two children were chosen by the emperor Domitian as his heirs. Perhaps there was almost an emperor of Rome that was brought up in a Christian household!

17   This term is from the word αποκαλυψις/*apokalupsis*, the first word of the Book of Revelation. It means "unveiling," "disclosure," or of course "revelation." Outside of the NT the word sometimes refers to the "uncovering" of a head (*BDAG*).

18   Mounce, p. 18.

19   George E. Ladd, "The Kingdom of God in the Jewish Apocryphal Literature" Part 3, *Bibliotheca Sacra*, 109:436 (Oct. 1952), p. 325.

20   In the same way, the living God contextualized Himself into humanity, being fully God He also became fully human, a male Jewish baby.

21   Beasley-Murray, p. 14.

22   Bauckham, *The Theology of the Book of Revelation*, pp. 7-8. (Dr. Richard Bauckham, Professor of New Testament at St. Mary's College, University of St. Andrews in Scotland, examines the Book of Revelation as well-designed literature. His insights into the theology of Revelation are valuable. This writer wishes, however, that Dr. Bauckham might admit that even though the prophecies of Revelation express profound theology, they are also prophecies awaiting historical fulfillment. They speak of things which truly "will take place after these things.")

23   Bauckham, *The Theology of the Book of Revelation*, pp. 9-12; Mounce, p. 24; and Beasley-Murray, pp. 12-29. Dr. G. R. Beasley-Murray taught New Testament at Southern Baptist Theological Seminary in Louisville, Kentucky, USA. Before

that he served as rector at Spurgeon's College in London. His commentary is thorough.

24 Beasley-Murray (p. 12) mentions the letter of guidance from Aristotle to Alexander the Great as an example. The letters of the NT could also be considered letters of guidance.

25 Beasley-Murray, p. 22.

26 The word "Preterist" is taken from a Latin word meaning "past" or "beyond."

27 This position is very difficult to defend. When in Rev. 22:20 John says "Yes, come Lord Jesus" he certainly did not mean "come quickly and destroy Jerusalem and its temple"! He was yearning for the coming of the Lord Jesus in which all evil will be destroyed, and the glory of the Lord will fill the earth as the waters fill the seas. He was not yearning for the "coming" of the Lord "in the clouds" to destroy Jerusalem that is hypothesized by some Preterists. The coming of the Lord Jesus described in this book did not happen in 70 AD when the army of General Titus destroyed Jerusalem.

28 See also Mark 13:29-30 and Luke 21:31-32.

29 Preterists do not understand that in biblical prophecy, promises made to one generation may be fulfilled only later, in the days of another generation. Deut. 18:15 was a promise, apparently spoken to the Jews of Moses' day. "The Lord your God will raise up from among you, from your brothers, a prophet like me for you, to him you must listen." However, that promise was not fulfilled until the Lord Jesus was born, many generations later. Likewise the "you" of Matt. 24:33-34 has not yet been fulfilled for any generation of Jews, but will someday, hopefully soon, be fulfilled. There is no need to make up an extra-biblical "cloud coming" in 70 AD.

30 See the discussion under 1:3 concerning this issue.

31 P. 18.

32 Pp. 42-43.

33 Mounce (p. 42) writes that often commentators who choose the Futurist view say that the seven letters symbolize seven ages in church history. That interpretation is invalid and not at all foundational to the Futurist view.

34 Mounce, pp. 39-41.

35 Stars are very large, so a hand that could hold seven of them would have to be unimaginably huge, and yet in the next verse the Lord places His hand upon John. It is better to take the idea that He holds the seven stars in His hand as a figure of speech.

36 Most of this discussion is taken from Bauckham's *The Theology of the Book of Revelation*, pp. 23-26 and 109-113.

37 *The Theology of the Book of Revelation*, p. 25.

38 These expressions were taken up by Jewish writers as well. Josephus calls God "the beginning and the end of all things" (*Antiquities* 8.280, quoted by Bauckham in *The Theology of the Book of Revelation*, p. 27).

39 Note the discussion of this four-fold expression in the section "The Interpretation of Numbers and Repetitions," and in the comments under 5:9.

40 Hemer, p. 142; and Bauckham, *The Theology of the Book of Revelation*, p. 110. Colin J. Hemer's commentary on Revelation 2 and 3 updates Ramsay's older work. Both men sought to provide deeper insight into these two chapters through careful research into the historical background of the seven cities.

41 Bauckham, *The Theology of the Book of Revelation*, pp. 110-113.

42 Bauckham, *The Theology of the Book of Revelation*, p. 140.

43 Collins, pp. 1253-1255.

44 Collins, p. 1256.

45 The spirits and the torches are counted together in 4:5 and the spirits, the horns and the eyes are counted together in 5:6.

46 ουαι/*ouai*

47 πνευμα/*pneuma*

48 The expression "the seven spirits of God" is discussed in the section entitled "Revelation and Systematic Theology" and in the discussion under 1:4.

49 ερχομαι/*erchomai*

50 Bauckham, *The Climax of Prophecy*, p. 34.

51 *The Climax of Prophecy*, p. 34.

52 This term, αρνιον/*arnion*, is used once about the second beast in 13:11. The term "lamb" is used 34 times in the NT.

53 P. 1286.

54 The understanding of what a planet is, and how many planets exist, in that era was quite different from today's understanding of those issues.

55 Note that the word "nine" (or "ninth" or "one ninth") is used 51 times in the OT, but only once in Revelation; the word "eleven" (or "eleventh" or "one eleventh") is used 34 times in the OT, but only once in the Book of Revelation; and the word "thirteen" (or "thirteenth" or "one thirteenth") is used 24 times in the OT and is not used at all in Revelation. Clearly the OT influenced the use of certain numbers, but not others, in Revelation.

56 *The Theology of the Book of Revelation*, p. 16.

57 The term Philo uses in "On the Creation" 102-103 is τελεσφορεω/*telesphoreō* (Collins, p. 1277). But note that Collins himself does not agree that the number seven points to "perfection."

58 δρακων/*drakōn*

59 διαβολος/*diabolos*

60 σατανας/*satanas*

61 *The Climax of Prophecy*, p. 36.

62 *The Climax of Prophecy*, pp. 22-29.

63 Pp. 1272-1273.

64 Collins, pp. 1272-1273.

65 Eusebius, in his *Church History*, written about the year 330 AD, makes three lists of writings: 1. writings that are recognized as in the canon, 2. writings whose place in the canon is disputed, and 3. rejected writings that are not in the canon.

He included the Book of Revelation in his list of recognized writings, and also, oddly, in his list of disputed writings. He did not include it in his list of rejected writings.

66   P. 39.

67   Quoted from Luther's 1522 Preface to the Book of Revelation. Translation from the American edition of *Luther's Works*, vol. 35 (St. Louis: Concordia, 1963), pp. 395-399.

68   Γραψον ουν/*grapson oun*

   α ειδες/*ha eides*

   και α εισιν/*kai ha eisin*

   και α μελλει γινεσθαι μετα ταυτα/*kai ha mellei ginesthai meta tauta*

69   και/*kai*

70   The *NIV, RSV, KJV*, the *NJKV*, the *NET*, and the *HCSB* all agree that *and* is the proper translation here.

71   *The Theology of the Book of Revelation*, p. 14.

72   Although often translated "servants," this word, δουλος/*doulos*, really does refer to the harsh and sinful idea that some human beings become the "property" of others. It is best translated *slaves*. In 10:7 and 11:18 the term is used concerning God's prophets. In 7:3 it is used of the 144,000 sealed of Israel, and in 19:5 it is used of those that fear God.

73   This expression, εν ταχει/*en tachei*, is also used in 22:6. A related term, ταχυ/*tachu*, is found in 2:5, 16; 3:11; 22:7, 12, 20, and is discussed in the endnote under 2:16. These two terms originate from the noun ταχος/*tachos*, which means "speed," so that εν ταχει/*en tachei* can be translated "with high speed" or *suddenly*. In Acts 22:18 and 25:4 this word can be translated "soon," but in Luke 18:8; Acts 12:7; Rom. 16:20; Rev. 1:1; and 22:6 the translation *suddenly* is more fitting. Thus we understand that the Word of God is not mistakenly saying that the Lord is returning soon, as in, during their lifetimes. Indeed, He did not come soon (in that normal sense of soon), but His coming will happen *suddenly*. It is also possible that in a prophetic sense, it will be "soon." Mounce (p. 65) says "in the prophetic outlook the end is always imminent." See the discussion on 1:3 for more about the concept of imminency.

74   The *He* here refers to Christ. Mounce (p. 64) observes that in the Gospel of John, Jesus Christ often takes what is from the Father and shows it to man, as in John 1:18; 5:19-23; 12:49; and 17:8. The expression *His angel* (του αγγελου αυτου/ *tou anggelou autou*) points to an unnamed *angel*. This interpretation is made very clear by the fact that in 22:16 we see that Jesus Himself sent *His angel* to testify to these things for the churches. The same *angel* is mentioned in 1:1 and 22:16, which both tell of the mediating role of that *angel*. In that way, those texts form "bookends" or "inclusio" for the whole book, suggesting that the entire book was revealed via the mediating work of that *angel*.

75   The verb σημαινω/*semainō* means "make known by signs or wonders." The term is especially appropriate because of the many signs and wonders in Revelation.

76 There are seven blessings in Revelation that use the word μακαριος/ *makarios*. This pronouncement of blessing is almost the same as what the Lord said in Luke 11:28. According to Bauckham (*The Climax of Prophecy*, p. 30), the seven blessings of the book are the essence of the purpose of the book. The blessings are given seven times because the happiness of everyone that obeys this book is a perfect happiness.

77 The verb τηρεω/*tēreō* can mean to *keep*, "obey," "guard," "hold," "fulfill," or "observe." In Mt. 19:17; 23:3; 28:20; Mrk. 7:9; Jn. 8:51, 52, 55; 14:15, 21, 23, 24; 15:10, 20; and Acts 15:5 it means "obey." It is used eleven times in the Book of Revelation. Nine of those passages concern commands or God's will, and in those passages the clear meaning is always "obey." In 3:10 ("keep you from the hour of testing") and 16:15 ("guards his clothing") it cannot mean "obey," but instead means *keep* or "guard."

78 The declaration of the nearness of the coming of Jesus Christ (ο γαρ καιρος εγγυς/*ho gar kairos enggus*) is repeated in Rev. 22:10 with terms that are almost the same. In Luke 21:31 the Kingdom of God is *near* (εγγυς/*enggus*) and in Heb. 8:13 "that which already became old and worn out is already *near* (εγγυς/ *enggus*) to its destruction." Other than these two uses about the last days this word is used in normal contexts (for instance Matt. 24:32 and Luke 19:11). See the endnote under 22:10 for more about this term.

79 εγγυς/*enggus*

80 The words *the province of* are added in the translation because this refers to the Roman *province*, not, of course, to the continent.

81 Ασια/*Asia*

82 The majority of the Greek manuscripts have the word *God* here, but three very ancient manuscripts lack that word. In either case, the sense of the passage remains the same.

83 This term, ερχομενος/*erchomenos*, uses the Present, not the Future Tense, so the word "will" is not used in this translation. For some reason this word is never used in the Future Tense in the whole Book of Revelation.

84 Ramsay, pp. 141-149.

85 Hughes (p. 18) mentions the completion of creation in *seven* days as support of the idea that the number *seven* suggests perfection.

86 Besides Rom. 1:7, Cranfield (p. 71) records 1 Cor. 1:3; 2 Cor. 1:2; Gal. 1:3; Eph. 1:2; Phil. 1:2; 2 Thess. 1:2; Titus 1:4 and Philem. 3.

87 A normal greeting in a letter would have the word χαιρειν/*chairein* ("greetings"), as in Acts 15:23; 23:26; and James 1:1, but here the word is χαρις/ *charis* (grace). This shift draws attention to the significant idea of *grace*.

88 The Jerusalem Targum is an "expanded translation" of the Hebrew Scriptures into Aramaic.

89 This is the "Tetragrammaton" which Christian Bibles often represent as LORD.

90 Beasley-Murray, p. 54. Mounce (p. 68) explains that the pagan god Zeus was sometimes called "Zeus who was, Zeus who is, and Zeus who will be."

91 Note the discussion of the *seven spirits* in the section entitled "Revelation and Systematic Theology."

92 According to Mounce (p. 69) this argument is not very strong because in Luke 9:26 and 1 Tim. 5:21 *God* the Father, the Lord Jesus and angels are all mentioned in parallel form. The observation of Mounce has to be weighed, but the two texts he brings up are not the same sort of formal blessing that we see here.

93 πρωτοτοκος/*prōtotokos*. This term, which literally means *firstborn*, is also used of the Lord *Jesus* in Col. 1:15 and 18. *Christ is firstborn from the dead*. Here the term *firstborn* indicates both preeminence and chronological priority. Although some people have been resurrected *from the dead*, He was the first to experience permanent resurrection. Normally this word has its simple and literal meaning of being the chronologically first one born in a family, but its use in the LXX in 2 Sam. 19:44 (verse 43 in our Bibles) shows that it can mean "first in importance" instead of "the one born first." Likewise in Ps. 88:28 (Ps. 89:27 in our Bibles), we read "I will also appoint him as my firstborn, the most exalted of the earth's kings." In the LXX of that verse πρωτοτοκος/*prōtotokos* is used.

94 The majority of the ancient Greek manuscripts read *washed* (from the word λουω/*louō*), but a few manuscripts read "freed" (from the word λυω/*luō*).

95 This also happens in 4:11; 5:9, 12; 7:10, etc.

96 The word here translated *Look* is ιδου/*idou*. It is actually an imperative form of the verb ειδον/*eidon*, which means "to see." The word ιδου/*idou* is used to draw attention to what follows. In older translations it is translated "Behold!" If a casual modern English translation were written it would probably use "Hey!" It occurs 26 times in the Book of Revelation. In this translation it is translated *look*, except in 4:1; 14:1, and 14. The word ιδου/*idou* is translated "see!" in those verses because those verses already have the verb *look* in them.

97 This word, φυλη/*phulē*, means "ethnic group," "tribe," or "people group." In the LXX it often referred to the twelve *tribes* of Israel. The word which is translated *earth* (γη/*gē*) often means the land of Israel, so that it is possible the intent of this sentence is "And all the tribes in the land of Israel are going to lament Him" meaning they will repent and believe in Him who was wounded by their ancestors. Thomas (pp. 78-79) prefers the meaning of *tribes* and *earth* mainly because Revelation often stresses all the *tribes* of the *earth* (as in 3:10; 6:10; 8:13; 11:10; 13:8, 12, 14; and 17:2), and not only the *tribes* of Israel. It is difficult to be sure which interpretation is correct, but the two possibilities that are mentioned are not too different.

98 In saying *Yes, amen*, John joins the Greek expression (ναι/*nai*) with the Hebrew expression (אָמֵן/αμην/*amēn*), just like in 1:4 "grace" is joined with "peace" (Morris, p. 50).

99 See also Matt. 24:30.

100 Jewish rabbis have said that the Law must be obeyed "from aleph to tau," or, in other words, from the first letter to the final letter (Beasley-Murray, p. 59).

101   Outside of Revelation, this term, παντοκρατωρ/*pantokratōr*, is only found in 2 Cor. 6:18. In Revelation, the expression "The Lord God Almighty" is used seven times, in 1:8; 4:8; 11:17; 15:3; 16:7; 19:6; and 21:22. (The expression here in 1:8 is broken up with the words *who is, and who was, and who is to come*.) Again we see the amazing intricacy of the Book of Revelation.

102   Hemer, p. 27.

103   Thomas, p. 87. Mounce, p. 75, notes that according to Eusebius (*Church History*, Book III, Chapter 20) John was later freed by the Emperor Nerva (96-98 AD) and was able to return to Ephesus.

104   Hemer, p. 28.

105   In addition to the words λογος/*logos* and μαρτυρια/*marturia* (word and testimony), the same Greek preposition, δια/*dia*, is used in each of these passages.

106   Other than four texts mentioning the "Seven Spirits," the word *Spirit* is used 14 times in Revelation about the Holy *Spirit*.

107   The expression *the Lord's Day* refers to Sunday in the Didache and in Modern Greek.

108   P. 76.

109   This rare expression, τη κυριακη ημερα/*tē kuriakē hēmera* is not the same Greek expression as "The Day of the Lord," η ημερα κυριου/*hē hēmera kuriou*, (as in 2 Pet. 3:10) which refers to the end of the age.

110   The command *write* (γραψον/*grapson*) is used 12 times in Revelation: 1:11, 19; 2:1, 8, 12, 18; 3:1, 7, 14; 14:13; 19:9; and 21:5. The repetition of the command clarifies that this book does not originate from man but from God.

111   According to Morris (p. 52), the expression *see the voice* was not used in the Greek literature of that time period, but its meaning is still clear.

112   According to the majority of ancient Greek manuscripts the word *seven* is here.

113   This word, ομοιος/*homoios*, here translated *like*, is used 19 times in this book, far more frequently than in the other books of the NT, perhaps because John is describing things for which he has insufficient vocabulary.

114   Of the seven letters, only the one to Laodicea does not begin with a characteristic taken from 1:13-18, but even in that case the characteristic is drawn from 1:5.

115   υιος/*huios*

116   According to some of the Church Fathers (Ignatius, for instance), the expression "Son of God" emphasizes that He is truly God, and the expression *Son of Man* emphasizes that He is truly man. However, there are scholars today that do not accept that understanding.

117   In the four Gospels we often see the expression ο υιος του ανθρωπου/*ho huios tou anthrōpou*, with the Greek definite articles, but in Rev. 1:13 the expression is υιον ανθρωπου/*huion anthrōpou*, without the Greek definite article.

118   Pp. 66-67.

119 Mounce (p. 78) is more certain that this *robe* refers to the Lord's role as priest, because this Greek expression is used six times for the clothing of the High Priest in the LXX, and only once of someone else's clothing.

120 Mounce, p. 78.

121 Thomas, p. 100.

122 The word here is και/*kai* which normally means "and" in the NT, but "that is" or "even" might be more fitting in this text.

123 This is similar to Dan. 10:6 where an angel had "eyes like a flaming torch."

124 Concerning this term (χαλκολιβανον/*chalkolibanon*) *BDAG* says, "Since the word is found nowhere independent of Revelation, the exact nature of this metal or alloy remains unknown." The word χαλκος/*chalkos* refers to copper, *bronze*, or brass. Hemer, p. 116, suggests that it probably refers to bronze, which is an alloy of copper and zinc. Hemer also states that the lack of information about this metal is probably due to the *bronze* workers' guild wanting to keep the details of χαλκολιβανον/*chalkolibanon* production a secret from their competitors.

125 Thomas p. 102.

126 This verb (εχω/*echō*) is the normal word for "to have," not "to hold." A different verb that means "to grasp" is used in 2:1.

127 This term, οψις/*opsis*, can mean *face* (John 11:44), "expression," or "appearance" (John 7:24).

128 At the transfiguration, John, along with Peter and James, bowed down just as John bowed in verse 1:17.

129 See for instance Josh. 5:14; Isa. 6:5; Ezek. 1:28; 3:23; 9:8; 11:13; 43:3; 44:4; Dan. 2:46; 8:17; 10:7-9; Matt. 17:6; Luke 5:8; and Acts 26:14.

130 εγω ειμι/*egō eimi*

131 See for instance Matt. 14:27; 22:32; Mark 6:50; Luke 22:70; John 6:20, 35, and 48.

132 The word *amen* is found in the Majority Text, though not in some of the oldest Greek texts.

133 See for instance Josh. 3:10; Ps. 42:2; and 84:2.

134 For instance in Matt. 16:16; Acts 14:15; and Rom. 9:26.

135 Beasley-Murray, p. 67.

136 Beasley-Murray (p. 68) quotes from the translation of Deut. 28:12 in The Jerusalem Targum.

137 α ειδες/*ha eides*

138 α εισιν/*ha eisin*

139 α μελλει γινεσθαι μετα ταυτα/*ha mellei ginesthai meta tauta*

140 αγγελος/*anggelos*

141 Also in Luke 7:24; 9:52; and James 2:25, the term αγγελος/*anggelos* refers to people that are sent, rather than heavenly beings.

142 Thomas, p. 118.

143 Mounce (p. 77) explains that in that time they did not yet have candles, so oil lamps were the easiest way to light up things at night. In Exod. 25:31-40 Moses was commanded to make a *golden* lampstand with *seven* lamps, and in Zech. 4:2 there was a lampstand with *seven* lamps.

144 P. 58.

145 The word "chiasm" is from the Greek letter χ, simply because this structure can be diagrammed as an X shape. In this case the fourth church is at the center of the X.

146 See the discussion concerning the imminent return of the Lord in the discussion and endnote under 1:3.

147 To the church in Smyrna He wrote "I know your afflictions and your poverty" and "I know the slander of those who say they are Jews and are not...." To the church in Pergamum He wrote, "I know where you live...."

148 There is a *very* slight change in the Greek word order in 2:2 and 2:13, but the same words are there.

149 In 2:10, the following italicized words are plural: "the devil will put some of *you* in prison *to test you*, and *you will suffer* persecution for ten days." In 2:13 only "in *your* city" is plural. In 2:23-25 the following are plural: "...I will repay each of *you* according to *your* deeds. Now I say to the rest of *you* in Thyatira, to *you* who do not hold to her teaching and have not learned Satan's so-called deep secrets (I will not impose any other burden on *you*): Only *hold on* to what *you have* until I come."

150 Strabo, *Geography* 14.1.24.

151 Ramsay, pp. 172-173.

152 By that time the harbor of Miletus, which Paul used in Acts 20:15-17, had become unusable due to the accumulation of silt deposited by the river that met the sea there. It was about 70 kilometers (40 miles) south of Ephesus.

153 "Artemis" became "Diana" in Latin.

154 "Cult Prostitution in New Testament Ephesus: A Reappraisal," S. M. Baugh, *Journal of the Evangelical Theological Society* 42 (1999): 443-60.

155 The Law of Moses provided something similar in Exod. 21:13-14; Num. 35:9-34; Deut. 4:41-43; and 19:1-13. 1 Kings 2:28-35 suggests that there was some hope of asylum in the temple in Jerusalem as well.

156 σωτηρια/*sōtēria*

157 Hemer, pp. 48-51.

158 See Clinton Arnold, *Ephesians, Power and Magic: the concept of power in Ephesians in light of its historical setting*, Cambridge University Press, 1989.

159 Thomas p. 129.

160 According to *BDAG*, the expression *this is what... says* (ταδε λεγει/*tade legei*) is an "introductory formula in the decrees of the Persian kings." These are formal statements by the King of Kings!

161 In the vision of Jesus in chapter one John saw that Jesus "had" in his right hand seven stars and that he "was" in the midst of the seven lampstands, but here in chapter 2 it is written that He *holds* the seven stars and that He *walks* among

the seven lampstands. What was said about the Lord Jesus in chapter one is made more active here in this text. "Had" becomes "holds," and "was" becomes "walks."

162 This word (κοπος/*kopos*) refers to *labor* that is so difficult that the worker perspires. The Ephesians really worked hard!

163 P. 88.

164 Four of the seven congregations got both praise and criticism from the Lord. The three congregations that are first praised, then criticized (Ephesus, Pergamum, and Thyatira) each have this exact same expression, *but I have against you that*, except that in 2:14 the congregation in Pergamum is told, "But I have a few things against you, that...."

165 These expressions, "mere intellectual assent" and "saving faith," are often used in the writings of Reformed theologians, but this writer does not accept them. As is clear in the Gospel of John, faith in Jesus Christ saves – there is no faith in Christ that does not save a person from eternal judgment.

166 The Majority Text includes the word ταχυς/*tachus*, here translated *suddenly*. See the endnote under 1:1 concerning related terms.

167 *The Climax of Prophecy*, p. 34.

168 This form is ερχομαι/*erchomai*, in the Present Tense, Middle, Indicative, first person, singular. In total, this word is used 36 times in the Book of Revelation, but this form is only used in 2:5, 16; 3:11; 16:15; 22:7, 12, and 20.

169 In a sense this is what happened to the temple in Ezek. 11:22-23.

170 Hemer, p. 56. Except for a brief period from 1090-1097 when it was under Turkish control, the city remained in the hands of people that considered themselves to be Christian until it fell to the Turks early in the 14th century.

171 Mounce, p. 89.

172 The word νικος/*nikos* means "victory," and λαος/*laos* means "people."

173 According to Eusebius, the *Nicolaitans* did not last long (Mounce, p. 89).

174 The verb translated *victor* here (νικαω/*nikaō*), is used 17 times in all of Revelation. It is used like this in each of the seven rewards passages of the seven messages. It means "win," "be victorious," or "conquer." See the explanation of this very significant concept in the Book of Revelation in the discussion of 5:5.

175 The majority of Greek manuscripts have the word *My*.

176 According to Mounce (p. 90), in 1 Enoch 24:4–25:6 and *The Testament of Levi* 18:11, Jewish apocalyptic literature, *the tree of life* was a reward for the righteous after judgment. Mounce also mentions 2 Esdras 8:52 and 2 Enoch 8:3.

177 *The tree of life* also is mentioned in Prov. 3:18; 11:30; 13:12; and 15:4 but the expression used in Proverbs is slightly different from that in Genesis. In Genesis the definite article is used but in Proverbs the definite article is not used.

178 The KJV uses the word "carnal" in 1 Cor. 3:1, the NIV uses the word "worldly." The Greek word is σαρκικος/*sarkikos*, which means "fleshly."

179 A word-for-word translation of this would be "the church of Smyrnaens...."

180 σμυρνα/*smurna*

181 Mounce, p. 91.

182 Pp. 59-60.

183 στεφανος/*stephanos*. See the endnote under 2:10 concerning this word.

184 Mounce (p.91) cites Tacitus, *Annals* iv. 55-56.

185 Hemer, p. 65.

186 Mounce, p. 91.

187 Polycarp's words were recorded in *The Martyrdom of Polycarp*, whose author is unknown. It seems to have been a letter sent from the congregation in Smyrna to the congregation of a place called Philomelium. Eusebius, who lived about 263-339 AD, accepted the document as genuine.

188 Pliny the Younger, *Letters*, X. 96-97.

189 Pliny used the Latin word *domine*, which is similar to κυριος/*kurios*, which is used by Christians to refer to the Lord Jesus, but also used by others to give honor to Caesar.

190 Twenty-five years before Pliny wrote this letter, the emperor Domitian initiated the persecution of Christians and the Book of Revelation was written.

191 Rumors that Christians were practicing cannibalism in their Holy Communion is almost certainly the background for these words of Pliny.

192 Unlike the Critical Text, the Majority Text has the words *deeds and*.

193 This word (θλιψις/*thlipsis*) is used in the NT for persecution (Matt. 24:9), the pain of childbirth (John 16:21), hunger (Acts 7:11), and trouble in the household (1 Cor. 7:28).

194 This word (πτωχεια/*ptōcheia*) is only used three times in the NT: here, in 2 Cor. 8:2, and in 2 Cor. 8:9. The other word for poverty, πενης/*penēs*, refers to the state of having no extra to spare, but this word πτωχεια/*ptōcheia* refers to people that have nothing at all. That was the situation for the congregation in Smyrna.

195 For instance, Beasley-Murray, p. 81.

196 Thomas, p. 163, lists the following verses: Matt. 6:19-20; 19:21; Luke 12:21; 2 Cor. 6:10; 1 Tim. 6:17-19; and James 2:5.

197 Persecution of Christians by Jews was not uncommon in the NT, as shown in Acts 13:50; 14:2, 5, 19; 17:5; 26:2; and 1 Thess. 2:14-15. Unfortunately, since then it has been people that call themselves Christians that have persecuted the Jews.

198 In Rom. 2:28-29 being a true Jew is being one spiritually rather than physically.

199 The word ινα/*hina* here is translated *so that*, and is usually followed by a purpose. But it can also speak of a result, as is the case here. The devil did not intend to test them; his purpose was to tempt them to deny Christ. But the result, in God's hand, was to test them. The word here translated *tested* is πειραζω/*peirazō*. It can also mean "tempt." The devil's purpose might have been to tempt them, but the result was that their faith was *tested*. The Lord will use for His own purposes the persecution that the devil brings upon believers.

200 The faithfulness that Christ asks for with the words *until death* (αχρι θανατου/*achri thanatou*) can have the meaning be faithful "as long as you live, until the moment of your death" (where *until* has to do with time, as in Rev. 2:25) or

be faithful "in persecution until they kill you" (where *until* has to do with degree, as in Acts 22:4 and Rev. 12:11).

201   Mounce, p. 93.

202   Ramsay, p. 206.

203   Thomas (pp. 169-70) gives some interpretations of *ten days* that show how diverse interpretations can become when the interpreter decides not to be limited to a simple normal interpretation:
   1. ten periods of persecution under the emperors of Rome
   2. ten years of persecution
   3. a long period of time
   4. a short period of time

204   This is the word στεφανος/*stephanos*, a *crown* or wreath given to bestow honor. The victorious ones in 2:10 and 3:11 are each given a στεφανος/*stephanos*. This term is also used in 4:4, 10; 6:2; 9:7; and 14:14. See the endnote under 12:3 concerning the term διαδημα/*diadēma*, which is also translated *crown*.

205   The double negative, ου μη/*ou mē*, appears in Rev. 2:11; 3:3, 5, 12; 7:16; 9:6; 15:4; 18:7, 14, 21, 22, 23 (twice); 21:25, and 27. It is used about 95 times in the entire NT, including passages like John 4:14; 6:35, 37; 10:28; 11:26; and Heb. 13:5. It always brings emphasis, and can frequently be translated "never ever."

206   The technical name of this figure of speech is "litotes." "It wasn't very clean" would mean it was very dirty, if the figure of speech litotes was used. "It wasn't cheap" would mean it was very expensive, if the figure of speech litotes was used (Thomas, p. 261). The same figure of speech is used in 3:5.

207   The word *Pergamum* (Περγαμος/*Pergamos*) originally meant "fortress." Later the name of the city was used for the new writing material that came to be known as περγαμενα/*pergamena*, which we call "parchment" (Mounce, p. 95; and Ramsay, p. 218).

208   Ramsay, p. 220, suggests another possible interpretation: the Roman Proconsul was given "the right of the sword" by Rome. He did not need to ask permission to have people executed by decapitation. Perhaps the Lord Jesus says He has the *sword* in order to deny that the Proconsul had any real power over life and death. However, in light of 2:16, this interpretation seems unlikely.

209   The Majority Text includes the words *your deeds and*, which are missing in the Critical Text. So, if the Majority Text is correct, the Lord says *I know your deeds* to each of the seven churches.

210   Hemer, pp. 82-84, explains that is it actually very difficult to determine which city was the capital of the province of Asia.

211   Morris, p. 67, and Mounce, p. 97.

212   The word σκανδαλον/*skandalon* literally means *trap*, but it is used here in a figurative sense of a trick that causes people to fail.

213   Note the comments on singular and plural verbs and pronouns in the introductory discussion on chapters 2 and 3.

214   Literally, "but if not" (ει δε μη/*ei de mē*).

215 This term (ταχυ/*tachu*) is similar to the word used in 1:1, and can be translated *suddenly*. This term is also used in 3:11; 11:14; 22:7, 12, and 20. According to the majority text, this term is also used in 2:5. See the explanation in the endnote under 1:1.

216 See the endnote under 2:5.

217 In the Majority Text the word *knows* is missing, but can be understood from the context. It is there in the Critical Text.

218 1 and 2 Maccabees concern the history of Israel between the Old and the New Testaments. These books are part of the Apocrypha. They are excluded from the Protestant Bible, but included in the Roman Catholic Bible. Even though these books are not a part of the Word of God, they can still be studied as historical records of men.

219 Mounce, p. 99.

220 Mounce (pp. 99-100) and Ramsay (p. 228) also mention this possibility, but note that none of those kinds of *white* stones have ever been found in the province of Asia. It was thought that there were no gladiator contests in Asia, but the discovery of a gradiators' graveyard in Ephesus has disproved that.

221 P. 201.

222 P. 229.

223 For some reason the word *Thyatira* here is plural. The literal translation would be "to the messenger of the among Thyatireans church." Translated more smoothly that might be "to the messenger of the church among the Thyatireans."

224 Ramsay, p. 243. Hemer, p. 107, notes that most of the literary references to *Thyatira* are about it being conquered, and that it reached its greatest prosperity in the second or third century AD. So at the time it received this message from the Lord it was an increasingly prosperous town that was benefiting from the Pax Romana, the peace that came from being a part of the Roman Empire.

225 Ramsay, p. 244, says that local inscriptions have been found there that refer to "wool-workers, linen-workers, makers of outer garments, dyers, leather-workers, tanners, potters, bakers, slave-dealers and bronze-smiths." From Acts 16:14 we know that Lydia, a seller of purple fabrics, was from *Thyatira*, but Ramsay reminds us that the ancients used the names of colors very loosely compared with modern standards. Lydia probably sold red fabrics, dyed red by the madder-root, which is common in that area. The only dye that produced what we would call purple was made from a certain shellfish, which was not found in the area of *Thyatira*, which was located about 73 kilometers (45 miles) from the coast.

226 Hemer. pp. 108-109.

227 As noted in the endnote under 1:15, the exact meaning of this term, χαλκολιβανον/*chalkolibanon*, is not known to us. However, it was surely well understood by the *bronze* workers of Thyatira.

228 The promise to the *Son* in Psalm 2 is adapted to become a promise to victors in Rev. 2:26-27.

229 The majority of the ancient Greek manuscripts, and the very early Alexandrinus, have the word *your* (σου/*sou*) here, so that it literally reads "that

woman of yours Jezebel," or *your wife Jezebel.* (The word γυνη/*gunē* used here can mean "woman" or *wife*, depending on the context.) If the reading of the majority of Greek manuscripts including the fifth century Alexandrinus is indeed correct, then the Lord is rebuking the "messenger" of Thyatira for allowing his own *wife* to teach those false doctrines! This would be in accord with the observation that the words *you* and *your* in this verse are singular. Note the comments on singular and plural verbs and pronouns in the introductory comments on chapters 2 and 3.

230   For some reason this verse echoes 2:14, in that the exact Greek words for *committing sexual immorality and eating meat sacrificed to idols* are used in this verse and in 2:14. Besides that, the word *teach* is used in both verses, though in different grammatical forms.

231   In the other letters the demand precedes the warning, but here the warning precedes the demand.

232   The word translated *bed*, κλινη/*klinē*, can also refer to a couch or a pallet. It is a place where someone reclines (κλινω/*klinō* is the verb "to recline"). She would suffer a sickness on her *bed*, just as she sinned on her *bed*.

233   In Greek this is emphatic. The literal translation is "and her children I will kill in death."

234   Mounce, pp. 105-106; Beasley-Murray, p. 92; Thomas, pp. 226-229 and Morris, p. 73.

235   Literally, "And the victor and the one who keeps My deeds...." The second "and" in this expression could also be translated "even," indicating that *the victor* and the one *who keeps* the Lord's *deeds* refer to the same people.

236   This word, ποιμαινω/*poimainō*, means *shepherd*, but the additional phrase *with an iron staff* makes it clear that His shepherding will not always be gentle! In the OT and the NT the idea of shepherding is sometimes a metaphor of ruling, as in 1 Chron. 11:2; Mic. 7:14; Jer. 23:2; and Matt. 2:6.

237   The words *this authority* are added to make the English sentence more clear. They are not in the original Greek.

238   P. 250.

239   Morris, pp. 74-75.

240   Beasley-Murray, pp. 93-94.

241   Thomas, p. 235.

242   The word *Sardis* here and in verse 4 is plural. Ramsay (p. 268) explains that at first the city was built high up on Mt. Tmolus, but later a lower city was built, so in effect there were two Sardises, and the plural form of the name endured, even though at the time of the writing of the Book of Revelation the upper city was no longer in use.

243   Hemer, pp. 129-130, explains that the mountain is subject to serious cracking and erosion, so that the ancient city had much more area than the present mountaintop site because most of it has crumbled away down the cliffs.

244   Hemer, p. 133.

245   Strabo, in his *Geography* (Book XIII 2:5), tells about *Sardis.*

246   According to the myth of King Midas, whose touch made things turn into pure gold, when Midas realized he would soon starve to death, he prayed to Dionysus, who told him to go wash in the springs of Pactolus. The legend says that when he did that, he was freed of his magical powers, and the river was enriched with gold sand, which was often mentioned in the ancient stories of that region. Hemer cites Ovid's *Metamorphoses*, 11.136-45, cf. 85-88 concerning that myth. In any case, the wealth of King Croesus was legendary (Hemer, pp. 130-131).

247   Hemer, p. 131. Hemer adds that this King Gyges (γυγες/*guges*) seems to be the source of the word Gog, mentioned in Ezek. and Rev. 20:8.

248   As the *Pax Romana* decayed, and raids and warfare increased, the need for a fortress high upon the mountain reemerged. In about 450 AD building materials from the lower city were used to build another fortress high upon Mount Tmolus, which was finally abandoned again in about 1425 AD, according to The Harvard Magazine, 1998, 03.

249   *The Histories* by Herodotus, Book 1, paragraph 84 (translated by G. C. Macaulay).

250   Book 7 chapter 2 of his *Cyropaedia*. This is Henry Graham Dakyns' translation.

251   Hemer, p. 133, reports that there are too many such stories for him to include in his commentary! That defeat was very significant for the Lydian kingdom and the Lydian people, because althought their culture reached back into the 2nd millennium BC, they never recovered their previous glory. There is no evidence of a distinct Lydian culture by the time of the writing of the Book of Revelation, but in the days of its greatest might, under King Croesus, the Kingdom of Lydia, with its capital in Sardis, covered the western half of what is now Turkey!

252   As recorded by Polybius in his *Histories*, Book VII, chapters 15-18.

253   This verb, γρηγορεω/*grēgoreō*, normally means "be alert," and may mean that here and in verse 3.

254   The Majority Text reads, *what remains which you are about to cast off*. The Critical Text reads "the things that remain which are about to die."

255   The Majority Text includes the words *upon you*.

256   The passage is literally "and you will not not know at what hour I will come upon you," so in order to show the emphasis which the double negative brings, "not know" is changed to the more emphatic *not know at all*.

257   Literally, "a few names."

258   The word *clothed* is not in the Greek, but it is supplied for clarity in the English.

259   Thomas p. 258.

260   The double negative is ου μη/*ou mē*. See the comments and endnote on 2:11, which also uses this form.

261   See the endnote under 2:11 concerning this figure is speech, which is called "litotes."

262   Lyall, pp. 60-61.

263   Mounce, p. 113.

264   Two related words, βιβλος/*biblos* and βιβλιον/*biblion*, are used to refer to the *book of life* in the NT. In the Book of Revelation the expression *book of life* is used six times.

265   Stanley, pp. 185-91 and Keil and Delitzsch, *Commentary on the Old Testament*, vol. 5, p. 285.

266   The word, ομολογεω/*homologeō*, used twice in Matt. 10:32, has a broad range of meaning, including "acknowledge," "promise," "admit something is true," "profess allegiance," and "praise," so it is possible the Lord is using two of these meanings in Matt. 10:32 in a word play.

267   The name of the city, Φιλαδελφεια/*Philadelpheia*, means "brotherly love."

268   Mounce, p. 115. Eumenes II was the older brother, Attalus II was the younger.

269   Hemer, p. 154, explains that this idea was first stated by Ramsey, and that the route of the roads in the area and the coinage of Philadelphia support this concept.

270   Pliny the Elder, in *Historia Naturalis* Book II, chapter 84, considered that earthquake to be the worst in human memory.

271   Mounce, p. 115, and Thomas, p. 271.

272   Beasley-Murray, p. 99.

273   There are many textual variants for this complicated verse, but this is the reading of the majority of manuscripts.

274   "The keys of death and Hades" in 1:18 speak of life and death, which is related to the *key of David*, which speaks of entrance into the Kingdom of God.

275   The Greek of this verse is somewhat complicated. It might literally be translated, "I know your deeds. Look! I have given before you an open door, which no one is able to shut it, because you have little strength, and you have kept My word, and not denied My name."

276   In 1 Cor. 16:9; 2 Cor. 2:12; and Col. 4:3 *open* doors seem to have that meaning. Other than "the opportunity to evangelize" the word *door* can be used for general opportunities (Luke 11:9), eternity (Matt. 24:33), the closeness of the Lord Jesus who is ready to fellowship with His people (Rev. 3:20), and Christ as Savior (Luke 13:24).

277   Compare this with John 8:44, where Jesus told the Jews that opposed Him, "you are from your father the devil, and you want to do the desires of your father...."

278   See the endnote that discusses Dan. 9:22-27 under the discussion of Rev. 11:2.

279   επι της οικουμενης ολης/*epi tēs oikoumenēs holēs*

280   τηρεω εκ/*tēreō ek*

281   In Daniel 11 there is a prophecy with a double fulfillment. That passage was fulfilled in the life of Antiochus Epiphanes, who ruled in the Middle East about 160 years before Christ was born, but the passage will also be fulfilled by someone

with the same character as Antiochus Ephiphanes, who will appear in the end times.

282   The word order (καγω σε τηρησω/*kagō se tērēsō*), in which a personal pronoun (εγω/*egō* in καγω/*kagō*) is used in the first part of the sentence, emphasizes the importance of the word εγω/*egō*. The grammar emphasizes that Christ will do the protecting.

283   See the discussion concerning this word, ερχομαι/*erchomai*, in the endnote under 2:5.

284   See the discussion concerning this word, ταχυ/*tachu*, in the endnote under 1:1.

285   This is the word στεφανος/*stephanos*. See the endnote under 2:10 concerning this word.

286   This would be translated literally, "The victor, I will make him...."

287   The Hebrew word *genizah* means "storage." These storage places were located in synagogues and cemeteries. The most famous *genizah* is the Cairo Genizah, located in a synagogue in Cairo. It contained about 200,000 documents or fragments that were written between 870 AD and 1880.

288   Beasley-Murray, p. 103.

289   The location was originally called "Diospolis," prior to the time when Antiochus II founded Laodicea there (Hemer, p. 180).

290   Concerning the actions of various men that Rome appointed over Laodicea, Hemer, pp. 202-203, writes that Sulla required the immediate payment of five years' worth of taxes, thought to be 20,000 talents. Before that was paid, Lucullus required a 25% tax on crops. Flaccus seized 9 kilograms (20 pounds) of gold from the Jews there. Soon afterwards, Cicero was so ashamed of this injustice that he declared that he and his staff there would not take anything away from the Laodiceans, not even hay or firewood!

291   Hemer, p. 202.

292   Mounce, p. 123 and Thomas, p. 298.

293   Hemer, p. 199.

294   Hemer, p. 193.

295   Beasley-Murray, p. 103 and Mounce, p. 123. In about the year 107 AD Tacitus, in Annals 14.26, wrote "One of the famous cities of Asia, Laodicea, was that same year overthrown by an earthquake, and, without any relief from us, recovered itself by its own resources." Hemer, p. 193, considers the possibility that contrary to custom, Rome decided not to offer help to *Laodicea*, but decides that it is more likely that Rome did offer financial assistance, but *Laodicea* proudly refused its aid.

296   Hemer, p. 194, notes the inscription that states that a man named Nicostratus paid for the construction of a stadium amphitheater whose arena was 275 meters (900 feet) long.

297   Hemer, pp. 196-199, gives a detailed explanation concerning evidence for the location of the medical school and the source of the famous "Phrygian powder."

After thorough examination of all the evidence, Hemer concludes that it is most likely that the school was in *Laodicea* and the "Phrygian powder" for eye salve came from *Laodicea*.

298 Mounce, p. 123.

299 The hot springs of Hierapolis are today known as Pamukkale, which means "Cotton Castle" in Turkish. Spilling over a high cliff, they have created a very beautiful white cliff with cascading pools formed by the calcium carbonate deposited from the hot water. The bright white calcium carbonate cliff is about a kilometer and a half wide, and 100 meters high (almost one mile wide and 300 feet high). That cliff can be seen clearly from *Laodicea*, about ten kilometers (six miles) away (Hemer, pp. 187-188).

300 Hemer, p. 277, notes that the pipes certainly would not have come from the area of Hierapolis.

301 Hemer, p. 189, explains that calcium carbonate tastes bad in water. He also says that if that water had been cold, the calcium carbonate would not have deposited itself on the inside walls of those stone pipes. It was lukewarm water, and it was full of calcium carbonate!

302 Hemer, p. 189.

303 Mounce, p. 123. Hemer, p. 183, quotes the Talmud, Shabbath 147b, "the wines and the baths of Phrygia have separated the twelve tribes of Israel," but also notes that the translation of that text is uncertain.

304 The words *faithful and true* are used four times in the Book of Revelation, two times about the Lord Jesus (in 3:14 and 19:11) and two times about the words of the Book of Revelation itself (21:5 and 22:6).

305 This term, αρχη/*archē*, can be translated "beginning" as in Matt. 19:4; 24:8; Mark 1:1; 10:6; 13:19; Luke 1:2; John 1:1; 2:11; 6:64 and Heb. 7:3. But it is translated "ruler" in Luke 12:11; 20:20; Rom. 8:38; 1 Cor. 15:24; Eph. 1:21; 3:10; 6:12; Col. 1:16; 2:10; 2:15; and Titus 3:1. If it points to an actual person, this word always means *ruler*, except in Rev. 21:6 and 22:13 (there the word must be translated "beginning" because it is contrasted with "ending") and maybe in Col. 1:18. Therefore the translation "beginning" does not have strong support, but the translation *ruler* fits with what is said about the Lord Jesus in the NT. (See also John 1:3, 1 Cor. 8:6, and Col. 1:15-16.)

306 We should be careful not to insert modern expressions like "cold-hearted" into this passage, because there are no biblical parallels for the idea of being spiritually *cold*, and no evidence that that figure of speech was used in that area and time period.

307 In Acts 18:25 and Rom. 12:11 the verb ζεω/*zeō* is used for having fervor; here in Rev. 3:15 the related adjective ζεστος/*zestos* is used.

308 In the normal pattern of the other messages of Revelation chapters two and three, the warning is given immediately after the demand, but in this message the warning is placed before the demand.

309 εμεω/*emeō*

310 According to Thomas (p. 311) their words, *'I am rich' and 'I have acquired wealth'* is a "hysteron-proteron," a figure of speech in which the order of a pair of expressions is changed, so that the thing that happened first (*I have acquired wealth*) is said after the thing that happened later (*I am rich*). Obviously they acquired their *wealth* first and then they were *rich*. The order of the expressions here emphasizes that they thought the *wealth* that they enjoyed was a result of their own labors. This literary device can also be seen in 4:11; 5:2, 5; and 10:9. In a few of these examples, some translations reverse the order of expressions so that the hysteron-proteron figure of speech is not apparent.

311 Hemer, p. 196.

312 Beasley-Murray (p. 106) connects the offer of *gold* here to salvation. He supports this interpretation with Isa. 55:1. But Isaiah is far from Revelation. As the near context, Rev. 22:17 is stronger as a supporting text. Also, in Isa. 55:1-3 it is emphasized that what is offered is offered to people "who do not have any money." That offer is made for those "without any money to buy." That same emphasis is not seen in Rev. 3:18-19. Those addressed in Laodicea are not offered salvation, because they already have it.

313 παιδευω/*paideuō*

314 παιδιον/*paidion*

315 This verb, δειπνεω/*deipneō*, means "to eat a meal," not just "to eat." The Lord is not saying He will have a hurried snack with them. Instead He is offering to enjoy a full meal with those in that congregation that will repent (Barclay, *The Revelation of John*, pp. 147-148).

316 Mounce (p. 129) explains that this table fellowship is already a symbol of the fellowship that will be enjoyed in the Kingdom of the Messiah. In 1 Enoch 62:14 this picture is given: "And with that Son of Man shall they eat and lie down and rise up for ever and ever."

317 Hemer, p. 202; and Mounce, p. 128.

318 In Rev. 3:21 there is only one throne, but in Matt. 19:28 there are 12 thrones, and in Rev. 4:4 there are 24 thrones. However, we should be careful about insisting that the design and number of thrones in heaven be clear to us now here on earth!

319 Beasley-Murray (p. 107) also mentions 2 Tim. 2:12 which says quite specifically, "if we endure, also we shall reign with Him...," and James 4:10 which says in a more general way, "Be humbled before the Lord, and He will lift you up."

320 Mounce, p. 131.

321 Many many times in this section of the Book of Revelation, the author uses the word και/*kai* to connect one sentence to the previous sentence. This word is normally translated *and*, but in some passages it could be translated "but" or even "therefore." In this translation it is translated as *and* if at all possible. This results in an odd English style, but it more accurately reflects the style of the original.

322 Morris, p. 86.

323 1 Enoch 14:25, and The Testimony of Levi 5:1. See also 3 Macc. 6:18.

324 θρονος/*thronos*

325 ιασπις/*iaspis*

326   σαρδιον/*sardion*

327   In Exod. 28:9 a different precious stone was engraved with the names of the sons of Israel.

328   According to the traditions of the Jews, the *elders* of Isa. 24:23 are the leaders of the people of Israel; according to some church traditions, the *twenty-four elders* in Rev. 4 come from the 12 tribes of the people of Israel and the 12 apostles, which is an interpretation supported by Rev. 21:12-14 (Beasley-Murray, p. 113). Beasley-Murray (p. 114) and Mounce (pp. 135-136) disagree, suggesting that the *elders* are angels.

329   This word, φωνη/*phōnē*, frequently means "voice" (as in Rev. 4:1), or "sound" (as in Rev. 18:22, "the sound of a millstone"), but in Rev. 19:6, which has "like the sound of strong thunders," this word is associated with *thunder*. However, it cannot mean *thunder* in this or the parallel passages, because *thunder* is already one of the elements of the lists. It seems to refer to other sounds of storms, and so is here translated *roaring*.

330   With these verses and others (Hab. 5:4-5; Joel 2:10; Mic. 1:4; Ps. 77:17-19; Ps. 114; and Heb. 12:26-27) Bauckham (*The Climax of Prophecy*, pp. 199-201) says there is a connection between earthquakes and the coming of the Lord Jesus to the earth.

331   The few oldest Greek manuscripts include "an earthquake" here, but the majority of manuscripts do not include that element.

332   *The Climax of Prophecy*, p. 8 and p. 202.

333   See also the comments on this structure in the discussion of 11:19.

334   In the original language the word is ως/*hōs*, which means *like*.

335   P. 89.

336   Morris, p. 90.

337   They are called ζωον/*zōon*, "living ones," a term related to the verb ζαω/*zaō*, "to live."

338   In 6:1, 3, 5 and 7 the same *creatures* have a task which is very different from what is written in 4:8. This is not a contradiction. This verse means that they do not *rest*, either *day or night*, and if they are not busy with another duty, they praise Him. This is similar to what is written in 1 Thess. 2:9 and 2 Thess. 3:8, that the Apostle Paul worked *day* and *night* as a tentmaker so as not to be a burden to those he served. If the Apostle Paul had an opportunity to preach the Word of God he would stop tent making to do so. So it is with the *creatures* who do not ask for a *rest*; they continuously praise God, unless they have a special assignment from God.

339   P. 360.

340   Mounce, p. 138.

341   βαλλω/*ballō*

342   See also Matt. 9:2; Mark 7:33; John 5:7; 18:11; and James 3:3.

343   See also Matt. 3:10; 4:6; 7:6; 13:47; John 8:7; 19:24; 21:6; Rev. 8:8; 12:4, 9, 13; 18:19, 21; and 20:15.

344 In the majority of Greek manuscripts, this expression is literally "the Lord and the God our, the Holy One." Some early manuscripts omit *the Holy One*, and some precede those words with "Oh Lord."

345 This is according to *EBC*, which also cites Alford. This would be another example of the figure of speech called "hysteron-proteron," in which the order of a pair of expressions is changed, so that the thing that happened first (*were created*) is said after the thing that happened later (*they exist*). Note the endnote under the discussion of 3:17 which discusses this figure of speech in Revelation.

346 Although Kittel (*Theological Dictionary of the New Testament*, 7:941) says an inheritance scroll might be sealed with six seals, Emmet Russell's article, "A Roman Law Parallel to Revelation Five," in *Bibliotheca Sacra* 115:459 (Jul 58) p. 260, refers to the Roman jurist Gaius, who says "for if the seals of seven witnesses are attached, the testamentary heir is entitled to demand possession in accordance with the will" (*Institutes of Roman Law* by Gaius, translated by Edward Poste).

347 Rengstorf (mentioned in Collins, p. 1275); Barclay, *The Revelation of John*, p. 166; and Thomas, p. 377.

348 Illustration from *A New Introduction to Greek*, third edition, by Alston Chase and Henry Phillips, Harvard University Press, Cambridge, 1965, p. 118.

349 Eph. 5:5 is very similar to Gal. 5:21.

350 This word, κατασφραγιζω/*katasphragizō*, means "to seal." In the ancient world signatures were not used to authenticate letters and other documents, but a seal was used, as in I Kings 21:8 and Neh. 9:38. Wealthy and powerful Greeks and Romans used signet rings each with a small carved precious or semi-precious stone to seal a letter (see also Gen. 41:42 and Esther 8:8). Earlier in Mesopotamia a small cylinder would be used to make a seal (as in Gen. 38:18). Merchandise that was sent was also sealed, to prevent tampering. The seal could not be broken by anyone without authorization. This term, with the prefix κατα/*kata*, is only used here in the whole NT, but the word σφραγιζω/*sphragizō* (without the prefix κατα/*kata*) is used also in Matt. 27:66; Rom. 15:28; Eph. 1:13; 4:30 and Rev. 22:10.

351 In Ezek. 2:9-10 there is also a *scroll* which has writing *on the front and back*.

352 Of course the *seals* must be broken before the *scroll* is opened. This is another example of the figure of speech called "hysteron-proteron," in which the order of a pair of expressions is changed. Note the endnote under the discussion of 3:17 which discusses this figure of speech in Revelation.

353 A word-for-word translation of the majority of Greek manuscripts would be "the Root of David, the Opener of the scroll and its seven seals." As in the very similar 5:2, this is an example of the figure of speech hysteron-proteron, in which the order of a pair of expressions is changed. Note the endnote under the discussion of 3:17.

354 νικαω/*nikaō*

355 Mounce, p. 134; and Beasley-Murray, p. 124.

356 The words *but looking as if it had been slain* are literally, "as having been slain."

357   This is the word αρνιον/*arnion*. In Revelation it is used metaphorically of Jesus Christ 28 or 29 times, depending on whether it is found in Rev. 6:9, where the manuscripts are quite divided.

358   In English the word "take" suggests that the recipient initiated the action, and the word "receive" suggests that the giver initiated the action. However, in this verse and in verses 8 and 9 the word λαμβανω/*lambanō* is used, which can mean either "take" or "receive." Thus there is an interesting ambiguity here. Did the Lord Jesus take *the scroll* from God, indicating initiative on the Lord Jesus' part, or did He receive it from God, indicating initiative from God? The Greek verb λαμβανω/*lambanō* gives no indication on this.

359   The tense used for these two verbs also emphasizes the importance of this event. He *came* uses the Aorist Tense, and *took* uses the Perfect Tense. At that moment He *took the scroll* and the result can still be felt, for example, in all the disasters described in the Book of Revelation.

360   Evidently this event is different from what is said in Matt. 28:18 and Phil. 2:9. Since He was raised from the dead, our Savior has been given the Name "Lord" and He has been lifted up. But until this moment, the Lord Jesus has not yet asked the Father for the nations as His inheritance.

361   This word, κιθαρα/*kithara*, is often translated "harp" or "lyre." This and related words are also used in 14:2; 15:2; and 18:22. J. Daryl Charles in "An Apocalyptic Tribute To The Lamb (Rev 5:1-14)" translates the word as *zither*. He writes, "The kithara, an instrument having from thirty to forty strings stretched over a shallow horizontal soundboard and played with the fingers or a plectrum, was related to the lyre and associated with hymns since the time of Homer" [*JETS* 34:4 (December 1991) p. 470].

362   This word, φιαλη/*phialē*, was used of bowls which are flat and shallow, which were used for drinking or for pouring out offerings (Mounce, p. 146). In this text the word is in the plural form.

363   The plural of the word αγιος/*hagios*, here translated *saints*, is used fourteen times in Revelation to refer to the people of God. It might also be translated "holy ones."

364   Morris, p. 98.

365   The word *us* is missing from three manuscripts, but present in the majority of manuscripts, including Sinaiticus, the oldest manuscript involved. The existence of the word *us* is significant here, because only the four creatures and the twenty-four elders are singing here. That means that the "them" of the following verse must refer to the four creatures and the elders, not all believers.

366   The word *language* is literally "tongue," γλωσσα/*glōssa*.

367   The word *nation* is εθνος/*ethnos*, which refers to an ethnic people group, not a sovereign country.

368   "New" in time is νεος/*neos*.

369   "New" in essence is καινος/*kainos*.

370   αξιος/*axios*

371 The term αξιος/*axios* is also used here. According to Mounce, p. 147, the saying *you are worthy* was also shouted when the people of the Roman Empire welcomed their emperor.

372 P. 148.

373 *The Climax of Prophecy*, p. 34.

374 Note the repetition from 1:6.

375 Note the repetition from 20:6.

376 The word ως/*hōs*, here translated *something like*, is present in Sinaiticus and the majority of manuscripts, but not in many of the older manuscripts.

377 P. 128.

378 Morris, p. 101. Morris notes the similarities between this text and 1 Chron. 29:10-12.

379 Mounce, p. 150.

380 Bauckham, *The Climax of Prophecy*, p. 14.

381 Ladd, p. 122.

382 These six arguments for the telescopic view are from *EBC* on Revelation.

383 See the endnote that discusses Dan. 9:22-27 under the discussion of Rev. 11:2.

384 P. 130.

385 Literally this is "...saying like the sound/voice of thunder...."

386 The majority of the Greek manuscripts include *and see* at the end of this verse and in the middle of verse 5.

387 Three of the four *riders are given* various kinds of authority. These expressions are examples of what is called "The Divine Passive," because it is most likely that God gives them that authority, but God is not mentioned. This is in accord with the general pattern we see in the Book of Revelation: little is said about God until in chapter 21 we read that He dwells among His people in the New Jerusalem. Note the comments on this in the section entitled "Revelation and Systematic Theology."

388 The *crown* here is a στεφανος/*stephanos*, a *crown* of victory and honor. It is not a διαδημα/*diadēma*, the kingly *crown*, which is in 19:12. See the endnotes under 2:10 and 12:3 concerning these two terms.

389 Beasley Murray, p. 131.

390 Literally, "And another horse of fire went out...."

391 This word, ζυγος/*zugos*, can mean "yoke" or *scale*. Here the meaning *scale* seems more appropriate, because of the following words about the price of *wheat* and *barley*.

392 A *denarius* was a Roman silver coin, and an average daily wage for a laborer.

393 *EBC* cites Beckwith for this figure.

394 *EBC* offers both explanations.

395 P. 132.

396 The word *voice* is not in the Greek, but is added in the translation for clarity.

397 This adjective, χλωρος/*chlōros*, means *green*, but it can refer to any *green* from that of grass (Rev. 8:7) to the greenish gray of a very sick person, according to *BDAG*. That sickly *green* seems to be intended here.

398 The words και εν θανατω/*kai en thanatō*, literally "and in (or "by") death," seem to mean *and with plague*, because θανατος/*thanatos*, although it normally means "death," can sometimes refer to deadly *plague*. Note that Job 27:14 mentions death by the *sword*, and lack of food (that is, *famine*), and the next verse says "death" will bury his survivor. The LXX translation of Job 27:14 uses εν θανατω/ *en thanatō* just like this verse in Rev. 6:8. Likewise Jer. 15:2-3 seems to speak of judgment by *plague*, the *sword*, and *famine*, and wild beasts, and uses θανατος/ *thanatos* to refer to *plague*.

399 The use of this word (μαρτυρια/*marturia*) in Revelation is interesting. Because of his *testimony*, John himself was exiled to Patmos (1:2, 9). The ones that were killed because of their *testimony* were crying out under the *altar* of God (6:9). After they are finished with their *testimony*, the two witnesses will be killed (11:7). There are those who defeat Satan with the blood of the Lord and the power of their *testimony* (12:11). Those holding on to their *testimony* are attacked by Satan (12:17). Finally, those who are martyred for their *testimony* for Jesus are going to reign with Him for a thousand years (20:4). In summary, the *testimony* about the Lord Jesus has unfathomable power, and it brings martyrdom along with rewards.

400 Though many manuscripts have *of the Lamb* here, many others read "of Jesus Christ," and the oldest have neither. If *of the Lamb* is not in the original reading, then the word "lamb" is used of Christ 28 times in the Book of Revelation.

401 The Imperfect Tense of εχω/*echō* here is translated *they were holding on to*.

402 According to Beasley-Murray (p. 135), Lev. 4:7; Phil. 2:17; and 2 Tim. 4:6 are some background verses relating to this text.

403 P. 157.

404 The term *Master* (δεσποτης/*despotēs*) refers to a *master* that has a slave (1 Tim. 6:1-2; 2 Tim. 2:21; Titus 2:9; and 1 Pet. 2:18). When this term is used of God (Luke 2:29) or of the Lord (2 Pet. 2:1; and Jude 4) it emphasizes His sovereignty.

405 Morris, p. 109.

406 1 Enoch is a non-canonical Jewish book. It is hard to know for sure when it was written, and it is possible that it was written after the Book of Revelation, but it is clear that these elements were not foreign to the writings of the Jewish people.

407 Beasley-Murray, p. 134.

408 Perhaps the word *robe* (στολη/*stolē*) refers to a kind of special clothing, because this word is used less than the word ιματιον/*himation*. The word *robe* (στολη/*stolē*) is only used in Mark 12:38 (clothing of the scribes); Mark 16:5 (clothing of the angels); Luke 15:22 (party clothing); Luke 20:46 (clothing of the scribes) and Rev. 6:11; 7:9, 13, and 14.

409 Because the Greek term αδελφος/*adelphos* can certainly include women, some recent translators have translated it "brothers and sisters." However, the Greek term αδελφοι/*adelphoi* does not stress the specific inclusion of women like

the expression "brothers and sisters" would. Therefore the translation *brothers* is retained, with the note that the Greek term here includes women.

410   A word-for-word translation would be "until they are fulfilled/completed even their fellow slaves and their brothers and those that are about to be killed, as also they."

411   Outside the canon of the Bible, note also 1 Enoch 47:4, "And the hearts of the holy were filled with joy; Because the number of the righteous had been offered, And the prayer of the righteous had been heard, And the blood of the righteous been required before the Lord of Spirits" (translated from the Ethiopian by R.H. Charles, 1906). That Jewish text also suggests that there is a fixed number of people that will be granted the privilege of martyrdom.

412   See the discussion about the "Reiteration View" and the "Telescoping View" in the discussion about the structure of this section.

413   *Sackcloth made of hair* is made from the wool of black sheep and used by people in mourning (Mounce, p. 161).

414   αστηρ/*astēr*

415   The majority of Greek manuscripts read *His* rather than "their."

416   In the ancient manuscripts there are no quotation marks, but because modern languages require quotation marks, the translator is forced to decide exactly which words are meant as quotations. Clearly, 6:16 has a quotation, but 6:17 could be a quotation, or it could be an explanation from John. It seems better to take 6:17 to be a part of the quotation, but one cannot be certain. Clearly, in 7:1 we return to the words of the Apostle John, and not a quotation from those "mighty" men.

417   *The Climax of Prophecy*, p. 31.

418   For instance Morris, pp. 176-177; Ladd, p. 191; Mounce, p. 270; and Beasley-Murray, p. 223.

419   Mounce, p. 168.

420   P. 170.

421   In the context of this discussion, Ezek. 47-48 is also significant.

422   Mounce, p. 169.

423   This translation, *After these things – and look! – a great multitude* is a word-for-word translation. The NIV reads "After this, I looked and there was before me a great multitude...." See the endnote under 1:7 concerning the translation of the word ιδου/*idou*.

424   Thomas, p. 488. Note the comments on this four-fold expression in 5:9.

425   The Greek noun here is σωτηρια/*sōtēria*, related to the verb σωζω/*sōzō*. That verb often translates the Hebrew ישע/*ysh'*, which although usually translated "to save," usually speaks of a physical deliverance, rescue, or *victory* for the people of God. The word σωτηρια/*sōtēria* is found in the LXX of Ps. 14:7; 20:5; 21:1, 5; and 53:6, all of which speak of *victory*.

426   Mounce, p. 173.

427 Just like the English word "lord," the word κυριος/*kurios* can certainly be used of the *Lord* Jesus or the *Lord* God, but it can also simply be a term of respect like *lord* or "sir." The respect John gives in this verse is also seen in Rev. 19:10 and 22:8-9 (Mounce, p. 173).

428 η θλιψις της μεγαλης/*hē thlipsis tēs megalēs*

429 But Mounce (p. 173) and Morris (p. 118) say they are believers who come out of the *Great Tribulation* because they die a normal death, not because they are killed because of their faith and testimony. However, it would seem that in that age, when persecution will be so intense, there would not be many faithful believers who would have the opportunity to live peaceful lives and die in peace.

430 It is true that Isa. 1:18 says, "If your sins are as scarlet, as snow they shall be made white; if they are red like purple, like wool they shall be." But even in that passage in Isaiah there is no mention of clothing being *made white*. It is better to connect this passage to the special status that martyrs have in the Book of Revelation, rather than to the forgiven status of all believers.

431 In Rev. 7:15 and 21:3 exactly the same verb is used, σκηνωσει/*skēnōsei* from σκηνοω/*skēnoō*.

432 Thomas, p. 501.

433 The words *the heat of* have been added to the translation for clarity. A literal translation would be "neither might fall upon them the sun."

434 The four parts of this promise were taken from a promise made to Israel in Isa. 49:10.

435 Note the endnote under 2:26-28 concerning shepherding.

436 These words, *in the middle of the throne* (ανα μεσον του θρονου/*ana meson tou thronou*), are different from those in Rev. 5:6, (εν μεσω του θρονου/*en mesō tou thronou*). Normally, ανα μεσον/*ana meson* means "in between." The same word is used in Matt. 13:25 "between"; Mark 7:31 "in the middle of"; and 1 Cor. 6:5 "from." The meaning of the words *in the middle of the throne* cannot be defined exactly, because we do not know the shape of *the throne*.

437 P. 176.

438 As was discussed in the comments concerning the structure of this section, some interpreters think that the series of seven trumpets is a repetition of what was given in chapter six and not a continuation; but in this text, 8:1-2, there is not even one indicator leading us to that conclusion. Seven angels are each given a trumpet to bring the judgments accompanying the opening of the last seal.

439 In the original language there is a definite article here, so it is translated *the seven angels*. Even so, which *angels* the author is speaking about is not clear. Maybe these *seven angels* are the same *seven angels* that will be given the bowls to pour out (15:6).

440 In Josh. 6:1-16 *seven trumpets* are blown by *seven* priests prior to the miraculous destruction of the walls of Jericho.

441 Beasley-Murray (p. 152) compares the opening of the seals and the sounding of the *trumpets* in Jewish literature. He says that only in the Book of Revelation

are seals opened in connection with the coming of Messiah, but in many Jewish writings a trumpet is blown in the context of the arrival of the Messiah.

442   In 1 Kings 17:1; 18:15; 2 Kings 3:14; and 5:16 "stand in front…" means "ready to serve…."

443   The word used in Exod. 27:3 can mean "copper," but it is probably a copper alloy that we might call "bronze," which is copper alloyed with some tin. In the ancient world the metals that were alloyed with copper could vary considerably, so Hebrew could use one word for what we would call "copper," "bronze," and "brass."

444   Bauckham, *The Climax of Prophecy*, p. 203.

445   Beasley-Murray, pp. 155-156.

446   The word "angel" is not in the Greek text, but *the first* is clearly *the first* of the seven angels mentioned in 8:2 and 8:6.

447   The eruption of Mount Vesuvius, its ash suddenly covering the city of Pompeii, happened about 20 years before Revelation was written. But what was the meaning of that disaster compared to the disaster here that ruins a third of the earth?

448   This expression, *living creatures*, is very different from the term used for the "four creatures" near the throne of God. The expression, *living creatures*, could also be translated "creatures that have life." The term creature here is κτισμα/*ktisma*. Note the endnote under 4:6 concerning the "four creatures."

449   This word, αψινθος/*apsinthos*, is a kind of plant that is very bitter. See Jer. 9:15 and 23:15.

450   Mounce, p. 187.

451   Literally, "and the day did not shine a third of it, and the night likewise."

452   This word (αετος/*aetos*) is only used five times in the NT. The use of this word in Matt. 24:28 and Luke 17:37, and comments in Aristotle and Pliny (according to *BDAG*), show that the word can include vultures who eat carrion. However, the αετος/*aetos* here in Rev. 8:13 and in Rev. 12:14 are strong fliers, and so the English translation *eagle* is appropriate.

453   See the comments on this expression in the discussion of 3:10.

454   This word (αβυσσος/*abussos*) is used nine times in the NT. In Luke 8:31 the demons are afraid of being thrown there, in Rom. 10:7 it is the place of the dead, and in Rev. 9:1, 2, 11; 11:7; 17:8; 20:1, and 3 there are demons there, and it is the place where Satan is thrown as punishment. It is possible this place is the same as the "prison" (φυλακη/*phulakē*) in 1 Pet. 3:19, which is in itself a rather mysterious text.

455   This word, καμινος/*kaminos*, can also mean "oven" or "kiln."

456   1 Enoch has a long explanation about the demons imprisoned in the pit of the *abyss* as punishment for their works that are mentioned in Gen. 6:1-7, where they are called "sons of God." Remember that 1 Enoch is not the Word of God, but only one book in the traditions of the Jewish people.

457   Mounce, (p. 194) quoted from Barclay.

458 Mounce (p. 194) observes that the similarities of these disasters to the plagues of Egypt are strengthened because in Exod. 8:22; 9:4, 26; 10:23; and 11:7 the people of Israel did not experience those plagues at all, just as here the sealed 144,000 are not harmed.

459 Mounce, p. 194; and Morris, pp. 126-127.

460 The Greek double negative ου μη/*ou mē* is here translated *certainly not*. See the endnote under 2:11 for more on the Greek double negative.

461 The Greek expression here is unique in the NT. Literally translated it would be "and the likenesses of the locusts were like horses...." See the endnote on the word *like*, ὅμοιος/*homoios*, under 1:13.

462 Mounce, p. 196.

463 Ladd, p. 133.

464 In the LXX of Job 26:6 and 28:22 this term, Αβαδδων/*Abaddōn*, is translated "destruction," and it is parallel with "death." In the OT this word often means the same as "sheol," which is the world of the dead. This term can be compared with the "world of the dead" (ἅδης/*hadēs*) in Rev. 1:18; 6:8; and 20:13, 14.

465 Beasley-Murray (p. 162) says there is another word (απωλεια/*apōleia*) which is normally used to translate the word *Abaddon*. Maybe the name *Apollyon* (Απολλυων/*Apolluōn*) was used here because it is close to the name of the god, Apollo. This change in translation is quite barbed, because a few of the Caesars of Rome (Caligula, Nero, and Domitian) liked to imitate the god Apollo. The god Apollo is sometimes symbolized as a locust, so this possibility is strong. If so, the Book of Revelation could be said to compare Caesar to *the angel of the abyss!*

466 Ladd, p. 136.

467 Those composite bows were invented on the steppes of Central Asia about 1500 BC. A composite bow is made of several materials like wood, horn and animal tendon that are glued together, making a stronger and more flexible bow.

468 Beasley-Murray, p. 164.

469 Literally, this could be translated "breastplates of fire color, of hyacinth color, and sulfurous," meaning those are the colors of their *breastplates* and not the materials of which they are made. So the colors of the *breastplates* are the colors of what comes out of the *mouths* of the *horses*.

470 Mounce, p. 202.

471 In 1 Sam. 16:14-15; 18:10; and 19:9 God sends demons to King Saul. So also in this passage, God sends demons in the form of *horses* and locusts/scorpions.

472 Mounce, p. 203.

473 Morris, p. 134.

474 The word *people* is not in the original, but was added because the English verb *harm* requires an object in this sentence.

475 The word *repent* (μετανοεω/*metanoeō*) is used six times in chapters two and three. Other than that, in the Book of Revelation this term is only used in 9:20, 21; 16:9, and 11.

476 A literal translation of the original would read "...repent of the deeds of their hands, that they would not worship demons...."

477 Mounce, p. 204.

478 In Acts 1:9 *clouds* covered the Lord Jesus from their view when He ascended to heaven. In Rev. 4:3 a *rainbow* surrounded God's throne. In Rev. 1:16 the face of Christ shone intensely like the *sun*. In Num. 14:14 the presence of God was made known by a *pillar of fire*.

479 This *scroll* is mentioned four times in this passage, sometimes as a *scroll* (βιβλιον/*biblion*), and sometimes as a "little scroll," (βιβλιδαριον/*biblidarion*). There are several textual variations among the Greek manuscripts for these terms.

480 Morris, p. 137.

481 The word *open* is in the form of a perfect participle, giving the impression that it is already *open* and will remain *open*.

482 The word here translated *voices* (φωνη/*phōnē*) can also mean "sound," and the word translated *spoke* (λαλεω/*laleō*) here and twice in verse 4 can also refer to inanimate things that making noise, so this might also be translated "the seven thunders sounded with their own sounds."

483 The word translated *it* is actually plural in the original, but it is better treated as a singular in English.

484 P. 139.

485 P. 143.

486 P. 7.

487 P. 209.

488 In the original language, Abram said, "I have raised my hand to the Lord God Most High, Creator of heaven and earth...." The words "and have taken an oath" are added by the NIV translators as clarification.

489 This word, φωνη/*phōnē*, often means "voice," but here seems to refer to the *sound* of the *trumpet*.

490 Ladd, p. 145. This "telescoping" understanding of the structure of this part of Revelation was explained at the beginning of this section.

491 μυστηριον/*mustērion*

492 Mounce, p. 212.

493 This is another example of the figure of speech hysteron-proteron. Note the endnote under the discussion of 3:17 which discusses this figure of speech.

494 Morris, p. 142; and Ladd, p. 147.

495 P. 175.

496 P. 216.

497 Note the comments on this four-fold expression in the discussion of 5:9.

498 This word, καλαμος/*kalamos*, means *reed*, but such reeds were often used as measuring rods. See for instance Ezek. 40:3, which uses this word in the LXX.

499 The word used is ναος/*naos*, which refers to the *temple* itself, but not the courtyards. The other word that might be used is ιερον/*hieron*, which also refers

to the *temple* but includes the courtyards. (In Luke 2:37, Anna never left the ιερον/*hieron*, but of course she was never allowed into the ναος/*naos*. In Luke 23:45 it is the curtain of the ναος/*naos* that is torn.) Often in the *NIV* when the word ιερον/*hieron* is used, it is translated "temple courts," but that gives the impression that it is only the courts. A better translation would be "temple precincts" or "temple complex." The word ναος/*naos* is used 45 times in the NT, and ιερον/*hieron* is used 72 times in the NT, but never in Revelation. So whenever you see the word *temple* in Revelation, it does indeed refer to the *temple* itself, excluding the courtyards.

500 P. 72.

501 P. 152.

502 *The Climax of Prophecy*, pp. 273-283.

503 *EBC*.

504 P. 277.

505 The word πλατεια/*plateia* can either mean *street* or "square."

506 More literally, this would be translated "from the peoples and tribes and tongues and nations." Note the comments on this four-fold expression in the discussion of 5:9.

507 See the comments on the expression *those who dwell upon the earth* in the discussion of 3:10.

508 Pp. 281-283.

509 The command *Come up here!* is almost the same as the command given to John in 4:1, except that in 4:1 it is singular, and here in 11:21 it is plural.

510 The majority of the Greek manuscripts say the *earthquake* happened *in that day*, but the oldest surviving manuscripts read "in that hour."

511 It underscores the uniqueness of this event that this is the only use of the term *tenth* in the entire book.

512 *The Climax of Prophecy*, pp. 278-279.

513 This transfer is also a theme in the OT, for example in Dan. 2:44 and Zech. 14:9.

514 Walvoord, p. 184; and Ladd, p. 160.

515 The majority of manuscripts read *before the throne of God*, but the oldest manuscripts read "before God."

516 This word, παντοκρατωρ/*pantokratōr*, is frequently used in the translation of expressions like "the Lord of Hosts" in the LXX.

517 This term ειληφας/*eilēphas*, from the word λαμβανω/*lambanō*, is in the Perfect Tense, because at the moment this will be said, it shall have already happened and the results will be ongoing (Morris, p. 153).

518 The verb translated *begun to reign* is the term εβασιλευσας/*ebasileusas*, which uses the Aorist Tense. Mounce (p. 231) mentions that this is what grammarians call an "inceptive aorist" meaning that it describes action that is just beginning. Because of this it is translated *begun to reign*.

519 Beasley-Murray, p. 189; Mounce, p. 231; and Bauckham, *The Theology of the Book of Revelation*, p. 29.

520 From the verb οργιζω/*orgizō*.

521 From the noun οργη/*orgē*.

522 The words *the time* are used only once in the original, but are repeated in the translation to make the meaning more clear.

523 Beasley-Murray, p. 190.

524 Ps. 2:1 and 2:5 are the background of this verse.

525 Ladd, p. 163.

526 There is a textual problem among the Greek manuscripts of this verse. The earliest manuscript and the majority of Greek manuscripts read *the covenant of the Lord*, one early manuscript reads "the covenant of God," and two early manuscripts read "His covenant."

527 The few oldest Greek manuscripts include "an earthquake" here, but the majority of manuscripts do not include that element.

528 Mounce, p. 232.

529 Mounce, p. 233.

530 Bauckham (*The Climax of Prophecy*, pp. 199-201) mentions these verses, as well as Joel 2:10; Mic. 1:4; Ps. 77:17-19; Ps. 114; and Heb. 12:26-27.

531 *The Climax of Prophecy*, pp. 8 and 202.

532 Other than that, Bauckham (*The Climax of Prophecy*, p. 31) notes that the creation of God is divided into four in 8:7-12; 14:7; and 16:2-9.

533 αβυσσος/*abussos*

534 αξιος/*axios*

535 βασιλευω/*basileuō*

536 γεμω/*gemō*

537 δρεπανον/*drepanon*

538 πορνεια/*porneia*

539 Note the use of this expression, ο κυριος ο θεος ο παντοκρατωρ/*ho Kurios ho Theos ho Pantokratōr*, in 1:8; 4:8; 11:17; 15:3; 16:7; 19:6; and 21:22, with very slight variation.

540 αστηρ/*astēr*

541 αληθινος/*alēthinos*

542 αριθμος/*arithmos*

543 βροντη/*brontē*

544 εικων/*eikōn*

545 δωδεκα/*dōdeka* or δεκαδυο/*dekaduo*

546 In the Critical Text, the word "twelve" occurs only 11 times. The problem is in 21:16. Those that hold to that text might also note that the word "three" is used four times, so that in that final vision (if "three" appearing four times is considered a twelve) the concept of twelve occurs 12 times in the Critical Text. To complicate matters, the word "twelfth" occurs once in that vision, in 21:20, so it is also true that in the Critical Text, the words "twelve" or "twelfth" occur twelve times!

547 πνευμα/*pneuma*

Bibliography

Barclay, William, *Letters to the Seven Churches*, Abingdon Press, New York, 1957.

―――, *The Revelation of John*, The Westminster Press, Philadelphia, 1976.

Bauckham, Richard, *The Climax of Prophecy*: Studies on the Book of Revelation, T & T Clark, Edinburgh, 1993.

―――, *The Theology of the Book of Revelation*, Cambridge University Press, Cambridge, 1993.

Baugh, S. M., "Cult Prostitution in New Testament Ephesus: A Reappraisal," *Journal of the Evangelical Theological Society* 42 (1999), pp. 443-460.

Baur, Danke, Arndt, and Gingrich, *A Greek-English Lexicon of the New Testament and Other Early Christian Literature*, University Of Chicago Press, Chicago, third edition, 2001.

Beasley-Murray, G. R., *Revelation*, William B. Eerdmans Publishing Company, Grand Rapids, 1978.

Bruce, F. F., *New Testament History*, Doubleday & Co., Garden City, 1969.

Collins, Adela Yarbro, "Numerical Symbolism in Jewish and Early Christian Apocalyptic Literature," *Aufstieg und Niedergang der romischen Welt*, W. Haase, ed., vol. 2/21/1, de Gruyter, New York/Berlin, 1984, pp. 1221-1287.

Cranfield, C.E.B., *A Critical and Exegetical Commentary on The Epistle to the Romans*, The International Critical Commentary, T. & T. Clark Limited, Edinburgh, 1975.

Hemer, Colin J., *The Letters to the Seven Churches of Asia in Their Local Setting*, William B. Eerdmans Publishing Company, Grand Rapids, 1986.

Hitchcock, Mark L., "A Critique of the Preterist View of 'Soon' and 'Near' in Revelation," *Bibliotheca Sacra* 163:652 (October-December 2006), pp. 467-478.

Johnson, Alan F., *Revelation*, Gaebelein, Frank E. (series editor), The Expositor's Bible Commentary, Zondervan, Grand Rapids, 1982.

Keil and Delitzsch, *Commentary on the Old Testament*, updated edition, Hendrickson Publishers, 1996.

Ladd, George Eldon, *A Commentary on the Revelation of John*, William B. Eerdmans Publishing Company, Grand Rapids, 1972.

———, "The Kingdom of God in the Jewish Apocryphal Literature" Part 3, *Bibliotheca Sacra*, 109:436 (Oct 52)

Lyall, Francis, *Slaves, Citizens, Sons*, Zondervan Publishing House, Grand Rapids, 1984.

Morris, Leon, *The Revelation of Saint John*, The Tyndale New Testament Commentaries, William B. Eerdmans Publishing Company, Grand Rapids, 1969.

Mounce, Robert H., *The Book of Revelation*, William B. Eerdmans Publishing Company, Grand Rapids, 1977.

Newell, William R., *Revelation: a Complete Commentary*, World Bible Publishers, Inc., Iowa Falls, Iowa, 1935.

Ramsay, William N., *The Letters to the Seven Churches of Asia and their place in the plan of the Apocalypse*, Hodder & Stoughton, London, 1904.

Ryrie, Charles Caldwell, *Revelation*, Moody Press, Chicago, 1968.

Stalker, James, "The Son of Man," in *The International Standard Bible Encyclopedia*, vol. v, pp. 2828-2830, 1929.

Stanley, Charles, *Eternal Security: Can You Be Sure?*, Thomas Nelson Publishers, Nashville, 1990.

Walvoord, John F., *The Revelation of Jesus Christ*, Moody Press, Chicago, 1966.

www.ingramcontent.com/pod-product-compliance
Lightning Source LLC
Chambersburg PA
CBHW062129160426
43191CB00013B/2243